A Wiggly Way Through England

Wandering the watershed in search of history, characters and cakes

by Richard Guise

A WIGGLY WAY THROUGH ENGLAND

Maps, drawings and photographs by Richard Guise

ISBN: 978-0-954-55874-1

PERMISSIONS:

Base for watershed map:

upload.wikimedia.org/wikipedia/commons/thumb/b/b0/Major.rivers.of.England.jpg. Used under the Creative Commons Attribution-Share Alike 3.0 Unported licence at http://creativecommons.org/licenses/by-sa/3.0/deed.en.

Base for route map:

Ordnance Survey data © Crown copyright and database rights 2010 Ordnance Survey. Used under the OS OpenData™ licence at www.ordnancesurvey.co.uk/oswebsite/opendata/docs/os-opendata-licence.pdf.

Let him that purposeth to travell, first begin where he was born, bred up and nurst, that's his own country.

(from *A Relation of a Short Survey of Twenty-Six Counties*, the account of a 1634 journey through England by 'a Captain, a Lieutenant and an Ancient', but whose authorship is unidentified)

To those friends
who accompanied, accommodated or sponsored me

ACKNOWLEDGEMENTS

For their support en route, thanks to John Allen, Lindsay Allen, Julie Challans, David Foster, Erica Foster, Edna Hanford, Gerald Hanford, Richard Mahoney, Wendy Mahoney, Kate Paterson, Tim Rodgers, Margaret Toon and Peter Toon.

For advice and comments, thanks to Nick Crane, Jim Faulkner and Richard Mahoney.

For outstanding support thoughout as always, thanks to Julie.

NOTES FROM THE AUTHOR

Some of the personal names used in this book are not the real ones.

For American Readers. This book is written in British English, where a 'watershed' is what an American would call a 'divide'. Somewhat confusingly, a 'watershed' in American English is exactly the opposite: what the English would call a 'catchment area' or a 'drainage basin'.

The path to Martin's Down, near Littlebredy, Dorset.

A busy sky above King Alfred's Tower on the Somerset/Wiltshire border.

Close-up of the white horse sculptured from the chalk of Roundway Hill, near Devizes, Wiltshire.

A Roman coin bearing the head of Constantine the Great sees the light of day for the first time in about 1,700 years, at a dig near Tetbury, Gloucestershire.

The eggs are priced but the view is free, near
Little Compton, Oxfordshire.

England's coldest days can also be some of the most
stunning, as here near Crick, Northamptonshire.

It's all quiet now at Naseby, Northamptonshire.

This lamb struggles to a better vantage point near
Husbands Bosworth, Leicestershire

Time for reflection by the Stratford Canal, near Lapworth, Warwickshire.

A classic English skyline at the Lickey Hills, Worcestershire.

Beneath the English Watershed pass many canal tunnels, as here on the Dudley Canal at Dudley, West Midlands.

The quiet village of Maer, Staffordshire, was a favourite spot for Charles Darwin.

An unusually empty A53 approaching Axe Edge, near the Staffordshire/Derbyshire border.

Journey's end: the deserted plateau at Kinder Scout, Derbyshire.

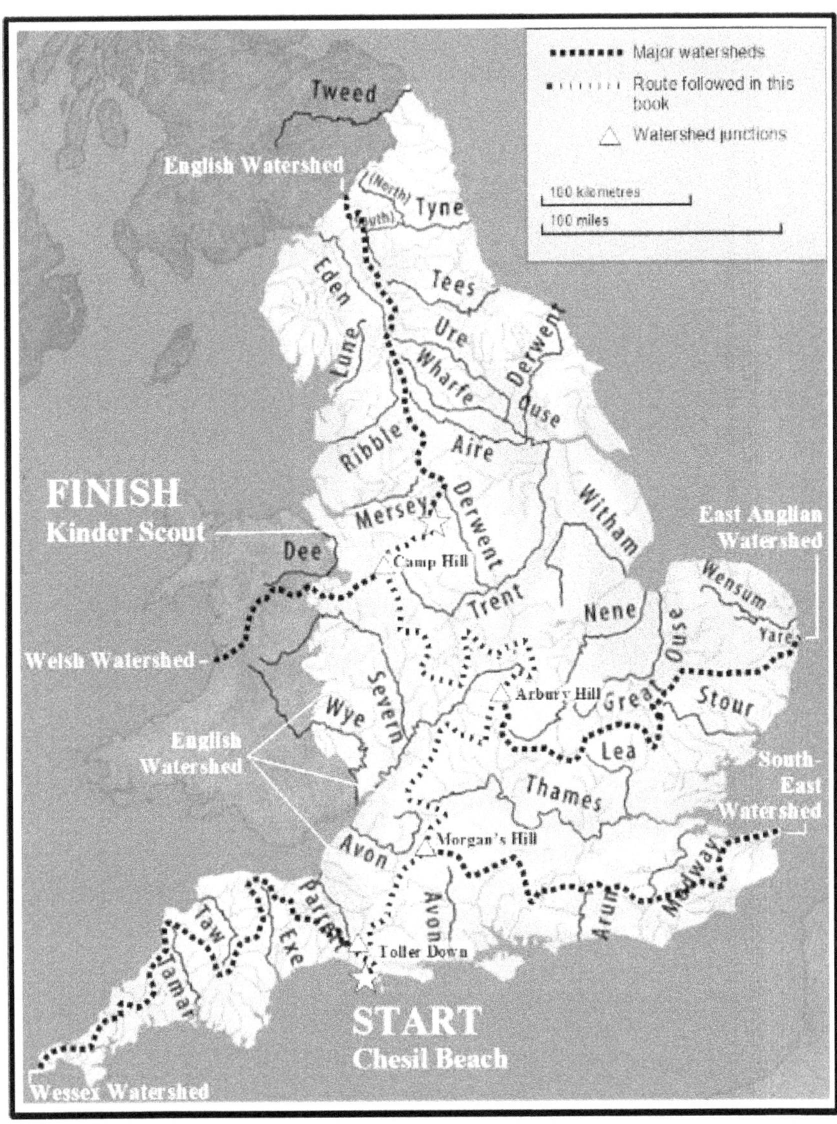

Map 1. Major Watersheds of England. Watersheds appear to be officially nameless and so the names shown here are those attributed by the author.

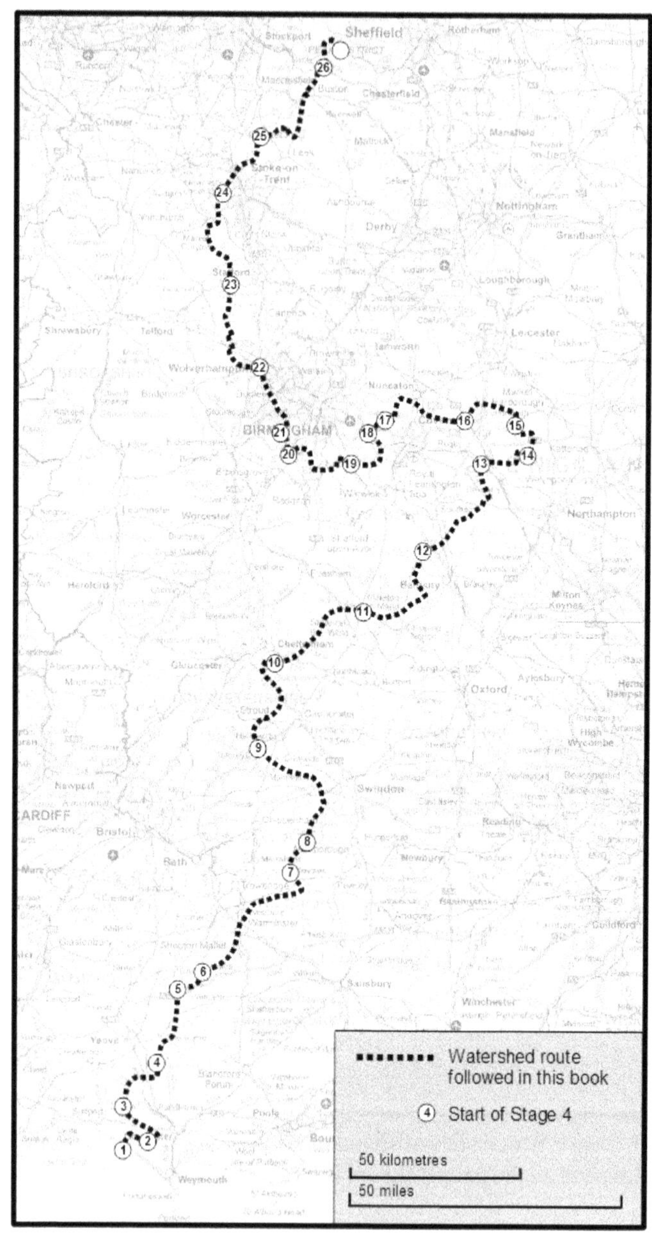

Map 2. Route followed in this book.

Contents

What, Why, Where...

What is a watershed?

Imagine you're a raindrop. You're hurtling towards the green fields of England and, after making one of them a tiny bit greener, you're keen to find your way back to the sea. But which way to turn? With gravity as your guide, you head downhill -- whichever way that is -- for downhill always leads to the sea. Eventually.

But while you finally flow into the huge swells of the Atlantic -- via the River Severn perhaps -- your neighbouring raindrop from all that time ago finds itself slipping into the chilly waters of the North Sea -- maybe past Spurn Head at the mouth of the Humber. So you both fell to earth close to the English watershed, an imaginary line that divides streams and rivers reaching the sea on our west coast from those heading to our east coast.

It's a wiggly affair, as the map shows. Skirting Salisbury Plain, negotiating the Cotswold Edge, wandering through the Midlands, lurching up onto the Pennines -- it looks pretty indecisive. Passing through picture-postcard villages, industrial estates, sleepy suburbs and historical battlefields, it does seem fiendishly fickle. But in its *raison d'être* it's quite constant: all Atlantic-bound streams to the left (if you're headed north), all those destined for the North Sea to the right.

There's a correction to make already. I glibly wrote '*the* English watershed' when it should have been *an* English watershed, for there are more than one. There are hundreds, millions -- an infinite number in fact. It's all a question of scale. Any watershed is always a watershed *between this and that.* Between one coast and another, between the catchment area of the Avon and that of the Nene, between this stream and that brook, and so on. Even in terms of coasts, there are three, for England has a south coast too of course, and therefore not only a watershed between the Atlantic and the North Sea, but also one between the Atlantic and the Channel and between the North Sea and the Channel.

Why follow a watershed route?

Britain is nowadays laced with long-distance, waymarked paths. While many of the tracks themselves have been around for centuries, it's only recently that so many have been strung together into the Jurassic Way, the

Heart of England Way and all their companion 'trails', with their carefully crafted logos and handy, pocket-sized guides. Likewise, since the 1980s Sustrans has been tracing out a national network of admirable, well-documented cycle routes.

This is all well and good. In dragging thousands from their Sunday papers and computer games out into the fresh air to follow the colourful signs to health and well-being, they've done a fine job. But I'm not one of those. I'm out here anyway. And actually I don't want to be told where to go, preferring to figure that out for myself. I don't really want to be with hundreds of others tramping up and down the High Peak Trail either. I'd rather it were just me, the hills and maybe a couple of mates. Some of us still prefer maps to GPSs too. With a map the landscape takes its rightful place of dominance, the route a thin thread across it, the reader a mere dot in the corner. This is how it should be.

Contrary and curmudgeonly? If so, I'm not the only one. If any of this sounds like you too, then following a watershed may be right up your street.

Some detailed mapwork is required beforehand -- and carefully tracing a line between the headwaters of streams can, I warn you, become addictive. Even from the map you'll see that your watershed route will take you through a merrily mixed bag of environments: hills and ridges yes, but also woods, leafy lanes and back streets. What it won't do -- in Britain at least -- is to route you via many main roads and conurbations, which have, over the centuries, followed the valleys and crowded around river crossing points.

As soon as you're out on foot or in the saddle, you'll begin to notice that watershed routes pull in more than their fair share of features that have themselves, for various reasons and over various periods, been attracted to these relatively high, relatively dry areas. Hill forts, burial mounds, farmland, airfields, racecourses, rail and canal tunnels, transmission masts, reservoirs -- in a sense, it's the flipside of our urban environment: the rejects from the valleys, but also the essential infrastructure that supports us. And, although you'll cross some of the well-signed, well-trodden long-distance trails -- even follow some of them for a while -- the overall route will be yours alone, a secret compact between you and the map. Throughout my own watershed route I saw not a single signpost announcing its existence.

Where?

You can trace a watershed route from anywhere to anywhere in Great Britain, but any long-distance route will eventually join up with one of the five major watersheds in southern Britain, as marked on the map. Try as I might, I've been unable to find any official names for them and so have taken the liberty of naming them myself: the Wessex Watershed, the South-East Watershed, the East Anglian Watershed, the Welsh Watershed and the longest of them all, the English Watershed.

They're not entirely 'secrets', of course. The most well-known is probably that stretch of the English Watershed along the crest of the Pennines, followed, more or less, by the Pennine Way. But, while many have walked -- and written about -- it, the majority seem to bow to the waymarking and stop (or start) just south of Kinder Scout in Derbyshire, the southern end of the Pennine Way. For this reason I also chose to finish at Kinder Scout -- but having approached from the opposite direction to everyone else, from the south.

Where to start though? Well, the English Watershed begins at Morgan's Hill in Wiltshire, but starting on the south coast seemed somehow more definitive. After tracing on the map a few watersheds from miscellaneous spots on the south coast, I found one that neither dithered too much in running parallel to the coast nor took me through the hazardous waste section of an oil refinery compound. It starts on Chesil Beach in Dorset, at East Bexington to be precise. No, I'd never heard of it either. As a bonus it led me straight into some stunning scenery.

How?

I'm a law-abiding citizen. The Countryside and Rights of Way Act (2000) gave access for walkers to 'open country', not the right to charge through any field, yard or garden they fancy. The laws of physics inhibit the breaching of hedges, walls and fences. Having plotted the watershed's path on large-scale maps, I identified the nearest means of feasible public access: an inviting mixture of footpaths, bridleways and roads.

Any walker knows that mile after mile of tarmac is hard on sole and soul alike. I therefore mixed walking and cycling. After all, this was no test of endurance, no attempt to follow the stringent rules of some challenge from the *Guinness Book of Records* -- Slowest Watershed Traverse on Foot? -- but simply an opportunity to experience this unique south-to-north trail slowly and under my own steam. My stately pedalling pace meets that spec as well.

When?

Arthritis, in its various forms, is quite a common disorder of the joints -- but its commonness in no way reduces the impact on sufferers. One of these was my dear old dad, a very active man in his prime, but effectively house-bound by arthritis in his later years. There is no cure, but **Arthritis Research UK** is a charity whose work aims to take the pain away from sufferers and help people to remain active. Half the net royalties from the sales of this book will be donated to that charity.

Being the wrong side of sixty myself, I listened to the testimony of my own joints and did not, therefore, undertake the 28 days that this journey eventually comprised all in one go. Far from it. Indeed, walking and cycling days were fitted in to match the schedule of those who accompanied me, accommodated me or helped out in other ways.

And finally...

One of the many lessons I've learned from my father is to enjoy life while I can. We all should. What more enjoyable adventure could there be for an Englishman than to travel through his homeland along a wandering line that guarantees to take in a kaleidoscopic variety of landscapes, of villages, towns and hostelries, of encounters and surprises -- all on a purposeful path just above, sometimes way above, the travails of day-to-day life? None, I think. In truth no other motivation is necessary.

However, to add spice to my serendipitous journey, I intended to undertake some research along the way. Quite literally add spice, for I hoped there might be the odd en-route opportunity to try a local cake or two. My specific cakely mission would be a straightforward one: to establish whether anywhere in England made better *locally named* cakes than the Bakewell Puddings of my native Derbyshire.

RGG, March 2013

Stage 1: Unextreme Sports

Chesil Beach to White Hill

February's gruel-grey sky hung low over Abbotsbury as we emerged early and eager to find the walking route to the beach. Although we weren't the only souls abroad in the little Dorset village that morning, the others seemed unusually keen to be done with their chores -- fetching the paper, seeing the children onto the bus -- and back indoors by the fire as soon as they could. Only a few paces down the lane beyond the village store, we were quite alone.

My companion for this first stage -- as for several of the others -- was my long-suffering partner Julie. Though I don't believe the suffering to be frequent, my winter wittering on the subject of 'the watershed project' would have tested the patience of a saint, even a saint partial to a good walk. Having hatched the idea the previous autumn and then, over the severest winter for two generations, planned how to achieve it, I was eager to be under way. Too eager, as it turned out, but we didn't know that yet. At the first hint of a window in the weather, we'd booked in for two nights at Peach's Bed and Breakfast, a choice that proved excellent for both small snippets of local information and larger snippets of locally sourced breakfast that had seen us on our way with little need for extra nourishment to weigh down our packs.

The 3-kilometre route to the beach at East Bexington wound between the bare, smooth slopes of Chapel Hill and the deep green woods of Abbotsbury Subtropical Gardens until before us rose a huge bank of browns and greens right where the sea should have been. This was Chesil Bank. In case we needed any convincing, the short stretch on pebbles between our track and the road confirmed that the bank itself is suited more to the SAS than to a pair of ageing ramblers. However, the heavily pitted shore-side road proved quite a find: a quiet lane between sheep-dotted hills and riffling surf, bordered here and there by the wispy dust-green of a tamarisk bush or the welcome yellow splash of an iris. With the low cloud now having headed north to leave hints of a watery sun, it seemed a perfect way to set out on an adventure.

*

While West Bexington, just out of sight along the shore, is a heaving metropolis of 130 inhabitants, East Bexington seemed to be just a farm of that name and an accessible stretch of beach. To the latter we descended for a first sip from the coffee flask. Yes, *de*scended, for the massive bulk of Chesil Bank had by now assumed the proportions of an ordinary shingle beach. But ordinary Chesil Beach is not.

From West Bay near Bridport the action of the sea over thousands of years has created a 29-kilometre shingle beach all the way to Portland, joining that former isle to the mainland and therefore making Chesil Beach a rare example of a geographical feature called a tombolo. From Abbotsbury onwards the beach becomes a bank so massive -- over 14 metres above mean sea level -- that all watercourses are diverted through a shallow lagoon, the Fleet, before they can finally enter the sea. This is one of the world's finest examples of a 'barrier beach'. And its name? 'Chesil' comes from the Old English '*ceosel*' meaning, unsurprisingly, shingle.

Looking out to sea, I concentrated on the sound of the pebbles as they rolled up and down the beach. Was there an echo? Hm, difficult to tell. On the sleeve of Martha and the Muffins' 1980 hit 'Echo Beach' is a map of this very shoreline. In any case, the beach in the lyrics is rumoured to be just a symbolic, faraway location. Turning to put the rustle of surf on pebbles behind me, I surveyed the low, crumbling cliffs for the reason I'd chosen this as a starting point. In truth, as already mentioned in the Introduction, I could have started anywhere on the Channel coast, since any point -- other than one actually on a watercourse -- can be regarded as being on a watershed, albeit a very local one. And yes, here was mine. Though virtually dry that day, the courses of two small streams clearly tumbled to the beach either side of a miniature headland. East of here other streams find their courses blocked by Chesil Bank, forcing them further eastwards to drain into the sea at Weymouth. To the west the first to merit the name 'river', the River Bride, flows more directly into the Channel at Burton Bradstock. But here at East Bexington, not only do these two streams sneak through, but also -- and crucially, given my intentions -- the watershed route sets off directly inland along a public bridleway.

Yes, *the* watershed route. For, having chosen the point of departure, I was now committed to only one route to Toller Down, where I'd pick up the Wessex Watershed, one route to Morgan's Hill, where the Watershed of England takes over, and one route to Kinder Scout in faraway Derbyshire.

'*I've* only committed to the first day, haven't I?' asked Julie, as I reminded her why we were at this particular point.

'Yes. You're shopping tomorrow, aren't you?'

'I am. So let's get today done then, before we're wrapped up in the mist.' So engrossed had I been with the shoreline that I'd completely failed to notice the disappearance of the southern horizon in a soupy swirl of white and grey.

As we regained the road, a single, sturdy walker -- the first we'd seen since Abbotsbury -- strode westward. Since she seemed both well-equipped and purposeful, as well as some thirty years younger than us, I was a little taken aback when she paused for a few words.

'Hallo,' she said, grinning with the confidence of a girl guide with all the badges. 'Chilly one today.'

'Let's hope the mist stays out to sea,' said Julie.

'Well, even if it comes ashore, you can't go wrong sticking to this path. Just keep the sea on your left -- well, mine anyway. For another five hundred and fifty miles or so.'

'Where are you going?' I asked.

'South-West Coast Path. Aren't you?'

We explained our plan. Looking us up and down, Girl Guide seemed to be assessing whether we were up to it. Whether I was, at least.

'Well,' she said. 'Take a tip from me. Don't try and do it all at once. Ten days at a time, that's my plan.'

'Blimey,' I said. 'We're only doing five days to start with. Some stages may be just a single day.'

'Ah, even more extreme than me. Or do I mean less extreme? Sounds like you're into unextreme sports. Ha.' This idea appealed to her so much she beat a roadside rock with her stick. 'Anyway, got to get on. Bridport beckons. Good luck with your waterworks.'

'Water*shed*.'

'Precisely.'

The South-West Coast Path starts just along the coast from here at Poole Harbour and ends, after an astonishing 1,014 kilometres, at Minehead in Somerset. Girl Guide, whose determined gait soon took her over a little hump and out of sight, must have been on day three or four. Our own path inland along a bridleway to the farm, however, was partially blocked by a small flock of sheep, the farmer and the trailer into which he and his dog were attempting to guide them. After a check via hand signals that it was all right for us to pass, our presence evidently disturbed the animals anyway and we left farmer and dog frustratingly farther back in their herding than when we'd arrived. Sorry.

*

What is now southern England was one day -- was for millions of days -- a seabed on which successive deposits of various materials were laid down one on top of the other. Naturally, the layer on top was the latest deposit. For millions of subsequent days, however, the whole caboodle was gradually tilted down towards the south-east and up towards the north-west, so that the subsequent actions of wind, rain, river and sea exposed not a neat sequence of young rocks followed by older rocks below, but rather a bewildering mixture of rocks at or near the surface, rocks laid down in quite different periods but now sitting cheek by jowl. Bewildering, that is, until you look at a geological map.

This reveals a series of easily discernible patterns. A dramatic band of deposits laid down in the Jurassic period, for example, stretches all the way from North Yorkshire to here in Dorset, where the sea has cut a cross-section through the sloping layers to form what is nowadays called the Jurassic Coast, a World Heritage Site. And we were on it. Our route inland, however, would soon take us onto the more easterly -- and therefore younger -- rocks from the Cretaceous period. While the Jurassic lands are dominated by one type of limestone (of which we'd see more further north), the Cretaceous lands are almost all about another: chalk.

One feature of chalk that was immediately brought home to us was its distinct tendency to form hills, in this case that paradise for ramblers, the Dorset Downs. Our ascent from the beach was particularly steep. And then steeper still. Pausing for breath among the bracken, bramble and gorse of Tulk's Hill, we turned to take in the view. The long, silver string of the Fleet tailed away towards Portland, but was then engulfed by the advancing mist. While our visible world was shrinking, the sound of waves breaking on the shingle seemed to have grown louder. Whether echoey or not, it's a significant sound. The prevailing wind is from the south-west (the right from our viewpoint) but, somewhat counter-intuitively, the sea has systematically sorted Chesil Beach's shingle from pebbles the size of peas at West Bay to those you can barely hold in one hand at Portland. In the west, therefore, the sound of surf rolling pebbles is a high-pitched whisper; here, towards the centre, a mid-pitched rustle; and in the east a low-pitched rumble. Even as we watched, however, Chesil Beach itself was swallowed up by the mist. Girl Guide would have to keep the sea on her left by sound rather than sight.

By the time we reached the embankment of the hill fort called Abbotsbury Castle -- confusingly so, as there's no such castle -- we too were quite enveloped in a February fog that shrank our world to some 30 metres in any direction. Not so unextreme after all. Although with some difficulty we managed to locate the ridge walk across Wears Hill and White Hill, part of the South Dorset Ridgeway, it was much like striding across the surface of a tiny green planet, at the bottom of its deep, damp atmosphere. Somewhere out there beyond the water droplets was, alas, 'the third best view in Britain', as recently selected by readers of *Country Life* magazine, but perhaps we should have taken the hint from the name of one of the houses we'd passed on the way up: Labour in Vain.

'I'm cold and wet and lost,' stated Julie.

'We're not lost,' I stressed, sounding more confident than I felt. 'And anyway, there's still things to see all around us.' Though her face was hidden inside a large, green hood, shiny with water droplets, Julie's posture told me she might be less than convinced.

'These humps on the left, for instance, are ancient burial mounds.' The hood looked left. 'And lying here on the chalk all around us are bits of the flint they'd have worked up into tools.' Hood down. Gloved hand picks up flint and casts it down again. From within the hood, no comment.

Desperate though I might have been to keep spirits up, this really was a classic ridge. From the neolithic to the Iron Age (approximately the last 4,000 years BC), with forests and marshland rendering Britain's valleys largely impassable, high, bare ridges along the watersheds offered relatively easy routes for communication. Trackways developed along these ridges, often linking defensive sites with 360-degree views over any source of danger. The sea being one of these sources, a location with (usually) such broad views to the south was doubly valuable and it's no surprise that the defensive site later called Abbotsbury Castle was constructed up here. It was first built in the Iron Age and, like the larger Maiden Castle a few miles to the east, occupied by the local Celtic tribe, the Durotriges. And yet, despite all its advantages, this site, like all Durotriges' territory, was taken over by the 2nd Legion of the advancing Roman army soon after 43 AD, offering less resistance than the far western and northern tribes in the Romans' new island colony.

Maybe their advance had been hidden in a fog similar to ours. For all we knew we could have circled our little planet several times, or even accidentally turned round and started walking in the opposite direction. Not that I mentioned the possibility to my damp companion. Mental note: a compass is worth its weight after all. Eventually, at the corner of a field, one signpost confirmed we were on the right track, for it marked the crossing of another long-distance path, the Macmillan Way. This is a coast-to-coast route created to raise public awareness of, and support for, the Macmillan Cancer Relief charity and running 467 kilometres from Boston, Lincolnshire, to its terminus just south of this spot.

At Bishop's Road, we dropped back down to Abbotsbury village -- and, thankfully, to the visible world.

*

Until chocolates began to arrive in tastefully plain packaging, Abbotsbury itself was what used to be called a 'chocolate-box village': all thatched roofs and cosy-looking pubs. In fact one of its thatches is claimed as the biggest in the world: that atop a medieval tithe barn linked to the now-ruined abbey from which the village gets its name. However, it was the two other chocolate-box images that warranted closer attention.

As for the pubs, the cosier choice was clearly the Ilchester Arms. Here we let a roaring fire burn the last of the mist from our memories, but my choice of bitter was, alas, 'off' on both our nights here and, having both asked for fish and chips with vegetables, were a tad surprised to be faced with cod, chips and... swede. Whether peas were also 'off' I don't know, but, having sampled this odd take on standard pub fare, Julie summed up our conclusion:

'I don't think it's a combination that will catch on.'

It wasn't until wandering back to the B&B on what had become a chilly, moonless winter's evening, that we experienced Abbotsbury's most startling feature -- and, oddly, one which no guidebook seems to mention: the village has no street lights at all. For townies such as us this meant a rare and glorious night sky so full of stars that we stood, faces lifted heavenwards, for a good ten minutes, totally transfixed. It appears that in 1944, when Abbotsbury found itself on a major route to ports of embarkation for D-Day, all its lamp standards had to be removed for American military vehicles to negotiate the village's tight bends -- and they were never replaced. Our landlady's confirmation that, by and large, the villagers can do very well without any street lighting is a timely one, for, at the time of writing, several pilot schemes to save money by switching off unnecessary lights are under way around the country. My vote goes to the big switch-off too.

Before the shops had closed, I'd kicked off my Cake Research Project (to establish whether anywhere in England made better locally named cakes than the Bakewell Puddings of my native Derbyshire) by popping into a local farm shop.

'Oh,' said the lady behind the counter, 'you should try our Dorset Knobs.' Each rolled 'r' confirmed her local credentials.

'Excuse me?'

'Knobs... well, they're half cake, half biscuit I suppose, but a word of advice.'

'I'm all ears.'

'Only eat 'em outdoors.'

Intrigued, I bought a packet for sustenance the next day.

Stage 2: Atacama of Cakes

White Hill to Powerstock Common

Dropping me the next morning at the point where we'd left the ridge, Julie didn't seem too disappointed to be missing what promised to be a brighter, drier day. She had before her, after all, a day's bargain-hunting in the two nearby towns of Weymouth and Dorchester. As I strode along the footpath to Portesham Hill, I too felt a tinge of excitement, for Stage 2 counted as another 'first day', the first on which I set out alone. Being lucky enough to feel relaxed either in or out of company, I even cast into the sharp Dorset air a joyous -- and probably tuneless -- rendition of the self-penned song, 'Awa' the Noo', which had signalled the start of all such recent journeys. After nervous glances in my direction, the heavily pregnant sheep beside the path soon returned to their munching, unimpressed.

Barely had I started out than I came across the first stone circle on the route. Though in scale it was less Stonehenge than stone rockery, I nevertheless drank in every word on the information board. Most of these features, it said, date from the neolithic period, but this one is relatively late, thought to have been put in place during the Bronze Age, and is so small that until recently you'd be hard pressed to see it at all, covered as it was by brambles. The board suggested that for its creators it held ritual rather than astronomical significance... though exactly what, of course, we just don't know.

Below me lay Portesham, which an Abbotsbury villager had told us some older locals pronounce 'Possum'. The siting of both villages, just below the chalk ridge, is typical of many along this part of the watershed route, coinciding with the level to which groundwater filters through the porous chalk before emerging as springs when it hits the older, impermeable clay beneath. A practical consequence for the walker is that the nearest pubs are often frustratingly off route and this stage, I already knew, would be entirely pub-free.

While the watershed line I'd traced on my Ordnance Survey map turned north, I'd already decided on a short diversion eastwards to Hardy's Monument, easily visible for miles around as the 'factory chimney' on Black Down. While nowadays I rarely read fiction (with more fascinating facts to learn than anyone can embrace in a single lifetime, what's the point?), as a teenager I enjoyed reading about the travails of other angst-ridden souls and Thomas Hardy's novels easily drew me in with their tortuous, fatalistic life stories and evocative Wessex landscapes.

As I approached the information board, a short woman with white hair and even whiter shoes was walking away from it. Stamping away actually.

'It's not the real Thomas Hardy, honey!' she shouted to no one in particular, but not to me, whom she ignored. As I reached the board, 'Honey' emerged from the undergrowth: a tall man, also white-haired and with a large camera slung around his neck.

'Uh?' he uttered.

'He's not the real one. He's some kinda sailor.'

By the time they reached me, I'd taken in the board's key information. On completion of this structure in 1845, Hardy the novelist would have been about five years old. This is a monument to Rear Admiral Sir Thomas Masterman Hardy, the one in Nelson's reputed 'Kiss me, Hardy' aboard HMS Victory, of which this Hardy had been commander at the Battle of Trafalgar in 1805. The famous phrase was not, as is sometimes implied, Nelson's last, for it's understood that before his death Nelson went on to discuss crucial operational matters with his close friend and colleague. Hardy's home was just down the hill at Portesham and when he died, 34 years later, having risen to become First Naval Lord at the Admiralty, this monument was erected through public subscription.

Honey and I nodded to each other. Brushing me aside, however, White Shoes made an accusing gesture at the board's drawing of the Admiral.

'There! See what I mean, honey?'

'He looks real enough to me,' he stated, raising an eyebrow toward me, but getting only a stare from his wife.

I offered some sympathy: 'Actually, I was expecting a monument to Thomas Hardy the novelist as well.' White Shoes turned, seeming to notice me for the first time, but said nothing. The tall grass rustled in the breeze.

'Um,' I went on, 'it's unusual to hear an American accent here in winter.'

Another stare.

'We're Canadian,' explained Honey.

'Oh, sorry. What an insult!'

'No problem. Are you a local?'

'Wrong accent for me too. No, I'm from Nottingham,' I said, choosing the nearest approximation that foreigners have usually heard of.

'Ah, as in Robin Hood,' he said, pulling the stress onto the 'Rob'. 'Now, he ain't real, right?'

'Well, the local tourist board seems to think he is.'

He laughed. 'Ah, that's because pounds sterling sure *are* real.'

'But a pound doesn't really weigh a pound.'

'Really?'

'Don't know actually. Just guessing.'

Whether this transatlantic banter was above the head of White Shoes or beneath her I couldn't tell, as she'd stamped off in the direction of their car. Honey cast me a confidential look.

'This admiral's put her in a bad mood for the morning now,' he said, turning to go.

Something I'd read popped into my head.

'There's a statue of Thomas Hardy in Dorchester.'

'The real one?'

'The real one.'

'Thanks,' he said, walking backwards to the car, where his wife was already tapping one white shoe. 'You have a real nice day, now.'

*

Whether my head was in a steamy novel or swotting up some schoolwork I can't remember, but for some reason, forty-odd years before, I'd opted out of the sixth-form field trip to Dorset. It's no wonder that the county's still the destination for so many school trips, for these hills are positively brimming over with geography and history. Hard on the heels of the previous day's tombolo and tumuli came today's dry valleys and barrows.

Before surface water permeated through rocks like chalk, it had formed valleys as normal, valleys that are now left either completely dry -- as in the Valley of Stones, which fell away to the left as I picked up the watershed again -- or supported occasional streams when the rains, usually winter rains, raised the water table high enough, as in nearby Winterbourne Abbas and Winterbourne Steepleton. The Valley of Stones gets its name from the ancient quarry from which, thousands of years ago, men transported most of the 'sarsen' (i.e. sandstone) stones used in West Dorset's stone circles.

As for the barrows, to reach these I needed to leave the road at the five-way junction above Littlebredy, where the River Bride rises, and head for another long ridge walk -- this time with fog-free views -- across Whatcombe Down and Martin Down. With the sky still bright, the distant farms and churches mere dots in the rolling green hills and a fresh westerly sweeping across the landscape, it felt a world away from the twenty-first century life that worries away in the valleys.

I was by no means the first to notice this remote atmosphere of the Downs, all the more remarkable for being so close to urban centres. Before this trip I'd read a vivid account of these hills by one Harold Massingham, a writer and ruralist more usually known as H.J. Massingham, whose prolific output in the 1930s included eloquent and informative guides to virtually the entire southern portion of my route. 'The unenclosed chalk landscape,' he wrote, '... bespeak[s] a calm, a remoteness from the tumult of our mortal days.' (Massingham H.J. *English Downland.*)

I might add, though, that the rolling, remote landscape also made it easy to imagine the time when these hilltops would have been the principal routes of our lives, the only link outward to the neighbouring tribe or inward for rare visitors with new ideas. Tripping over more graves helped too.

My map appeared to be sprinkled with snowflakes around here, so numerous are the symbols for barrows or tumuli or burial mounds -- all the same thing. Seeking them out on the ground, I identified round barrows, long barrows, bank barrows and bell barrows. None shaped like a wheel, alas. Probably the most impressive was the Long Bredy bank barrow, which towers above the living and measures nearly 200 metres in length, the second longest in Britain. It features, apparently, a mysterious V-shaped notch in the summit -- the mystery being that no one knows what it was for -- but, the wind having now strengthened, instead of blundering around to find the notch I settled down in the lee of the mound for some lunch. Out came the knobs.

When I was a student, one of the dafter challenges we set ourselves one evening was to see who could eat the most unadorned cream crackers without taking in liquid. Eight, nine, do you think? I remember barely managing two. Well, compared to the Dorset Knob, a cream cracker is a positive peatbog of moisture. Dry? The Dorset Knob is the Atacama of cakes. While shaped like a cake, it's as dry as a biscuit. Drier than most in fact. As I broke one of them open, the whole thing disintegrated in my hands, a gust of wind carrying it instantly towards Dorchester. The next one I did manage to get into my mouth, but found it took the bulk of my precious bottle of water to prevent lockjaw. Reading the packet, I learnt that Dorset farming folk used to pour hot tea and sugar on them at breakfast. 'Used to' I noted: that would be before they starting selling their entire production of knobs to gullible outsiders like me.

Fortunately I'd also bagged some marmalade sandwiches at breakfast and so, duly sustained, I dropped down from the downs back to twenty-first-century reality in the shape of the roaring A35. Quite why, in southern England, 'down' is usually up had puzzled me until I discovered that the Old English '*dūn*' means 'hill'. So does the Celtic '*brez*', so that Breedon on the Hill in Leicestershire, for example, means 'hill hill on the hill'.

*

Another down that was down and a longer down that was up brought me to a road junction called Two Gates, where two more uses to which we've put these high ridges over the years coincide. Roman roads are traditionally thought of as straight lines, orientated from viewpoint to viewpoint and ignoring the intervening relief. But in some places they too clung to high, dry ground and the wandering east-west minor road I'd just joined follows the line of the Roman route between two neighbouring *civitas* capitals, Durnovaria and Isca: Dorchester and Exeter, still county towns of neighbouring counties today. Though not a major route, this road would have been quite a different animal from the ridge-based trackways of the pre-Roman Britons and would probably have been the first paved and properly drained road the local tribes had ever seen.

The other, more modern use is the first example of what were to become familiar features all along the watershed route -- indeed, they regularly helped me pick out the way ahead: transmission masts. Naturally favouring the high ground, their most recent incarnation has been as mobile phone masts. Over the thirty years to 2011, Britain moved from having no commercial mobile phone network at all to hosting about 52,000 'base stations', of which two-thirds are on existing structures. By 2011 these supported more mobile phones than there were people.

On this stage, however, I was constantly drawn back to the distant past and the last prehistoric feature of the day was the most spectacular. Just along the old Roman road lies the magnificent fortified site of Eggardon Hill. By the time I'd staggered up the footpath that breaches its outer bank, I was astonished that I'd never heard of this magnificent place before. Astonished too by the view, today unimpeded by mist and some 70 years earlier described by Massingham as comprising 'tumbled dark-haired Devon' to the south-west, 'the sombre limestone ranges' of Somerset to the north, 'the mid-Dorset backbone' to the north-east and the sea to the south. (From Massingham H.J. *English Downland.*) All this still rang true.

So, as above Abbotsbury, the Iron-Age builders had made use of a hilltop that gave them almost 360-degree views but once again, although the site includes two earlier Bronze-Age barrows, nothing else of what lay within the hill fort remains. 'Fort', however, is a rather misleading term, since such settlements were less the homes of garrisons than homes for all local members of a tribe, fortified simply because of the threats of the time.

Having made the most of the southward views, for my guess was that this would be my last sea view from the watershed route until the Cotswolds, I returned to the lane and headed north to a rendezvous with Julie on the edge of Powerstock Common. While the watershed cuts straight across this ancient woodland, I could not, the route being blocked by the line of a disused railway. Earmarked for closure by Dr Beeching in 1963, this Bridport branch of the former Great Western Railway proved to have some unexpected staying power, surviving until 1975, when its demise made it one of the very last victims of the doctor's report. Showing even more longevity was Toller Porcorum station, a mile to the east, for it actually still exists... but not here. After being carefully dismantled, it was rebuilt as part of the Dart Valley Railway in Devon.

Biscuits aside, this had been an excellent day's walk. Having also met with success on her bargain-hunting in Weymouth and Dorchester, Julie was in good humour too as she picked me up and whisked us both to the first of three overnights with friends in the village of Leigh (pronounced 'Lie'), a few miles to the north. The tales of Leigh, Sir Walter Raleigh and a baby quail named Lazarus, however, are best left till after Stage 3.

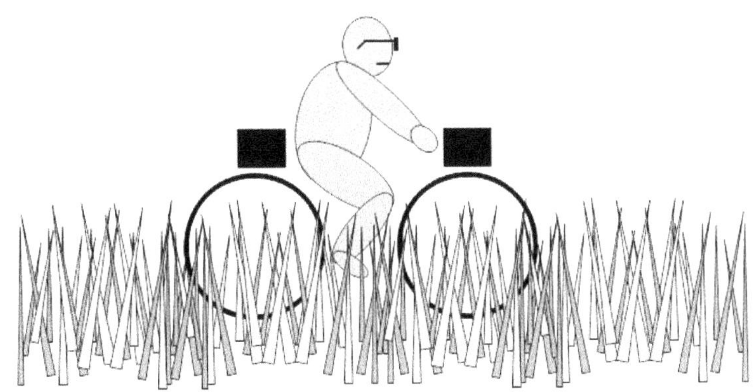

Stage 3: Lazarus the Quail

Powerstock Common to Blackmore Vale

The next day had been nominated my first cycling day -- a decision whose wisdom I'd already begun to question while pushing Tetley the bike up a second hill after only a quarter of an hour. While the watershed swung westwards from Powerstock Common to avoid the headwaters of the eastbound River Hooke, the lane most closely following it forged a dark, serpentine route through woodlands still dripping extravagantly with overnight rain. While a helicopter buzzed to and fro overhead, down in my dark brown tunnel I was making painfully slow progress, taking in with each short breath the heavy smell of sodden undergrowth.

Now and then I emerged on one of the bare hilltops that lay scattered about the woods like the tonsures of so many monks. At one, the eastern horizon was festooned with pylons: the BBC's World Service transmitter on Rampisham Down. I counted thirty-one. At another, emerging from the trees to the west was a spectacular view over the small town of Beaminster (pronounced 'Bemster'), surrounded by its cosy patchwork of fields and small farms. The owner of one of these, actor Martin Clunes, has described Dorset as an idyllic location in which to bring up a family. This is sentiment would have resonated with another parent whose visits to the county with her own children inspired a series of books that have sold an astonishing one hundred million copies in the 70 years since first being published: the 'Famous Five' stories of Enid Blyton. A few of those copies swallowed up my own pocket money.

Julian, Dick, Anne and George (nor forgetting Timmy the dog) would doubtless have found something suspicious in the name of the junction from which I was admiring the Dorset landscape that morning, but 'Dirty Gate' was notable only for the absence of any gate at all. It was here that my route headed off-road. Pushing Tetley along a rough track with more views over Beaminster to the left and hilltop fields to the right, I came across two damp tents strung out on a hedge and two damp gents energetically wringing out socks. Unable to think of anything but the obvious, I asked it.

'Hello. Rainy night?'

'Just a bit,' panted the balder of the two.

'Where are you walking?'

'Were about to start Hadrian's Wall.' This wasn't among the answers I was expecting. 'Third mate pulled out. Doing Wessex Ridgeway instead.' Seeing my raised eyebrows, he went on: 'Weren't literally stood with boot on wall. Few days notice. Change of plan.'

'How long's the Ridgeway?'

His friend, who had longer hair as well as slightly longer sentences, stepped in.

'It's about sixty miles end to end. This is day two of three. What about you?'

Unlike with Girl Guide on Chesil Beach, my attempted explanation this time produced only blank looks and resumed packing.

'In fact your ridgeway's probably following the watershed that comes up from Land's End,' I said, finally blathering to a full stop.

'Except it's not,' said Baldy. 'Not always. Crossed lots of streams yesterday. Watershed doesn't cross streams.'

'Oh, exactly,' I said, taken aback that they'd got the picture after all.

'Wet socks. Incident at babbling brook. Must get on. Your track turns right into the field up there. Stay dry.'

*

Turn right I did, stay dry I did not. Where the map showed a neat dashed line, red on white (a bridleway), the ground revealed a field of tall, dense grass, glistening with moisture and falling away steeply before rising to Toller Down beyond. Ideal on horseback, impossible on a bike. By the time I'd squelched past Kitwhistle Farm, the lower halves of both Tetley and myself were dripping wet. With a significant objective just a few hundred metres away, though, it was with head held high that I pedalled along the lane to the junction.

Not a road or rail junction, but a watershed junction. For here, just to the south of the A356, at the end of a track where a large, new barn stands on top of the ridge, is where my little local watershed from Chesil Beach finally joined one of the biggies marked on the map at the start of this book. En route from Land's End, the Wessex Watershed, dividing rivers bound for the Bristol Channel from those flowing to the English Channel, had zig-zagged across the Cornwall and Devon and, most recently, squeezed between the headwaters of the northbound Parrett and the southbound Axe before charging along the A356 itself to this spot. And right on cue the landscape opened out to the north for the first time since Eggardon Hill. Under a grey sky, the gentle green folds of the North Dorset Downs fell away towards the flat silver of Sutton Bingham Reservoir, straddling the border with Somerset, the dark misty shades of Yeovil beyond. My first sighting of a stream bound for the Atlantic was that forming the little valley below Urless Farm: the Yeo. From here on I'd be with the big boys, heading for the country's major watershed junction at Morgan's Hill in Wiltshire, about 80 kilometres away as the crow flies -- but a good many more as the watershed wiggles.

A more immediate target was lunch. Weary from uphill pushes and damp from cross-field trudges, I felt a spot of sustenance was in order. It had not escaped my notice that thus far no inn had graced my daily wanderings with its convenient presence. This was about to change, as the village of Evershot found its way onto the signposts. However, it was in order to see a particular sign, one of the old fingerposts that are still liberally sprinkled across the English countryside, that I first took a small diversion. It stood at a T-junction near Benville Bridge.

Now, when you read the word 'fingerposts' just now, did your mind automatically conjured up a black and white structure with black directions painted on a white background? This one was different. While the structure was the same, the directions were white on *red*. Indeed, village names and distances apart, the entire structure was red. There aren't many of these red posts left and the story goes something like this. When prison wardens, like almost all our ancestors, were less literate than we are now, in need of special help were those officers tasked with shepherding offenders across open country to the south-coast ports for transportation. The relevant signposts en route were therefore painted red. Now, when I first learned of this explanation, I swallowed it hook, line and fingerpost. It fell to my friend Levi, now resident in these parts, to point out its flaw. If the whole signpost were painted red, in what way could it help those unable to read the directions? Which way did it point them? Either the originals bore only a single red 'finger' or the whole tale is a load of Dorset baloney.

*

Evershot is a classic Dorset village, part of a classic estate (like Abbotsbury, the Ilchester estate), with classic Thomas Hardy connections and a classic pub, The Acorn Inn. Inside its classic bar, next to a classic skittle alley, sat a classically bewhiskered Dorset gentleman who, in a classic Dorset accent, responded to my request for advice on a tipple likely to revive a weary cyclist.

'You'd best be 'avin' a pint o' this cider from the barrel. Real cider they call it. Keep an eye on the barmaid, mind, she's new. Mek sure she leaves the bits at the bottom fer me. Best bits they are.'

Whether the accent was genuine or an in-joke with his fellow drinkers was immaterial to me, for the advice was spot on. After a draught or two of The Acorn's misty scrumpy and the return of life to the my legs, my gaze was drawn to an item which, even more than the skittles, the drink or the drinkers, marked this out as a pub that could be nowhere but England. Filling most of one wall was a large blackboard, bearing data both neatly written and colourfully presented. Its heading read 'Yard of Ale Records'.

Now, a yard glass of ale usually contains about 2.5 pints (about 1.4 litres). The times taken by customers to drain such a glass, as recorded on The Acorn Inn's blackboard, fell mostly between one and three minutes. Impressive enough in my view. The shortest time though was that posted by one Jamie (of England) on 27th July 2007. On that day this doyen among drinkers downed two-and-a-half pints of ale in an almost unbelievable 10 seconds. That's one zero. As long as it took me to type this sentence.

And yet it wasn't even this stunning record that made the board so typically English. It was the three letters entered against several names in place of a time: for example against Maxine (of

France) and Cameron (of England). The letters were 'P.I.A.', translated in a footnote as 'Puked in Action'.

Where else would you find such gruesome failure recorded with such meticulous honour?

*

Evershot's Thomas Hardy connections include the inn itself, represented in *Tess of the D'Urbervilles* as The Sow and Acorn, where Tess spent the night, and, more surprisingly, a building I passed on my way out of the village called Summer Lodge. Set back from the road, it's now a hotel but as a private house in the nineteenth century it was enlarged by Thomas Hardy the architect. No, this is not a third TH but the very same person as the author: it's a rare novelist that doesn't need a day job and in his early years this was Hardy's.

The breezy run eastwards along what would for me be the last of the Dorset Downs and then north into Blackmore Vale was uneventful, though featured yet more northward views along the next day's route, beyond Sherborne and up to Wincanton in Somerset. While this first day's cycling had clocked up less than 30 kilometres, it was nevertheless a slightly aching cyclist that trudged onto the gravelled drive of a smallholding in the village of Leigh, to be welcomed by Julie, who'd dropped me off at Powerstock Common and by our friends Kate and Levi, who were graciously putting us up for three nights.

*

Over 400 years before, Queen Elizabeth I had presented some of her land in Blackmore Vale to the soldier and explorer Sir Walter Raleigh, one of her favourites at the time and a West Country man. Raleigh's period in the queen's favour, however, was soon to be over since, having failed to ask her permission before marrying one of her ladies-in-waiting, he found himself in the Tower of London. Also short-lived was his ownership of much of the land in the vale, but one of his properties, a farm in Leigh, was eventually to find its way into the caring hands of Kate and Levi.

The farmhouse itself, believed to have been built shortly after Raleigh sold the land on which it still stands, is a solid, homely building, at the centre of which sits a large kitchen, at the centre of which stands a handsome table, at the centre of which that evening was placed a huge tajine. Delicious though Kate's cooking was, it was not the centre of attention, for this honour fell to a transparent box on the Aga. In the box were about twenty little animals the size of large bees, half of them also the colour of bees, the other half bright yellow. Rolling around, testing their springy legs and perfecting their sharp, plaintive squeaks, these were two-day-old quails.

The quails' location on the Aga, I should stress, was away from the source of heat, but sufficiently warm for their temporary home. Plan A had actually been for Kate and Levi to join us on Chesil Beach for the first day's walk, but this bouncy batch of babies had intervened. Being a townie, I'd never seen a quail before, young or old, alive or dead, and was astonished at how tiny they were.

'Three didn't hatch out,' said Kate after we'd eaten, 'but we left the eggs in a bag anyway.'

'In fact,' added Levi, jumping up, 'I'd forgotten. I'd better go and throw them out.'

Two minutes later he was back, cradling in his hands a very, very tiny bird, feathers all matted, eyes closed and legs dangling in the wrong direction -- but clearly alive.

'Late arrival! Quick -- open the box!'

Lazarus, as he was instantly named, was placed carefully among his brothers and sisters, but another two minutes later Levi was issuing more urgent instructions:

'Open the box again! They're trying to eat him! Small plastic dish! Quick! No, wait. Holes in the dish! Yes, good. Back in!'

So Lazarus spent the night in a small intensive care ward within the already quite intensive care ward of his siblings. The next morning he'd opened his eyes and gained the use of one of his legs. The day after he gained most of the use of the other leg and was released to explore the outer box. On the third day Lazarus died. Though he didn't rise again, Kate and Levi felt that he'd had as comfortable and interesting a short life as anyone could have offered.

And who could argue?

*

While it boasts a sizeable population of over five hundred, Leigh no longer has a pub and so our after-dinner exercise had us walking over to the neighbouring village of Chetnole. As if I needed it, we'd already been out on the district's dense network of public footpaths before dark to Leigh's highest point, where lie the remains of something vary rare in England: something that, I have to admit, I'd never even heard of. It was a mizmaze.

What's the difference between a maze and a labyrinth? A most significant one apparently. While a maze is a complex pattern with branches at which decisions have to be made, a labyrinth is exactly the opposite: a pattern that, however intricate, comprises a single path leading inexorably from the edge to the centre. Now it gets complicated. A mizmaze is a pattern cut in turf, i.e. much smaller in scale than the famous hedge mazes around the world, and there are only eight of them left in England -- or fewer, depending on definitions. However, the mizmaze patterns that remain intact look remarkably like labyrinths, begging the question: are they mazes at all?

In the case of the 700-year-old mizmaze at Leigh, however, this question is academic since, as I was disappointed to discover, what's left is neither a maze nor a labyrinth, but simply a mound in the corner of a field. We were 200 years too late, for the pattern of paths had apparently already eroded by 1800. Like another disappointing Dorset 'sight' I'd passed after Evershot, what seems to keep the Leigh mizmaze in local guide books is the hint that some supernatural goings-on have been linked to it. With the mizmaze it's an alleged link to a witches' coven, while at the other it's said that the ghost of a murderer who 'sold his soul to the devil' wanders nearby. The latter, a stone post called the 'Cross and Hand' on Batcombe Hill, had turned out to be, well, just an old post: no cross, no hand and of course, no ghost. The simple fact that no one knows its original purpose seems to have shifted someone's imagination into overdrive. Well, I suppose the pages of the Dorset tourist guides have to be filled with something.

Much more worthy of close attention is The Chetnole Inn. Opposite the churchyard, next to open fields, with low-beamed bars, rough wooden tables and friendly staff, what more could you want from an English pub? Oh yes, they also keep some beer. As a free house, it usually has a good choice of real ales, confirmed Levi, recommending the Butcombe Bitter -- and stirringly bitter it was: as refreshing a pint as you could want after a brisk walk.

Since he and Kate had only recently moved to Dorset from the same Leicestershire village Julie and I call home, we were keen to know how they were finding life down here.

'Instantly accepted, I think you'd say,' commented Kate. 'There's none of that "natives and newcomers" thing you get up your way. Everyone seems to be treated the same in Leigh. Mind you, most seem to have been incomers at some point anyway.'

'One thing's odd,' said Levi. 'You know how, in Leicestershire, everyone's keen to stress they live in a village, even if it's really a suburb or even a town -- trying to keep the property prices up, I suppose -- well, down here, it's the opposite. You came through Beaminster today, didn't you?'

'Saw it from the hill. Small place in the valley?'

'Yes. No more than three thousand people, half the size of the village you two live in, but they call it a town. Towns have status round here.'

'In America it'd be a city,' I added.

'In America everything's a city.'

*

While villages across the country are racing to turn off street lighting to save energy, no such problem exists here as it's never been installed; hence we were glad to have brought torches and umbrellas as we wandered back along the lane to Leigh in single-file, but still nattering.

'Julie!' called Kate from the front. 'That cruise we went on wasn't with Saga, was it?'

'Course not,' she called back, 'we're not that old yet. Why?'

'Well, with us having an Aga in our kitchen here, Levi was wondering if he's now got through three of the four ages of man.'

'What are they?'

'Lager, Aga, Saga and gaga.'

A voice from the back: 'And with much more of this Dorset rain seeping into my head, I'll soon have ticked the last one off too.'

*

('The Four Ages of Man' are from the *Tottering-By Gently* cartoon strip by Annie Tempest.)

Stage 4: Equipment Failure

Blackmore Vale to Jack White's Gibbet

At least the timing was good.

There are cyclists who mend punctures in a matter of minutes, their ride barely interrupted. To repair my last one, however, had taken about four days. My special habit is, after mending the first puncture, to create a second while forcing the tube back inside the rim. So spotting this one before breakfast came as something of a relief, giving me two hours and three encouraging spectators -- just enough to get the job done.

That the steady Dorset rain had also set in again before departure from Leigh alerted me to don the appropriate waterproofs in Kate and Levi's warm, dry kitchen. Waterproof by name, water-permeable by nature. By the time I'd pulled into a bus shelter at Longburton, no part of me was remotely dry and, more ominously, the damp had started to creep over the plastic-encased maps on my handlebars as surely as an incoming tide over a sandbank.

Having only recently bought the map case, I found in its permeability yet more grist to my anti-equipment mill. Some people love sports equipment. The French, for instance, wouldn't consider taking up any activity that didn't offer endless kit-buying opportunities, especially if the kit *de rigeur* changes with every season. Personally I'd prefer a pastime that requires no equipment at all. Meditation is good, walking not bad. Shame that bike rides require some kind of bike.

Having dried as much of me as decently feasible in a public shelter and then swaddled the maps in a towel, I packed up and resumed the traverse of Blackmore Vale under thinning, rising clouds. It's essentially a clay vale mixed in with better-drained areas of limestone, the same limestone that forms much of the vast Jurassic ridge stretching from the Dorset coast (just west of my starting point), via the Cotswolds and the East Midlands to Yorkshire. Turning right on the Sturminster Newton Road opened up a view over the east of the vale, a low, rolling landscape drained by the Caundle Brook and given over mostly to pasture -- deep green, twinkling pasture that morning. Taking a left in North Wootton along the narrow lane to Haydon presented a similar scene to the west, with clearing skies coming in from the lower Yeo valley in Somerset. While at first counter-intuitive, the fact that the watershed route should cross a vale at all is therefore explained: not every stream rises in uplands. As would become clear further into the journey, sometimes there simply aren't any real hills around at all.

Just a mile or two beyond the woods that began to close in from the north lay the main town serving this part of Blackmore Vale: Sherborne. While locals are proud to remind visitors that Sherborne has not one, but two castles, neither would have been much use when this area was invaded...

*

When was the last successful invasion of England? 1066? That's what I used to think... until, brushing up on my English history, I was reminded of a more recent one. Since joining the Wessex Watershed at Toller Down, I'd also been following, more or less, the route taken by a foreign army marching and riding out of the west towards their target: London. The year was 1688.

It reads like the plot of a soap opera written while the character-naming committee was on holiday.

Catholic King Charles had been forgiven by his Protestant subjects for the excesses of his father, also Charles, but the younger Charles failed to produce an heir. So when this Charles died, his younger brother James, another Catholic, became king. Charles had, however, produced an illegitimate son, also James, and, cheesed off by the accession of his uncle, James the bastard led a rebellion, only to be easily defeated by James the king, who then proceeded to behave a little like his father Charles by suppressing his Protestant subjects. However, as he'd been equally unsuccessful in the male heir department, they were prepared to await his demise... until his queen, Mary, unexpectedly produced a baby boy. Despite rumours that she'd simply been handed the baby, the latter, also named James, duly took his place as first in line to the throne. It gets even more complicated...

Noticing that all Charleses and Jameses seemed to end up Catholics, the English Protestants scoured the family tree for another name. They didn't have to scour far. The king's late sister Mary had married William, a Dutch Protestant, also now deceased, but the couple had had a son, another William and another Protestant, who had married another Mary, yet another Protestant and, strangely enough, a daughter of James the king, to boot. Well, a man with two kings for uncles and a princess for a wife sounded royal enough to the English, who promptly invited William and Mary to leave the Netherlands, invade England and be jointly crowned. They accepted. Glorious!

But is invasion by invitation really an invasion at all? Well, for two reasons it seems to me that it is. Firstly, unless the Netherlands has moved in the last three hundred years, the shortest route from there to London is straight up the Thames estuary, not via the back door, i.e. Devon. Secondly, it's documented that William of Orange landed in Brixham with fifty warships, 7,000 horses and an army of about 20,000 men: rather more than needed to serve tea and biscuits en route. The apparent fact that there was little opposition between Devon and the capital doesn't mean that England hadn't been invaded, just that the English knew which side their bread was buttered.

William's army made its way to London in several contingents and by several routes, but at a number of locations the routes converged, creating temporary HQs, and one of these was Sherborne, where William himself lodged with Lord Bristol. The reason that neither of Sherborne's castles would have been of much use against the invading army is that, while the old twelfth-century castle had recently been destroyed by the Parliamentarians in the Civil War, the new one, though built for Sir Walter Raleigh, was occupied by the Digby family. And, far from resisting the would-be king, the Digbys actually invited William over to the castle and entertained him.

*

Reminders of the 1600s seem to come thick and fast around here. Pedalling through Purse Caundle, I found it difficult to associate this unnervingly quiet and pristine village with the all-action life of one of its sons, Peter Mews, born here in 1619.

An Oxford graduate, Mews was made a Royalist captain in the Civil War, in which he received about thirty wounds, was taken prisoner and eventually escaped to Holland. Here, in Scotland and in England, as a master of disguise he became a valuable secret agent for the Royalists, at one point just avoiding being hanged -- but then, somewhat incongruously, was appointed Bishop of Bath and Wells and subsequently of Winchester. When the Duke of Monmouth ('James the bastard' in the soap opera plot) led a revolt, Mews went back to war on the side of the king, but then pleaded for clemency for the rebel. Buried in Winchester Cathedral, Peter

Mews led a life that seems less soap opera than swashbuckling film script: 'The Battling Bishop'?

*

Just as I crossed my first county boundary, from Dorset into Somerset, I set eyes on something for the first time in England: a cowboy. Two cowboys, to be precise. While I've seen cattle herded on foot, from a Land Rover and from a quad bike, never had I witnessed this. In Somerset's very first field, just after the bridge over the Yeo, a slow-moving herd of Friesians was being squeezed towards the gate onto the road by one eager sheepdog and two lads on horseback. The wild west of England.

You're quite right: on the watershed route I shouldn't really be crossing a river. But an empty water bottle had prompted a diversion to the nearest settlement and this was Milborne Port. Now, even I could see that here the Yeo was barely wide enough to accommodate a Pooh stick, let alone any commercial craft, and so why the 'Port'? While too heavy to carry around with me, at home the *Oxford Dictionary of British Place Names* is always close by and it reveals that 'port' is Old English not only for 'harbour', but also for 'gate' and 'market town'.

'I've just arrived in this port through that port. Could you tell me where the port is?'

Maybe no one asked directions in those days. The days in question were between the fifth and eleventh centuries when the vast majority of current English place names were coined by the Angles, Saxons and Jutes, the invading Germanic tribes whose languages developed here into 'Anglo-Saxon', referred to by the dictionary as 'Old English'. Other places with Old English names that I'd already encountered include Evershot ('wild boar corner'), Leigh ('clearing') and Sherborne ('bright stream'). However, other origins do crop up in this part of the country: for example, Frome is Celtic for 'brisk' and Toller Porcorum combines the Celtic for 'hollow stream' with the Latin for 'of the pigs'). In the case of Latin suffixes (Porcorum, Intrinseca, Magna, Parva and so on), the origin almost always turns out not to be Roman, as I would have guessed, but medieval, being ecclesiastical suffixes to distinguish two places of the same name. In one local instance, however, the admirable dictionary admits defeat. While it raises a few possibilities, it simply does not know what's meant by Purse Caundle.

*

One of the many sounds that people will associate with a journey through the English countryside is the timeless banter that accompanies cricket commentary on the BBC's *Test Match Special*. Whether from a car radio or, until the spread of earphones, from the speaker of a transistor, the jovial tones of Johnners, Aggers and their chums have regularly swum into and out of my hearing for more years than I care to remember. As I took a short break on the village green at Charlton Horethorne, the memory of one commentary in particular popped into my head.

Being in England, rain stops play at some point in almost every home test, giving the commentators ample opportunity to follow virtually any train of thought that occurs. One wet afternoon a few years ago (I think India were England's opponents), one of them mentioned that he'd recently spent the night in a Norfolk village whose name sounded as if it should be that of an English cricket captain -- Melton Constable -- and wondered if any listeners had come across any similar place names. This seemed to strike a chord, for scores of calls, e-mails and texts filled the rainy afternoon with improbable teams featuring such fictional players as Kingsley Green, Roydon Hamlet and Winfrith Newburgh. (Having been unable to track down any reference to this broadcast, I offer these examples just from memory -- they may not be the ones actually used on the BBC.)

Well, Charlton Horethorne seemed to me like a very plausible captain of a fictional WCC (Watershed Cricket Club). A casual glance at my rapidly drying map immediately threw up his wicket-keeper from a village just north of here: Bratton Seymour. The next four hundred miles revealed, player by player, the whole team and, for any reader with a similarly warped imagination, here it is, in sequence of the batting line-up:

1. Charlton Musgrove (Somerset), steady opening bat and reliable slip fieldsman.

2. Baddesley Clinton (Warwickshire), aggressive opening bat.

3. Charlton Horethorne (Somerset), captain and accomplished all-rounder.

4. Miles Green (Staffordshire), specialist batsman.

5. Sibford Gower (Oxfordshire), David's cousin, similar style.

6. 'Fenny' Compton (Warwickshire), Denis's low-lying grandson and would-be all-rounder.

7. Bratton Seymour (Somerset), reliable wicket-keeper and less reliable lower-order batsman.

8. Rushton Spencer (Staffordshire), seam bowler, past his prime.

9. Scot Hay (Staffordshire), seam bowler and dangerous big hitter.

10. 'Maiden' Bradley (Wiltshire), relentless spin bowler renowned for bowling maidens.

11. Clyffe Pypard (Wiltshire), fast seamer but hopeless with the bat. A classic number eleven.

*

While pushing Tetley up Charlton Hill to regain the line of the watershed on the ridge, I was reminded by the name of a house that, though now north of Dorset, I was still well within the south-west as far as pronunciation was concerned. It was called 'Charn'

Hill. Though both Dorset and Somerset have lost their 'shire' suffix, their names have a similar origin: the 'set' in both is from the Old English 'sǣte' (settlers), being those around Dorchester and Somerton respectively.

Such trivia would have been of little interest to another man struggling up the same escarpment 360 years before. Yes, that makes it those busy 1600s yet again. This time it was 1651 and the third and final phase of the Civil War had ended with the Battle of Worcester, a decisive defeat for Charles, son of the executed Charles I and yet, while declared Charles II in Edinburgh, by no means king in the *de facto* English republic. Having escaped with his life from the battle, he set out on a long and circuitous route which eventually ended six weeks later with his safe arrival in France. The route of the would-be king's flight through England is well documented and has been commemorated in a waymarked path of nearly a thousand kilometres. At Charlton Hill, he would have been en route from Trent House near Sherborne, where he'd been in hiding for some time, to his eventual embarkation at Shoreham in Sussex. Included on the waymarker of the Monarch's Way is a representation of the *Surprise*, the vessel on which Charles was to cross the Channel; and here at the top of the hill, where our routes diverged, was my first sighting of it. The first of many, as it turned out.

The brow of the hill brought my own surprise: a view of the destination not of today's stage, but of the next. Protruding from a distant wooded hill, some 15 kilometres to the north, was the tiny stick that must have been King Alfred's Tower, on the border of Somerset and Wiltshire. In a long-distance bike ride along the west coast of Scotland, I'd become familiar with taking in from the top of mountain passes a panorama of the challenges to come. Here in this gentler landscape it was not what I'd expected, but had no time to dwell on this as an invigorating but hazardous freewheel down the escarpment's dip slope soon brought me to the village of Holton whose pub seemed pre-destined to be a late lunch stop, lying as it was in the shelter of Hunger Hill.

*

Since the recession that began in 2007, British pubs had been closing at an alarming rate, including some that had survived for centuries. By the time of this journey, while the number of closures had fallen to less than fifty a week nationwide, the effects of the recession were still clear on those that had survived. I'm talking the contentious issue of trendification.

Although the English pub has for years depended on the traditional male drinker as a mainstay of its business, this had recently been a declining market and, adaptability being the survivor's watchword, new markets have been sought. Even before the recession pub food -- beyond the cellophane-wrapped cheese roll in a glass case on the bar -- had become the norm, rather than the exception it had been in my childhood. Now the decor had come under scrutiny. For some reason, red floral carpets and worn, leather-seated benches appeal neither to the under-forties nor to that huge, previously untapped market: the English woman.

Although I'd never set foot in the Old Inn before, I instantly knew it'd just had the typical makeover of a 'gastro-pub', as inns specialising in food had become known. Bland grey walls, tasteful pictures, comfy chairs and even, where the reassuring set of wooden hand pumps should have been, an array of tall, shiny metal tubes dominating the bar.

'Hello,' I said to the smart young barman, as I flung my helmet onto the pristine bench. 'Do you do snacks?'

He lifted a tastefully printed menu from the rack.

'We do courgette potato cake, sir, with cucumber raita, ...'

My hungry heart sank.

'... seared scallop, chorizo and grapefruit salad, ...'

My head drooped.

'... a very fine seafood risotto, ...'

'Wait, let me look.' Right at the bottom was a dish free from foreign words. 'Ham, egg and chips please.'

Hearing other customers arriving, I diplomatically slid my cycling gear under the table, the better to remain inconspicuous. Not, however, inconspicuous enough. Entering with some gusto, a large gentleman a little older than me settled at a bar stool and ordered his usual before glancing in my direction.

'Got two rocket trout last night,' he said, in a standard Home Counties accent and as though we'd known each other all our lives.

'Do you mean rainbow trout?' I asked. It was the obvious response.

'What? No, trout from Rocket.'

'Is that a village near here?'

'What are you talking about? Two trout from Rocket the fisherman. They'll make a tasty meal tonight.' With this he examined me more closely. 'Sorry, old chap, thought you were someone else.'

By this time my food had arrived, as had the trout-owner's drink.

'What are you drinking?' he asked me.

'Bitter. Not sure which to be honest.'

'Ah, when I come in here I always have one of my "five a day".'

'Fruit juice?'

I received a withering look.

'Cider, man! Actually I think a pint may count as two of my five a day.'

*

Despite its trendification, the Old Inn at Holton dished up an excellent ham, egg and chips to see me safely and literally up Hunger Hill and on a long excursion off the watershed to catch a train from Castle Cary back to the warm, dry kitchen at Leigh. A rather muddy Tetley was garaged once again in the back of the car, as my temporarily mud-free boots were extracted for the next day: a short walking stage. Short but not straightforward, as it turned out.

Stage 5: Battling Against Somerset

Jack White's Gibbet to Alfred's Tower

'Bye! Do talk to strangers.'

To meet the demands of Julie's usual parting exhortation would today be harder than usual, the iffy weather keeping those with any sense indoors. As she drove away from the junction called Jack White's Gibbet I raised my umbrella, for today's stage would be on foot, and looked around. No gibbet... unless Jack had been strung up on a 'Give Way' sign or a telegraph pole.

I'd finally managed to push myself out of the 1600s and it was now 1730. A hot Wednesday in August to be precise. Carrying an urgent letter for a local gentleman, one Robert Sutton called in for refreshment at the Sun public house, just down the road from here in Wincanton. There he got into an animated conversation with Jack White on the subject of recent crime in the area: footpads, attacks on the mail coaches, the new judge at Taunton assizes... After far too much drink, Sutton finally remembered his mission and, now accompanied by White, re-emerged on the road and set off westwards. Neither would ever return.

Soon, overcome by heat and drink, White collapsed under a

hedge and fell asleep, but before long, lost without his guide, Sutton returned, aroused White and they continued as far as this very crossroads, just south of Bratton Seymour. Here they met two ladies and an incident occurred, the details of which remain a mystery, but the result of which was that one of the men once again lay in a ditch, but this time it was Sutton and he was not asleep but dead and mutilated by the hands of Jack White. At Taunton Assizes, White was found guilty and, in an unusual judgement, condemned to be hung in chains at the scene of the murder. Whether he died before or after he was strung up on the gibbet as a deterrent to others is unknown. To this day the junction is called Jack White's Gibbet.

Until I came across this case I'd confused a gibbet with a gallows. While a gallows was a structure on which someone was hanged (until dead), a gibbet was one on which they were hung (already dead) as a deterrent to others. One verb, two meanings, two past tenses. The tale also added a gruesome feature to my mental list of those more likely to be seen on a watershed than elsewhere, although spotting an actual gibbet in England is nowadays unlikely -- the last recorded gibbeting being in 1832.

Jack White's body would certainly have been seen for miles around as the land falls away from this low hill in all directions. Skipping on and off the grass verge to avoid heavy traffic, I too fell away as quickly as I could down the A371 as far as the Holbrook House roundabout.

*

Mallet, Shrapnel and Farewell. A vivid threat of more violence? An eccentric firm of solicitors? No, these are just some of the people who, over 700 years, lived on the estate that is now Holbrook House Hotel. By the time he lived here in the early nineteenth century, Major General Henry Shrapnel had already invented the horrendous anti-personnel device that bears his name. It was beside the hotel that I finally escaped the rather less horrendous but still uncomfortable A371.

From here the watershed -- and I -- wandered around the northern outskirts of Wincanton, one of those small English towns whose name is widely known but whose location many would be hard pressed to pinpoint. Its familiarity is founded on two local businesses.

The name of one you've probably seen out of the corner of your eye on Britain's motorway network: the blue and white logo of Wincanton plc, 'a leader in delivering supply chain solutions' -- or, in everyday English, a transport company. It was in the eighties and nineties that this type of commerce-speak seeped into Britain from America. Working in the marketing department of a multi-national, I saw it happen before my own eyes. One day we were selling computer equipment, the next we were 'delivering network solutions' -- to people who didn't even know they had 'network problems' to be solved. In today's Britain, if you don't 'deliver' something in the course of your job, you're nobody. Whether the irony is appreciated by people who actually do deliver something -- Wincanton's truck drivers, for example -- I don't know. At any rate, the company isn't actually based in Wincanton any more; they've moved up the road to Chippenham.

The other may ring a bell from television: *Racing from Wincanton*. The fact that the racecourse is bang on the watershed is no coincidence, since the last news that punters want to hear is 'Racing cancelled due to waterlogged course'. It was not a race day when I passed by. Or tried to pass by...

*

While the course itself was out of bounds, I didn't particularly want to battle with the traffic on another main road out of Wincanton and so had opted for a path that my Ordnance Survey map showed cutting across to the north of the racecourse through Moorhayes Farm. As I approached the farm, a short man with a long stick was heading into the fields and, not wanting either to trespass or to encounter any dogs, I checked my route with him. As it happened, he told me, I was wrong. The path actually went off at a crossroads just up the lane from the farm, came back down the old railway and only then set off over the hill. However, so far as he was concerned, I could take the farmyard route if I wanted.

'The way's clear,' he stressed, 'and there's no dog.'

So, as Mr Stick entered the field, I crossed the farmyard -- only to find the route beyond definitively barred by a barbed-wire fence. Turning back, I found myself staring at an equally definitive contradiction of his other assertion, in the form of a dog the size of a goat barely twenty metres away and now barking frantically at yet another gullible hiker sent to his gruesome death by nice Mr Stick. Fortunately, the headline-writers on the Wincanton Bugle would have to find another story that week, as the slavering hound was already at the limit of his taut chain.

Heart beating fast nevertheless, I scurried out of the farmyard pretty sharpish and continued up the lane while cardiac normality returned. With nothing, however, that could be described as a crossroads appearing either on map or ground, I turned back after about half a mile, to trudge back down the lane towards the outskirts of Wincanton, umbrella raised against a sharp shower. With three black marks against his name, Mr Stick, now renamed Mr Mud, can think himself lucky he made no further appearance. I'd wasted about an hour.

And yet he deserved only teo of the black marks. Back home a few days later I once again looked up the website that I'd used for my maps and, better late than never, learnt a useful lesson. While the Ordnance Survey's own site had recently withdrawn the most useful scales from public access, www.streetmap.co.uk still had them and it was their 1:50,000 scale that I'd used for all my maps, printing out each day's route and covering it with notes before setting out. While this 1:50,000 scale showed the public footpath crossing the farmyard, the more detailed 1:25,000, evidently more up-to-date, showed exactly what Mr Stick had described. I'd just been too lazy to walk far enough. Lesson learnt: different scales, different revisions.

Somerset 1 Guise 0.

*

Still cursing the locals on the day, though, I eventually did cross the disused railway (the old Somerset and Dorset or, as it was perhaps not entirely affectionately known, the 'Slow and Dirty') before dodging the traffic again on the main road past the racecourse. Surprisingly for a non-race day, it seemed to be humming with activity, the reason for which was soon revealed by its hoardings: of course, this being the twenty-first century, Wincanton is 'more than just a racecourse'.

Quieter lanes and paths awaited and it was in the shelter of low willows beside a gurgling brook that I settled down to my packed lunch, the highlight of which was a huge slice of Kate's home-made Dorset Apple Cake. Nothing could have offered a greater contrast to the dusty Dorset Knob of Day Two. This was a rich sponge cake, speckled with small pieces of apple and ground almond and topped with sprinkled sugar. Springy as a Dorset meadow, it melted in the mouth as a good cake should. Strictly speaking, of course, watershed picnics should not take place beside watercourses, but this brook, bound for the North Sea, was only yards from the watershed itself. Well fed and watered, I emerged into a drier afternoon, the sky clearing to reveal once again the protrusion of King Alfred's Tower from a woody horizon. This time, however, it was only about 3 kilometres away.

Not only the weather but also the path had improved. Up to now I hadn't been particularly impressed by Somerset County Council's maintenance of their public footpaths: compared with Dorset's, they seemed abnormally overgrown, with dilapidated stiles and waymarking that was either vague, worn-out or simply absent. From the suitably named Walk Farm onwards, however, all this changed. Paths were wider, undergrowth beaten back, waymarks freshly nailed, stiles and gates positively shining. For this I offered thanks to a sixteenth-century poet.

*

Born in London, John Leland's early life was, for a well-educated man of the time, not particularly remarkable, except for a short term of imprisonment following some unwise remarks whilst a student at Cambridge. Variously a linguist, poet, antiquarian and chaplain, Leland had reached the age of about thirty-five before he suddenly took an interest in local history and geography. It was to become an all-encompassing passion. Over six years and about five journeys, he traversed southern Britain again and again, making copious notes on what he observed, eventually presenting them to King Henry VIII in a volume called *New Year's Gift*.

Self-effacement was clearly not among Leland's palette of characteristics, for in the book he revealed to his king that: 'there is almoste nother cape, nor bay, haven, creke or peers, river or confluence of rivers, breches, watchies, lakes, meres, fenny waters, montagnes, valleis, mores, hethes, forestes, chases, wooddes, cities, burges, castelles, principale manor placis, monasteries, and colleges, but I have seene them.' (from Leland, John *Leland's Itinerary in England* (1907, G. Bell and Sons)). That certainly knocks my own little wanderings into a cocked hat.

Most of Leland's itinerary is not known in detail, but here in Somerset a 45-kilometre trail follows an approximation of one local section and it's that which I'd joined, along a stretch that coincides with another part of the familiar Macmillan Way, from Abbotsbury to Boston. Together we entered Newpark Wood, part of the vast Stourhead Estate, whose ownership is shared by the National Trust and the Hoare family, resident here since the early eighteenth century.

At first the way was obvious. Following two parallel wheel tracks that pierced deep into the dark greens of the mixed woodland, I was soon panting as the route became steeper. But by the time the track had begun to fork, the trail's little round waymarkers had gone AWOL and I found myself peering at a map of too small a scale, in light too dull, among trees too identical. In a mischievous piece of bad timing, King Alfred's Tower, which had dominated the view northward for so long, had now decided to to disappear just when it was needed. However, knowing that it stood on top of the hill I was climbing, I decided at each unmarked fork to select the steeper option. Little good it did me. Even though I was eventually within earshot of the road, my path had started an ominous descent. Somewhere above me Julie would be waiting in a car park, but since my mobile signal had also made its excuses and left, I was unable to let her know how close I was.

Backtrack, reselect, retry. Backtrack, reselect, retry. Just as my latest route was about to go the way of the others, i.e. downhill, I spotted through a gap in the undergrowth the unmistakable shimmer of puddle on tarmac. Ignoring all paths now, I ploughed a straight furrow through damp fern and prickly bramble to emerge, sodden, muddy and scratched, onto a narrow country lane.

Somerset 1 Guise 1.

After shaking unwanted pieces of the county from my not-very waterproof, I looked around, hoping to figure out where I'd emerged... when it suddenly became clear that no figuring out was required. So massive was the base of the tower beyond the trees that I'd taken it to be part of the forest behind. So tall was the structure before which my neck muscles strained as I walked into the clearing that 'incongruous' wouldn't really do it justice. It seemed to be an object from another universe altogether. It was, finally, King Alfred's Tower.

*

One of the Hoare family was known (whether to himself or others is not clear) as Henry the Magnificent and it was he who, to celebrate the end of the Seven Years' War in 1763, conceived this unusual triangular folly, which, at fifty metres, soars way above the treetops. Magnificent though Henry Hoare may have been, he was in his own eyes nothing in comparison to King Alfred of Wessex and England.

In the ninth century, so the story goes, one Ivar the Boneless arrived on a mission to avenge the death of his father Ragnar Hairy-Breeches. Ivar was just one of many Danish Vikings who had begun incursions on the east coast. Bit by bit much of England fell, but the kingdom of the West Saxons, Wessex, stretching across most of southern England, put up sterner resistance. Under King Alfred, only in his early twenties at the time, they just held on when attacked in 871 and even managed to defeat the Vikings four years later in a naval battle. This proved to be just a respite as the Danes, by then under King Guthrum, finally occupied Wessex in 878. But Alfred had survived. From a secret hideout in the Somerset marshes, he led an effective resistance movement, which reputedly included one particular coup in which Alfred himself managed to glean key military intelligence by inveigling his way into a Danish council of war, disguised as a minstrel quietly playing the harp in the corner. It's believed that at this very spot, where the tower was subsequently built in his name, Alfred rallied his Wessex troops prior to the Battle of Ethandun, an encounter that was to prove a decisive victory over the Danes.

Henry the Magnificent's fulsome inscription above the tower's door is intended to leave us in no doubt as to Alfred's own magnificence:

ALFRED THE GREAT
AD 879 on this Summit
Erected his Standard
Against Danish Invaders

To him We owe The Origin of Juries
The Establishment of a Militia
The Creation of a Naval Force
ALFRED The Light of a Benighted Age
Was a Philosopher and a Christian
The Father of his People
The Founder of the English
MONARCHY and LIBERTY

Having checked in with Julie, and paid my money to the quietly spoken curator, I climbed the 206 steps to the summit. While dominated by the woodland of the Stourhead Estate, the view to the south-west over Somerset's rich green pasture showed how short a distance I'd walked today, while the opposite view (tricky though the concept of 'opposite' is in a triangular tower) revealed the rolling Wiltshire hills that would characterise the next stage's rather longer stint by bike. These were still the same chalk lands as in Dorset but it's in Wiltshire that Massingham, that most poetic fan of the English downland, believes that 'the true, the aboriginal upper chalk emerges in its natural soil and purest outlines' (Massingham H.J. *English Downland*).

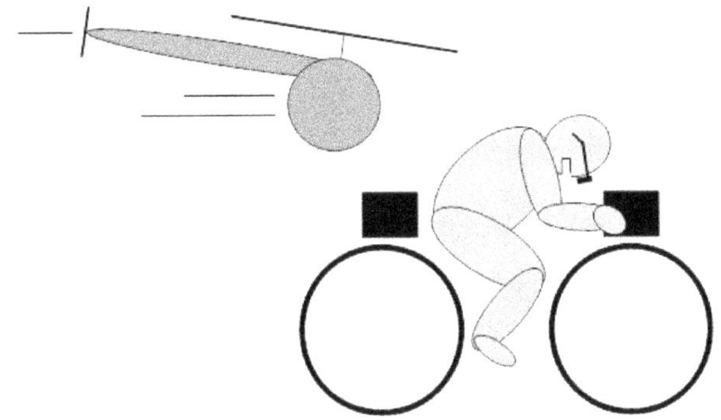

Stage 6: Prohibited Activities

Alfred's Tower to Devizes Market Place

By the time I stood once more before Henry Hoare's folly, a spring breaking records for its dryness (notwithstanding my own damp experiences) had come and gone, a wet early summer that blighted both Wimbledon and Lord's had belatedly brought the English countryside to life and now, in August, all seemed normal once again. Unless you're young, fit and free from responsibility, I can strongly recommend breaking up such a journey into bite-sized chunks to make it a long-term project. Not only does such a relaxed approach spread the pleasure, it also minimises the pain. As I pedalled away from the tower and onto the road, I detected no creaks at all from the old knees. In the hush of the woods, the only sounds were Tetley's tyres and my own breathing.

The morning was cool and dry, a busy sky draping the fields in alternate sheets of grey and gold. A morning, in other words, that could have been designed for cycling through the English countryside. Making rapid progress along Wiltshire's narrow lanes, I'd soon ticked off the four standard corn crops: wheat, barley, oats and maize, all approaching harvest time, but still with bare patches of cracked soil bearing witness to the earlier drought. Had Oscar

Hammerstein been penning the lyrics not for *Oklahoma!* but for *Wiltshire!*, the corn would have been only as high as a cyclist's eye. Nevertheless beyond one field of maize (Hammerstein's 'corn') I could clearly spy a Marilyn...

On the one hand it's among the things that make us human; on the other it can get obsessive to the point of weirdness. Such is categorisation: the urge to impose some kind of order on the chaos we see around us by devising categories into which bits and pieces of the natural world can safely be slotted. In 1891 Sir Hugh Munro placed all Scottish mountain peaks over 3,000 feet into a new, imaginary pigeon hole, creating 283 'Munros'. About a hundred years later, Alan Dawson created a new pigeon hole for hills, with a much lower threshold but for a wider geographical area -- and metricated to boot: hills in the British Isles of at least 150 metres in *relative* height, i.e. relative to the surrounding topography. With more than a nod in the direction of Sir Hugh Munro, these are called 'Marilyns' and, to be honest, they turn out to be what the rest of us would call simply a prominent hill. There are 2,009 of them, of which 176 are in England. Surprisingly this watershed route takes in just three Marilyns and, as I approached Maiden Bradley, what I was looking at was the first of them: Long Knoll, a green ridge of chalk grassland rising above all the arable land -- but with no cyclable route across it. (The section of the English Watershed that continues north of my destination, Kinder Scout, contains several more Marilyns.)

Bang on the watershed too lies Maiden Bradley, two hundred years ago a busy village at the junction of the London-Barnstaple and Bath-Poole coaching routes but now, at least on this weekday morning, as quiet as a sleeping dormouse. No village in England, however, is without someone dodgy lurking in its past and here lurked Richard Jennings. Living in the sixteenth century, Jennings' claim to infamy lies in his complete unsuitability for the job of local prior, of which he was the last. First, claiming to have obtained a Papal Indulgence for his unchastity, he exercised his new-found licence with, shall we say, an excess of enthusiasm, asserting that in every case the lady involved had been single and that he subsequently found her a good husband. And second, Jennings' eye for the main chance was equally well focussed on finance for it can have been no coincidence that shortly before the dissolution of the monasteries (and priories), he suddenly found it in his heart to offer the priory's farms on long leases at low rents -- but for unusually large payments up-front. While Maiden Bradley's priory did not survive Henry VIII's dissolution and now lies in ruin, it's no surprise that Jennings not only survived but managed to find a comfortable living in Gloucestershire, where he doubtless honed his negotiating skills ready for a coming encounter with St Peter.

Four hundred years on and the dubious activities of the rich and powerful seem still to be with us. Dismounting to push Tetley up a steep hill near Horningsham, I entered the dark, woody domain of the Longleat Estate, home since Richard Jennings's days to the Thynn family, since 1966 to the exotic animals of Longleat Safari Park and more recently -- and more interestingly, I suggest -- to a number of the Marquess of Bath's infamous 'wifelets'. That number is about seventy... and counting.

The polyamorous lifestyle of Alexander Thynn, the 7th Marquess, has been scarcely concealed by the Marquess himself and well documented in the press, who had sunk their teeth into the latest episode just weeks before this ride. The nose of a well-proportioned lady with the remarkably appropriate name of Trudi Juggernauth-Sharma, believed to be wifelet number 68, allegedly came into close physical contact with the fist of Amanda Doyle, an Irish singer and also a wifelet (sequential number unknown), after an exchange of words about the prospects of Mr Thynn, 79 at the time, fathering a child with Ms Doyle. After the police had been called, the tabloids predictably began a debate on which big cats were the more dangerous: those roaming the Marquess's park or those roaming his bedrooms.

*

Emerging from the woods at Picket Post Gate, I pulled up to look around. Rising from the clay vale on my left (the west) were the bare slopes of an isolated chalk hill, ironically named Cley Hill on my map, which also confirmed that the watershed ran across the top of it. Once again, the lack of any legally cyclable route doing the same spared me the effort. However, no elevation was needed to notice that the distant landscape to the north was the first I'd seen without any hills at all: this was the Vale of Malmesbury and, being drained by the Atlantic-bound River Avon (the 'Bristol Avon'), meant that my route must be to the north-east, where all that could be seen were the suburbs of Warminster. A fast road led me away from these as far as a tiny hamlet called Halfway (halfway to Westbury, I'd guess), from where the singular track that was to feel the weight of Tetley's tyres for the next four hours cut away from the main road.

It was an inauspicious start: a 'No Through Road' sign leading to a litter-spattered lane that rapidly degenerated into an overgrown dirt track. Before long, however, the undergrowth fell away, the metalled surface returned and I was admiring a classic dry valley to the south-east from the steep slopes of Upton Cow Down. Beside the track a noticeboard had been hammered in, then another and then a whole gaggle of them, each telling me in a slightly different way that I shouldn't even think of venturing down into the dry valley, for that side, the right, was part of the Salisbury Plain 'Danger Area' and this was the Imber Range Perimeter Track.

On a geological map the band of chalk that winds its way up from the English Channel here spreads out like an Hiroshima cloud to form the great chalk plateau of Salisbury Plain, at 780 square kilometres the largest area of chalk grassland in Europe. Just as in the Dorset Downs, prehistoric man seems to have loved these high, open places, erecting Stonehenge on the eastern side of the plain and, later, many Iron-Age hill forts or 'camps' here on the western perimeter. This is followed by the Wessex Watershed, since the plain itself slopes gradually south-eastward and is eventually drained by the southbound River Wylye and the Hampshire Avon. From medieval times this grassland was largely used for grazing sheep, but the year 1898 saw its first recorded use for army exercises and now the Ministry of Defence owns about half the plain, making it the largest military training area in the UK, about a quarter of the land being permanently closed to the public.

From my vantage point on Upton Cow Down, there lay to the east no public road or path for twelve kilometres -- a long way in England -- and yet the landscape was certainly not empty. In the foreground a sloping field of wheat awaited the combine, across the valley a line of black cattle wandered to the corner of their field and beyond them a cluster of buildings huddled around the edge of ragged woodland. The horizon, however, did look bleak: a billowing desert of grey/brown scrub dotted here and there with a dark green patch of bushes. They say that with little human occupation Salisbury Plain is nowadays a haven for wildlife -- except, one would think, those parts that get blown up. From time to time wild life of a different type has been permitted to encroach on the plain, for in the 1960s it was used as a film location for both the Beatles' *Help!* (at Knighton Down near Larkhill) and Dave Clark's *Catch Us If You Can.*

Being a conscientious citizen, before proceeding along the Imber Range Perimeter Track I examined the noticeboards to learn what I must not do here. Among the many and varied banned activities, I was told quite categorically that I must not:

ply my bicycle for hire,

ride an unlit tricycle during the hours of darkness,

fly at an altitude of less than 30,000 feet,

accidentally leave any aircraft on military land,

remove any humus,

remove any cross-bow,

use any animal for the purpose of advertisement,

address any assembly of persons,

affix a bill on any erection,

deface any cattle grid, or even

loiter.

Trying to envisage how I might make practical use of an animal for the purpose of advertisement ('Buy this book or I shoot the hamster'?), but trying even harder to expunge from my mind the picture of anyone affixing anything at all to an erection, I remounted and pedalled on. Frankly I couldn't foresee my causing any problem to the authorities, especially as the signs along the right of the track soon changed their wording from 'Military Firing Range: Keep Out' to 'Danger: Impact Area: Keep Out'. As if to underline the immediacy of this threat, a large helicopter kept constant station about a kilometre into the 'impact area' to the right. It was all I could do not to pedal with my neck permanently craning towards the left.

Actually, once I'd got used to the thrum of the chopper's rotor blades, I did direct my attention to the left, for here was to be seen a series of spectacular views. Immediately at the foot of the ridge lay the surprisingly large town of Westbury (surprising to me as I'd never even heard of it), which from this angle seemed to consist almost entirely of trading estates. Beyond this the hill-free landscape I'd glimpsed before had transformed into a billowing blanket of woodland and pasture that reached almost to an horizon that, on this clear August noontime, must have lay a good forty kilometres away. Almost but not quite, for in the far, far distance I could just make out a low line of blue-grey hills, which must have been my first view of that corner of England which would soon loom large in my days: the Cotswolds.

As I illegally loitered to admire this panorama with the help of a sip or two from my flask of coffee, a shiny man in a shiny white track suit, and sporting a single shiny earring, jogged up from behind.

'Fine morning, eh?' he panted, crunching to a stop, hands on hips.

'Yes, indeed.'

'Not as good as winter though. (Pant) Come up here in the snow. (Pant) Everything white, even the white horse. Ha! (Pant) Can't see it, you see.'

'What white horse?'

'That white horse,' said Panter, pointing.

Taller than me, he was also standing on the raised verge. Joining him, I could just see in the corner of a field facing away from us what must have been the ear and eye of a white horse revealed from the grass.

'Westbury White Horse,' he said. '(Pant) What most people come here for. (Pant) See you.'

With that he panted away.

I'd known some white horses were coming up but hadn't realised they'd be so big -- nor so recent. Of Britain's twenty-four such hill figures, thirteen have been carved from the thin layer of grass covering Wiltshire's chalk downland, of which eight are still visible. Restored in 1778, this one above Westbury is the oldest of those eight. The newest was done as recently as 1999.

Panter was right about the visitors. Just before the hill fort that stood above the horse a road joined the track and the sun had brought forth quite a crowd, including an ice-cream seller and three men who, rather like giant, drunken locusts, were staggering towards the edge of the ridge with rigid contraptions attached to their backs. One after the other, they dipped out of sight below the edge before soaring up over our heads, dramatically transformed from awkward insects into swooping masters of the sky beneath their hang-gliders.

In the middle of the car park, but ignored by the motorists, stood a huge stone and, licking a very welcome ice cream, I pushed Tetley over to examine it. It turns out that the battle against the Danes for which Alfred had mustered the Wessex troops on the site of his later eponymous tower, took place somewhere around here, for the 'Ethandun' in the Battle of Ethandun of 878 is thought to have been the modern-day village of Edington, just down in the valley from here. If so, Alfred must have taken more or less the same route as I'd followed that morning. This stone commemorating the event had been unveiled eleven years before by none other than the Marquess of Bath, he of the seventy wifelets.

Defeat for the Danes at Ethandun led to a treaty that left Wessex as the last of the free Anglo-Saxon kingdoms and to the supremacy of a Wessex dynasty in the unified England that eventually emerged. The last Earl of Wessex to hold the English crown was none other than King Harold, who fell at Hastings in 1066. Allegiance to the old kingdom is still strong in south-west England, culturally and even politically, with a movement arguing for some devolution of power to a reconstituted Wessex, and after some 900 years the title Earl of Wessex has recently been revived and given to the current Prince Edward.

*

Beyond the car park the perimeter track resumed its solitary route eastwards, accompanied by red flags indicating that a military exercise was under way, a fact confirmed when I had to stand aside to let three heavily armoured trucks rattle by. Though they were camouflaged, the camouflage's context was not the green hills of

Wiltshire but the yellow deserts of Central Asia, a location for England's defence that would have baffled Alfred as much as it does some of us who paid for the paint job.

A feature not merely camouflaged but actually invisible was passed just short of Gore Cross: the line of England's 'prime meridian'. Now, like me you may well have believed that this title fell to the line of zero degrees that passes through Greenwich and was chosen as the world's longitudinal datum in 1884. However, according to geographer and broadcaster Nick Crane, a subsequent decision of 1938 allocated the title of 'England's prime meridian' to 2 degrees west, since it passes through the greatest length of the country's territory, starting as it does at Berwick-upon-Tweed. Possessed of this fact, Crane proceeded to walk it, writing up his journey in *Two Degrees West* (1999, Viking). Since the straight line of England's prime meridian is to the wiggly line of England's prime watershed as the rod of Asclepius to its entwining serpent, I was destined to cross Crane's route several times -- and this was the first.

Headed due south, Crane had climbed up to Salisbury Plain from the village of West Lavington and it's here that he'd stayed with a Belgian lady who'd observed that, while it may seem quite normal in England for someone to follow religiously a route carved in the abstract, this would be regarded in Belgium as extremely odd. Maybe all nationalities but the English would agree. Well, for my own part, all I can say is that to blaze a trail that probably no one else has tried, whatever its reasoning, is definitely a life-enhancing experience that I'd recommend to anyone.

As if to confirm the point, at Redhorn Hill I obeyed the imperative of the watershed, leaving the perimeter track that most others up here would follow and, via an exhilarating, brake-squealing freewheel, dropped into the Vale of Pewsey, where the route squeezed me between the headwaters of the Channel-bound Avon and the those of the Atlantic-bound Semington Brook. Down in the vale, a headwind soon got up to remind my legs of the 60 kilometres they'd pedalled today and so I was particularly happy to pull over with the excuse of yet another roadside memorial to examine. And quite a rarity this one turned out to be: commemorating neither king nor soldier nor sailor, but a road-builder of over 240 years before. More than a little weather-worn, it read:

> This Monument from a general Sense of Gratitude was erected to the Memory of JAMES LONG Late of Wedhampton Esqr. Whose publick Spirit & Benevolence which he ever exercised for the service of Mankind were remarkably exerted in planning promoting and compleating this New Road An: Dom: 1768 By which a former tedious, and dangerous Way over the adjacent Hill is avoided To the great Pleasure and convenience of Travellers.

I especially admire the abandon with which the grateful authors scattered their capital letters. Expressing my own thanks to Mr Long, it was with great pleasure and convenience that I finally pulled into the cobbled yard of the Black Swan at Devizes.

*

The origins of both town and name lie with Devizes castle, originally built in the eleventh century as the *castrum ad divisas*, that is to say 'the castle at the boundaries' of three local manors. Early in its history it had an important prisoner to look after.

You could say there were a few issues between Robert Curthose and his family. Although 'Curthose' ('short stockings') was just a nickname, the fact that his father, William the Conqueror, regularly derided young Robert helped it stick. In Robert's twenties, William issued a warrant for his arrest following a failed attempt by his son to seize William's own castle at Rouen after, it is said, a fight with his two younger brothers, William (Rufus) and Henry, had led to only Robert being punished. Relations between father and son, already poor, reached a new low when the two found themselves on opposite sides in battle and Robert managed to unhorse and wound William before recognising his own father. It could have been no surprise then when William bequeathed the kingdom of England not to his eldest son but to William Rufus, leaving the duchy of Normandy to Robert. Mortgaging the duchy to Rufus, Robert disappeared on the First Crusade, only to return to find the English throne occupied by his youngest brother Henry following Rufus' death in an apparent accident. After Robert had led a failed invasion of England, Henry led a successful invasion of Normandy and, capturing Robert, had him incarcerated for twenty long years here at Devizes Castle. Eventually Robert was moved to Cardiff Castle, where he died, a victim not only of sibling rivalry but of his own temper and ineptitude.

Over the years, while the castle's significance waned, the market that grew up under its protection thrived, trading at first in wool and wheat, later in specialist textiles like serge and felt and later still in cattle and horses. Today Devizes is a fine example of a West Country market town whose essence has survived more or less intact, with an astonishing 500 or more listed buildings in a town of just 11,000 inhabitants.

As Julie and I walked out across the market square, Devizes somehow felt more French than English, with its elegant hotels, imposing banks, and nicely proportioned town hall. Even the market cross contained a panel telling the type of quirky tale that might have come straight from medieval France. In this very market place in 1753, accused of withholding money that she owed to her friends, a woman named Ruth Pierce rashly wished that, if she'd not in fact already paid it, she should drop down dead. At which point she did exactly that and, in case anyone was still in doubt as to the culprit, the coroner subsequently issued an official statement that Ms Pierce had been killed by 'the vengeance of God' (Haycock, Lorna *Devizes* (2000, The History Press)).

Vengeance was also the main theme of the locals' conversation in the inn where we slaked our thirst that balmy summer's evening on the excellent Farmer's Glory, from the local Wadworth's brewery right there at the bottom of the Market Place. For two successive nights now, in other towns and cities up and down England, rioters and looters had been causing midsummer mayhem.

'Bring in the army,' suggested one man younger than you'd normally associate with such forthright views. 'Hit 'em hard before they've got any namby-pamby lawyers to protect 'em.'

'Round up their parents as well,' suggested a middle-aged woman. 'Ten-year-olds out on the street at night? What are they thinking?'

'Is there still some remote island out in the empire that we can send 'em all to?' A man of around sixty. 'They don't deserve to live in England.'

Whether agreeing with the sentiments or not, we were a little concerned that the atmosphere in the bar was getting a bit too belligerent and were therefore relieved when another young man brought a smile to everyone's faces.

'I 'ear they've even been riotin' at Tesco's in Chippenham,' he said. 'What are they after? Free bacon?'

Stage 7: Watershed Junction

Devizes Market Place to Cherhill White Horse

Aware that my cake research project hadn't yet generated any taste test in Wiltshire, Julie and I had the previous evening interrogated the town's confectioners on the subject of 'Wiltshire Devizes pie', to whose existence the internet had drawn my attention. Nope, they'd said as one, never heard of it. Nor had our host, but the next morning he did set us up for the day in both food and mood.

After placing before us two full, 12-inch breakfasts (that is, plates a foot in diameter stacked with four rashers of bacon, two sausages, two fried eggs, a black pudding, a few spoonfuls of mushrooms and a generous dollop of beans), the manager at the Black Swan answered Julie's question as to why there was a huge metal grille across the centre of the bar.

'Ah well,' he explained, 'we once had a problem with some guests who nipped downstairs at night and helped themselves to the stock behind the bar. Mind you, even this gate didn't stop everyone. You won't believe this, but on another night two chaps squeezed into the dumb waiter upstairs and let themselves down into the bar that way.'

'Did you catch them?' asked Julie.

'Couldn't help it. They were daft as well as drunk. With no one left upstairs to press the button, they had no way of getting back up and so we found them in the morning still locked down here in the bar. We just called the police, saying they could take their time as the villains were already both incarcerated and incapacitated.'

*

While the previous day had involved my longest daily distance so far, today would involve the shortest, but would be most significant nevertheless. With Tetley trussed up in the car and Julie off to do some shopping, I'd donned my boots again and was soon puffing up Roundway Hill.

On the way out of Devizes I'd crossed the Kennet and Avon Canal, one of England's most vital inland waterways, connecting the Thames navigation via the River Kennet at Newbury to the Severn Estuary, via the River Avon at Bath. While the canal's summit lies some distance to the east, the stretch through Devizes was the last to be completed, in 1810, for it incorporates the remarkable Caen Hill Locks, a flight of sixteen in a line climbing up to the town from the west and usually taking over five hours to navigate.

Roundway Down has at least two claims to fame. In 1643, it was the scene of a Royalist victory in the Civil War when William Waller's Parliamentary troops, who'd been besieging Royalist Devizes, were almost completely annihilated by Henry Wilmot's reinforcements arriving from Oxford. For two years Devizes managed to remain in Royalist hands, but after Cromwell's men finally marched into town in 1645, Parliament, remembering the humiliation of Roundway Down, ordered that the castle be destroyed. And secondly it's home to Wiltshire's latest white horse, which I'd seen from the opposite hill the previous afternoon.

With such attractions, as well as being a Site of Special Scientific Interest for its butterflies, you'd have thought the local council would have encouraged visitors to Roundway Down. You'd think wrong. It seems to be a complete secret. For the benefit of any would-be visitor without a map, I can reveal that you leave the A361 by the Travelodge on the road with the 'No Entry' sign (ignore it: it doesn't mean you); go through the signless Roundway village, turn right at the signless fork, pull into the unsigned car park, walk through the unmarked gate and admire the anonymous chalky shape in the ground, for this is the Devizes White Horse. Admittedly an information board does reveal what you've just seen -- but only as you leave the site. Amazing.

*

Setting off along the bridleway, I was soon reminded that Roundway Down has yet another tale to tell. It was in these hills in the late 1970s and 1980s that sophisticated, large-scale patterns began to appear overnight in ripening corn...

Aliens, suggested the tabloids.

Across light years of space to Wiltshire? asked the voices of reason.

They're attracted by the vibes.

Why do they flatten corn?

Done by the flying saucers' feet.

Spacecraft that are always gone by the morning?

Er, yes.

Eventually, after thirteen years, two lads named Doug and Dave owned up to their jape and went on to demonstrate how easy it was. You tie one end of a rope to a fixed point and the other to a board, which you use to flatten the crops. The clue was in the timing. These 'crop circles' tended to appear on Saturday mornings... and thoughout England Friday night is traditionally pub night. Doug and Dave acknowledged that, of course, they hadn't done them all, but that others must been inspired to copy them. However, some people had invested too much emotion and energy into believing the circles constituted evidence of extra-terrestrials, whether the lads had confessed or not, and accused the devious drinking duo of being yet more conspirators in cahoots with the government to hide the truth that aliens had landed. Some still do.

A four-by-four pulled up beside me.

''Scuse me,' said the driver, an ordinary-looking chap in his forties. 'Do you know where the crop circles are?'

'What?' I asked, a little taken aback. 'I thought they were exposed as a joke years ago.'

'Oh, that's what they'd like us to think. No, it was on the internet yesterday. Another set due to be done last night around here somewhere.'

'You mean the aliens have a website where they announce their landings?'

He narrowed his eyes.

'You don't believe in 'em, do you? Fair enough,' he sighed, releasing the handbrake. 'But I bet you there's a fresh lot round here somewhere.'

And, you know what? It turned out he was right. The confirmation that some folks were still at it first came with a notice pinned to a fence just along the track. It read:

Below is an honesty box. We would be grateful if you could make a contribution (suggested amount £2 per person). Crop circles damage a significant amount of corn, both from the circle itself and visitors. Donations go a long way towards recouping this and mean that we don't have to resort to 'mowing out' the formation or harvesting early.

It was signed by the farmer. Well, I never! If you can't beat 'em, join 'em. Just two quid though? That sounded a paltry amount for wilful criminal damage, even it it did have the benefit of making fun of the gullible.

*

The reason I'd made a point of taking my time to walk this stage lay on the northern horizon: a pair of masts that marked the summit of Morgan's Hill. Named after John Morgan, a murderer hanged and then hung on a gibbet here in 1720, it held a different significance for me, for here lies the junction of England's three longest watersheds: the Wessex Watershed, the South-East Watershed and the English Watershed. As if to remind me of its likely significance to England's prehistoric forebears too, ancient burial mounds had once again begun to populate the edges of the route.

Having crossed the busy lane from Bishops Cannings to Blackland by the club house of a golf course, I sat down for a break in the lee of a small copse, beneath the chug-chug-chug of a microlight. With so many reminders of our distant ancestors around, I wondered what an inhabitant pausing in the same spot 4,000 years ago would have made of the view today. While the overall lie of the land -- rolling downs separated by dry valleys -- would probably have looked quite familiar, some features would surely have astounded him (or her): a person in a flying machine, shiny carts rushing at incredible speed along a wide black path, huge buildings with impossibly straight walls. And yet, with one exception, he would nevertheless probably recognise their purpose: transport and shelter. The exception lay immediately in front of me. Why, my Bronze Age friend might ask me, are those men pushing a little white stone down a hole with sticks and then pulling it out again? I'm sorry, I'd have to reply, this is something that leaves me equally perplexed.

Pulling myself up again, I took a diversion of about 100 metres from the bridleway to the brow of an anonymous field of grass that formed Morgan's Hill Watershed Junction. The spot deserved the capital letters. My passage along the Wessex Watershed, which had approached from the west and which I'd followed from Toller Down in Dorset, was now at an end. A raindrop falling on the south side of this field might still seep towards the English Channel but might also find its way to the shores of the North Sea along England's east coast, for here lay the start of the South-East Watershed, which finishes at North Foreland in Kent. While another raindrop falling on the north side of the field had a different choice again: the North Sea or the Atlantic, for setting off in this direction was my new companion, the guiding line from here to the start of the Pennines in far-off Derbyshire: the line of the English Watershed.

With chalk still underfoot, though, no flowing water was visible to confirm all of this, only the lie of the land. The low ridge by which I'd arrived was clear enough and the continuing ridge that constituted the first few kilometres of the English Watershed clearer still as it strode north-eastwards across the hilltops, the town of Calne in the valley to its left. The South-East watershed, however, was obscured by a prominent clump of trees that occupies the southern outlier of Morgan's Hill. Never mind, I knew the junction was here, although by now it came as little surprise that no information board was present to reveal it to the world. In fact it made Morgan's Hill that little bit more special for me. In recognising its significance, though, I was by no means alone.

*

Robert Hippisley Cox, born in 1857, was a former lieutenant in the Coldstream Guards and, more to the point, a keen observer of the English landscape which, as the cover of one of his books notes, 'he noticed disappearing at speed around him' (Hippisley

Cox, Robert *The Green Roads of England* (2010, The Lost Library)). In that book, first published in 1914, Cox puts forward the thesis that the great watersheds of England not only offered prehistoric man suitable individual sites for hill forts, burial mounds and the like but also formed a systematic network of routes of communication. The reader, of both Cox's book and, I hope, this one can be left in no doubt as to the advantages to our ancestors of ridge-top trackways in terms of dry, walkable terrain, of defensible locations and, crucially, of predictable, visible routes many years before the introduction of maps. This area was and is their major junction. Nowadays we know it not from the name of the hill at which the watersheds actually meet but from the name of a village in the valley below. At the centre of this landscape rich in neolithic and early Bronze Age features lies a UNESCO World Heritage Site: Avebury.

Down there you find not only the three Avebury stone circles (including the largest stone circle in Europe), the Avebury henge (a circular bank and internal ditch) and two avenues of paired stones, but also Silbury Hill (an artificial chalk mound, the tallest man-made prehistoric mound in Europe), and the West Kennet Long Barrow, as well as many other barrows. Not far away to the south lies Stonehenge. This was clearly an area of huge importance in prehistory. And it lies not only beside the junction of the three major watersheds of England, but also not far from the junction of the English Watershed with the Ridgeway, an ancient trackway that coincides for the most part with the Icknield Way, running from Wiltshire to East Anglia, largely along watersheds but also crossing the Thames at Goring. There must surely be a connection between the location of such important prehistoric remains and the watershed network. I was standing, I felt sure, at the major meeting point of what was to become southern England. Eventually, perhaps, Morgan's Hill Junction itself will be more widely recognised.

*

With renewed energy I dropped back down to the bridleway and headed north-east with Kinder Scout on my mind. It was a broad and well-worn track; part of another Roman road in fact, that from Londinium to Aquae Sulis, London to Bath. In modern-day footpath terms it's also the White Horse Trail and the Wessex Ridgeway, that long-distance route from Lyme Regis which the two damp campers on Toller Down had been sampling. Having kept largely to the south of my Wessex Watershed route, it had eventually rejoined the latter on the edge of Salisbury Plain, but just short of the A4 we parted company again, the Wessex Ridgeway heading east towards Avebury while the watershed continued northwards.

Having an appointment in the village of Cherhill with Julie (and, as explained below, with some bare buttocks), I had no choice but to brave the A4 traffic for a noisy mile or two. A significant mile or two, though, for beyond a stand of trees on the left, among the folding foothills below the obelisk that marked Cherhill Down, lay not only the nimble figure of the Cherhill White Horse, a little over 200 years old, but also, less than twenty-four hours old, a series of neat, saucer-shaped depressions in the dusty, ripening wheat: those crop circles of internet rumour, right before me and as large as life. Larger than I imagined in fact: scale was provided by a figure in a black coat, twice as high as the wheat but wandering around a circle whose diameter must have been a good five times his height. Japes they may be, but extinct they ain't.

So it was with a sense of the day's task almost complete that I disappeared into the bar of the ironically named Black Horse at Cherhill (which I here discovered to be pronounced 'Cherrill'). I should stress right now that the buttocks that would round off the day were nothing to do with Julie; indeed were not even live ones, but rather formed a prominent feature in a painting I knew to be hanging in the pub. Unfortunately it turned out not to be in the bar but in the dining area and so it was with a certain self-consciousness that I sidled past two late lady lunchers, offering them a rather sheepish smile, before briefly examining the renowned naked flesh and then, with a tad more aplomb, the explanatory notice to one side.

Long before the height of England's coaching era in the eighteenth century, the principal route from London to Bath had shifted down from the Romans' alignment to this road through Cherhill village. While the turnpike system had generated funds to reduce the physical hazards of long-distance travel in England, bringing this spot within a day's journey of the capital by 1750, the threat from one's fellow men remained. Attacks by highwaymen for the purposes of theft were still far too frequent and one such gang of brigands that operated from this very village was infamous for a peculiar *modus operandi*: the so-called Cherhill Gang did their dastardly deeds naked. While the shocking effect on their victims could only have helped their cause, it's also said that they chose to operate in the buff in order to protect their identities.

After undertaking her own examination of the painting, which depicted in graphic detail one such attack on a coach, Julie gave expression to the thought that had also occurred to me:

'There's a flaw in this plan.'

Stage 8: Edge of Empire

Cherhill White Horse to Trouble House

After many idle hours -- too many, to be honest -- spent browsing maps of Britain, one lesson I'd learnt is that an area surrounded by a series of inward-pointing dead-ends is most probably a mountain; possibly a moor or a heath. Ever since I'd plotted the watershed route across this particular tract of Wiltshire, I'd wondered which was the case here. While liberally laced with footpaths and bridleways, a good forty square kilometres supported no road at all beyond the little yellow stick to the hamlet of Yatesbury along which I was pedalling at nine o'clock sharp, after another pleasant evening in Devizes.

The most prominent features of the landscape hereabouts were ruins: huge sheds with gaping windows, low empty buildings with curved roofs, weed-engulfed concrete huts. These were the remains of RAF Yatesbury -- or, to go back to its origins, RFC Yatesbury, for what I was cycling through was that very rare find: the visible site of a World War One airfield, established before even the RAF existed, when the fledgling wing of Britain's air defences was the Royal Flying Corps. During World War Two, from which most of the ruins originate, Yatesbury was home to a radio training school and spread over both sides of the road. Nowadays the east side is still an airstrip, hosting the microlights I'd seen chugging overhead the day before, while on the day I cycled past, the western side was partly a building site for new flats and partly still a cobwebbed home to the ghosts of past conflicts.

Just beyond the overgrown entrance to the last air-raid shelter, the metalled road ran out and a cinder surface took over. A little further and this gave way to two weedy wheel tracks, then this to a single path thigh-high with grass sodden from overnight rain. Once again I'd fallen into the trap laid by those neat, red dashed lines on the map. Bridleway my foot! Whatever occupied the empty quarter ahead -- and it looked like just fields to me -- there was no way any sane person would attempt to cross it today on horseback, let alone on foot with a bike slung over one shoulder. Beckoning from the west lay an escape route down the slope to Compton Bassett and reluctantly I responded. However, not only was the diversion a pleasant one, passing through the little settlements strung along the spring line at the edge of the clay vale, but it also brought me past a grave that bears a name with a rare quality.

Beeton, Bradshaw, Fowler, Hansard, Wisden... what have these names in common? As author or publisher, each is used as shorthand for a specific publication in preference to its title. On a humble headstone in the churchyard of St Peter's at Clyffe Pypard is inscribed another. Born in Leipzig in 1902, the man buried here was twice excluded from his profession by matters beyond his control: first, as a Jew by the Nazis and then, after having settled in England, as a German by the British. Happily the latter internment lasted only a few months, and it was after the war that, over a period of 23 years, his vast reference book was published in a total of forty-six volumes. His specialist subject was the history of architecture, his work was called *The Buildings of England* and his name was Nikolaus Pevsner. The county-by-county guide is usually known simply as 'Pevsner'. The plain headstone is of blue slate and records first Lola Pevsner and then her husband Nikolaus, who died in 1983.

On leaving the little churchyard, I was in the saddle barely a minute before dismounting to start the back-bending trudge back up to the chalk ridge at the intriguingly named hill of Clyffe Hanging. From here civilisation, in the form of roads and lanes, had returned to the downs, but this was to be my final farewell to the chalk lands that had carried most of the watershed line -- and me -- all the way from White Hill near Chesil Beach, for the best part of seven travelling days. For here at Bincknoll (pronounced 'Binnol'), while the chalk downs marched on north-eastwards to form the Chiltern Hills and ultimately the low sea cliffs of far-off Norfolk, the watershed and I made a northward dash across greensand and clay towards Gloucestershire and the Cotswolds.

In doing so I felt I was leaving southern England behind and edging into the Midlands. For one thing the sprawling outskirts of the biggest town I'd seen en route so far half-covered the vale below: less-than-beautiful Swindon. And next, in short order, I crossed Brunel's Great Western railway from Paddington and then the east-west route that, to me at least, acts as the psychological frontier of southern England: the M4 motorway.

French motorway drivers are kept alert by regular brown signs extolling the virtues of the town accessed from the next junction: 'Nimportouville: her chateau, her glass-blowing, her fabrication of pencil-sharpeners'. With the strange exception of compulsive river naming, Britain's Highways Agency seems reluctant to draw motorists' attention away from the traffic towards such trivia. After this stage I wrote to the agency suggesting that hereabouts, between Hook and Ballard's Ash, another exception would be justified: 'English Watershed', together with a little graphic showing the parting of the waters, just as on the equivalent sign beside the *autoroute* near Langres in France, highlighting the watershed between the country's north and south coasts.

Weekenders from London would probably be relieved to learn that they've finally escaped the Thames basin. (While the Highways Agency acknowledged my 'unusual' idea, nothing seems to have come of it.)

Back on the bike, I was simply relieved that it was lunchtime and pulled into Hook's Bolingbroke Arms.

*

While many references across England to the name Bolingbroke allude to Henry of Bolingbroke, a.k.a. Henry IV, this inn derives its name from the Viscounts Bolingbroke, lords of the manor at Lydiard House, over the fields to the east. Lording it at the bar this lunchtime, however, was a young man, a student I'd wager, who was regaling the barman with a blow-by-blow account of the activities that had thus far illuminated his summer vacation. He had a local accent.

"Ad to drive virtually to the Welsh border for Cas's wedding. We all got wrecked o' course. Then it was straight up to London for Kev's do. Strewth, we wus well trashed. You know Kev, don't you?'

Whether the barman knew Kev was to remain unknown, since he was busy serving customers, offering just the occasional grunt to confirm his attention to the intoxicating narrative.

'Only got one night's kip at 'ome before it was down to Brighton and Nick 'n' Trish's, where oh my god did we get 'ammered. Just made it back last night and o' course tomorra's the flight to Bordeaux. What's that ginger bird's name?'

The barman seemed unacquainted with the ginger bird.

'Well, she's marryin' Baz over there and we're all bein' put up in a barn. Christ, will we get... get...'

'Sozzled?' The suggestion came from a well-dressed man waiting to be served.

'Wha'?' said the proud imbiber, turning round.

'You haven't used "sozzled" yet.'

'Is that what they call it in France then?'

'I don't think so.'

'Well, anyway I 'spect we'll be totally... unconscious.'

Let's hope he came round long enough to dip into a thesaurus before the Christmas vacation.

*

In a similar quest for original descriptions with which to enliven Britain's sometimes repetitive weather forecasts, that morning's BBC forecaster had predicted another band of rain would 'romping across' England from the north. As I pedalled through the northernmost reaches of rural Wiltshire, the rain and I seemed to be romping ominously towards each other. As the dark northern horizon and the lower portion of a mud-coloured sky were merging into one messy morass, wild life was busy choosing the best places to sit out the storm. A stoat made a hasty 90-degree turn just short of my front wheel, birds of prey ceased their swoops to take up positions in the trees and two red deer huddled in the corner of a field. Not wild admittedly, but deer are farmed hereabouts.

As for me, though buildings were few and far between along these quiet lanes, should the heavens have opened shelter would have been close at hand in the form of the dense woodlands flanking one side of the road or another. These were the remains of an old hunting territory, the Forest of Braydon, still reputed to include examples of the rare 'wild service tree', whose fruit, the chequer, is believed to be the source of the pattern of the same name and therefore of the game 'chequers' -- and indeed the pub name. Not feeling inclined to delay, I didn't search even the fringes of the forest for this rarity but rather pressed on urgently, one eye constantly on the glowering sky. Soon after Five Lanes, a crossroads that had only four, I turned right and onto a route more significant than it looked.

Today just a modest, rutted track, this was once one of the major roads of Roman Britain. Stretching over 350 kilometres from Isca to Lindum (Exeter to Lincoln) and at one time effectively the frontier of the Roman Empire itself, it was the Fosse Way, named after the ditch (Latin *fossa*) that ran parallel to it. Had I been bouncing along here some 2,000 years before, the land to my right, now occupied by a field of solar panels, would have been regarded as the very edge of civilisation, forming a remote part of the greatest empire the world had ever seen; while to my left, beyond today's barbed-wire fence, lay land controlled (or at least threatened) by the barbarians -- in this case the Welsh. Actually, the term 'barbarian' originates not with the Romans but with the Greeks, and Welsh didn't emerge as an identifiable nationality until after the Romans left... but you get my drift.

Remarkably, this stretch of the Fosse Way is still a boundary today: between Wiltshire (on the old imperial side) and Gloucestershire (on the Celtic side). What's remarkable is not so much that an ancient frontier has become a modern one, but that an English county boundary is, for a short distance, not the usual wayward, wandering line but as straight as a die. From Ilchester to Lincoln (293 kilometres) the Fosse Way never veers more than 10 kilometres from a straight line.

In leaving Wiltshire I was, according to its new slogan, leaving the county 'where everybody matters'. Quite why some English counties have suddenly felt the need for a slogan I'm not sure. After all, with county residents unable to buy their services elsewhere, local government is a classic monopoly with nothing to gain from advertising. Perhaps Wiltshire's public relations chief had recently holidayed in the USA, where such glib self-promotion is thought normal. Sometimes, though, it can raise a laugh. The weirdest local government slogan I ever heard was in Australia, where a local TV commercial boldly declared 'South Australia -- you're in it!' Gloucestershire, thankfully, seems to have bucked the trend and eschewed slogans altogether. Mind you, they must have been tempted by an obvious dig at their neighbours: 'Gloucestershire, where only *we* matter'.

Despite the gentle gradients, in entering Gloucestershire I was also entering the fringes of the hills that would dominate my route for some days to come: land famed for its sheep and for being at one time the wealthiest area in all England, the Cotswolds. Across England there are a number of 'wolds', the term coming from the Old English *wald* ('high forest land') and, since it's thought that 'Cot' is from the personal name Cōd, as the day's ride drew to a close I was entering the Forest of Cod.

*

If you found yourself in seventeenth-century France and in urgent need of breaching a wall, you might get hold of a *petard.* This was a small metal box containing a few pounds of gunpowder, activated by lighting a slow-burning fuse. Should you fail to retreat with sufficient alacrity, the explosion may well lift you off the ground along with the wall. You will have been hoist with your own petard. This, metaphorically, was what happened to me at The Trouble House.

Having looped around from its general north-westerly orientation to run parallel to the A433 for a while, the watershed passed temptingly close to an inn of that name a mile or two outside Tetbury and convenient for my usual afternoon pick-up. After 55 kilometres in the saddle, I'd been visualising a happy half-hour with a pint and a notebook in The Trouble House, named after local disturbances in the Civil War, and therefore the ETA I'd texted to Julie, who'd be driving from about 30 minutes away, was half an hour later than the time I actually pulled into the pub car park.

The empty pub car park. Next to the closed pub. England's

relatively new, liberal opening hours are not actually compulsory after all. And so, as dollops of rain finally started to fall, Tetley and I huddled against the unforgiving Trouble House wall awaiting rescue. A *petard* would have been handy.

*

A day's break -- of sorts -- had been planned, partly to benefit from the outstanding hospitality of Julie's parents in Chipping Sodbury. Awaiting the damp and weary cyclist was an unusual greeting:

'Come in,' called Gerald from the kitchen. 'I've been preparing some leg oil for you.'

'What?'

'It says "Wadworth's 6X" on the bottle.'

'Ah.'

'And Julie says you're trying out local cakes as you go,' added Edna. 'So try this. It's Sodbury Loaf Cake.'

Placed next to the beer was a generous wedge, whose distinguishing visual feature was its dark brown topping, rough with nuts. Is it a loaf or is it a cake? Definitely a cake. Is it better than a Dorset Apple Cake? Well, it's more crumbly, more sticky (that's the dates) and the topping, brown fudge made from treacle and walnuts, is especially delicious. There's a local tale, which I've been unable to verify, that Sodbury Loaf Cake was a special favourite of Queen Mary (mother of George VI) when staying at nearby Badminton House during World War Two. If so, I expect she'd have fancied this little research project herself. Right now I'd got two contenders out front, neck and neck -- or crumb and crumb.

While Chipping Sodbury itself lies some way off the watershed route, it's a classic example of a Cotswold market town, with its wide high street flanked by Tudor, Georgian and Victorian buildings -- or facades, since not all its frontages match the premises behind. Surprisingly little has changed since the turn of the twentieth century, the period depicted in most of the huge old photographs that Gerald showed me in the town hall. The original reason for the wide high street so typical of this part of England was, of course, the town's market. First present in the thirteenth century, it thrived for many years as a cattle, sheep and wool market and still, in one form or another, regularly nudges the parked cars out of the way today. In fact 'Chipping', which also appears in Chippings Norton, Camden and Warden -- none far away -- comes from the Old English *cēping* (market), from which we also get 'shopping'. While Chipping Sodbury is 'the market at Soppa's fort', I couldn't help wishing that old Cōd of Cotswolds fame had founded his own market town to give us the pleasure of visiting Chipping Cod.

Shopping, however, was not the other reason for the day's break from cycling and walking. Julie and I would be spending it, quite literally, on our knees.

*

The Barn Called 'The Barn': A Day at the Dig

Getting on for two thousand years ago, somewhere in the vicinity of modern-day Tetbury, a man called Mettus dies and one of his descendants has an engraved tombstone made in his memory. Fast forward to the 1840s and a farmhand's shift in a Gloucestershire field is interrupted by the clunk of a heavy stone against the plough. Having rescued Mettus's memorial, however, the farmer seems to have promptly forgotten about it. Fast forward another 150 years and the owner of Nesley Farm takes an enquiring look at this old piece of limestone and decides to invite the county council to investigate. Cue archaeologists, 'geophys' experts and an exhaustive study of aerial photographs in the county archive. The word goes out:

'Dig!'

Now slow forward just three more years and two visitors, booted, bucketed and betrowelled, trundle into Nesley Farm's yard, to be greeted by a short, bright-eyed woman, full of jollity and freckles.

'Welcome to Nesley Farm Roman Excavation. Are you volunteers?'

'We are,' I confirmed.

'Beginners?'

'First-timers.'

'Well, there's the barn we call 'The Barn', where there are some other beginners. See you there in five minutes.'

The barn called 'The Barn' contained a giant table of trays, which in turn contained, literally, hundreds of bones, flints, coins and pottery pieces. Standing by the table were three display boards and, standing by these, two middle-aged ladies whose boots were as clean as ours, that is to say several stages cleaner than those worn by Freckles.

'Hi,' said Julie.

'G'day,' said the fairer-haired lady. 'Come far?'

'Leicestershire,' I said, slightly bending the truth but hoping to imply that we'd made some effort to be here. It was still early morning. What about you?'

'Wagga Wagga. 'Stralia.'

These two ladies, it turned out, were well into a four-month tour of Europe and, rather than doing just the museums and the stately homes, had scoured the Web for more out-of-the way spots. Today a field in Tetbury, tomorrow a B & B in Okehampton.

After Freckles had filled us all in on the background and

given the health and safety talk (don't get over-tired, do wear a hat, don't fall into holes, do respect the bones), we were led out into a field swaying gold with wheat and bobbing blue with a dozen denim-clad bottoms in the middle of the broad, crop-free zone where lay 'Trench One'.

Now, to twenty-first-century Britons that aren't already archaeologists, ninety-nine per cent of what we know about the subject comes from Mick, Phil, Tony and their mates in Channel Four's *Time Team* (TT). So, to Julie and me, the nature of the excavation, with its half-revealed stone walls, red-and-white marker posts and crouching occupants, all earnestly scraping away at their sections, was not really a surprise. What was quite astonishing, however, was how shallow it was. The sturdy remains of what must have been a substantial Roman building had been lying here for centuries just inches from the stony surface of the field. To walk in or out of the trench didn't even require a break in your stride.

Pretty soon we'd been allocated our sections and were busily scraping away like good 'uns. Well, in my case, not too busily at first as my main fear was of of discarding some artefact of immeasurable national significance.

'Is this sharp enough to be a flint tool?' I asked my kneeling neighbour, a lanky man with the knowledgeable air of a retired Chemistry teacher. He gave it a cursory glance.

'It's just a stone.'

Scrape scrape.

'What about this? Is it a bone?'

'It's a stick,' said Lanky. 'Here's a tip, son. Take a look in the trays and you'll see what to look out for.' Son? Thank you, sir.

The rules of engagement were that you scraped away horizontally at the sticky, stony soil with your trowel (archaeological, twelve quid from the internet; not garden, three quid from Wilkinson's), putting anything interesting in a tray and everything else in a bucket. The bucket loads went to a spoil heap, while the tray went into the barn called 'The Barn'. After fifteen minutes Julie, who was my other neighbour, had trayed several pieces of smooth terracotta and Lanky a fragment of Roman oyster plus a couple of sheep's teeth. The contribution from yours truly was exactly zilch. I'm sure I'd have been much more productive sharing a cosy tent with TT's rosy-cheeked historical researcher Helen, but she didn't seem to be around.

Scrape scrape.

After another fifteen minutes there arose a trench conversation about kneelers.

'Yours looks luxurious,' Julie's other neighbour told her.

'It's made from memory foam,' explained Julie. 'I use it in the garden and it remembers what shape my knees are. Not cheap though.'

'These knee pads are pretty expensive too,' contributed Lanky. 'Don't blow away when you stand up and you don't need to keep shifting them either.'

Having had my attention redirected to my own knees, which were currently separated from the crusty remains of the greatest empire known to man by a sliver of cheap rubber about as thick as an air mail envelope, I decided to get up and wander around. Over at the higher edge of the field stood Freckles who, it turns out, had been one of the site's air photo interpreters and was now filling the role of Stewart, TT's landscape investigator, that's to say staring with furrowed brow into the middle distance, one hand shading eyes, the other resting on hips. I joined her.

'Seen something interesting?'

'Well,' said Freckles, 'the geophys clearly shows a road, or at least a track, going past the building you're excavating, through here and then... apparently nowhere.'

'On the Knoydart peninsula in Scotland there's a road that goes from nowhere to nowhere.' This revelation seeming not particularly useful, I filled the silence with another question. 'Isn't there another Roman road nearby then?'

'There's a road that went to the Severn crossing.'

'So the Severn Bridge wasn't the first crossing round here?'

'By no means. The Romans crossed the river, either by ford or ferry, at Arlingham, only about twelve miles over there.'

'But the road through this field doesn't go there?'

'Wrong direction. But it probably led to another road that did.'

'Probably?'

'Lots of work still to be done.'

'How long will you be excavating here?'

'Oh, as long as the farmer lets us -- or until we find a mosaic floor.'

'Then what?'

Freckles laughed.

'If we do, he probably won't have any choice!'

Well, we didn't turn up any mosaic on our shift, but what we did scrape down to was a wall, which happened to by under my own section and explained the discrepancy between the finds in the neighbouring sections, inside rooms, and their absence from mine, on the wall that divided them. The find of the day, however, came in the afternoon and was heralded by a hesitant cry from a few yards away:

'C..coi.. coin... COIN!'

The voice had a French accent, for the finder was a dessert manufacturer from Clermont Ferrand. As we creaked and stumbled over to his corner of the trench, two muddy French thumbs brushed Cotswold dirt from the angular profile of Flavius Valerius Aurelius Constantinus Augustus, better known as Constantine the Great, Emperor of Rome from 306 to 337 A.D. Many centuries ago, near the edge of the empire, someone had heard the clink of a coin as it dropped into the dark crevice of a wall. Maybe they dropped a whole purseful and recovered all but one. Here we were by that same wall, the empire long gone and many other claims to these hills having also come and gone in the meantime: ten soiled scrapers patting the back of the man who now lifted the same coin into the daylight once again, holding it up to our gaze and to the Gloucestershire sunshine.

*

Later on, while applying more 'leg oil' -- this time with 'Wickwar Brewery' on the bottle -- I tried to pigeon-hole archaeological digs as a potential leisure activity. There are only three types. Was it:

a) something right up my street (like maps and Marmite sandwiches) or

b) something I can see the point of, but just not my thing (like skiing and Shakespeare) or

c) something that, to me, seems completely pointless (like God and graffiti)?

Type b, I think. For a while it'd been quite addictive: bum up, head down, lost in my own square metre of mud with just a trowel, a brush and a bucket for friends. But in the end such hedonism doesn't really justify the stiff back and wind-lashed ears.

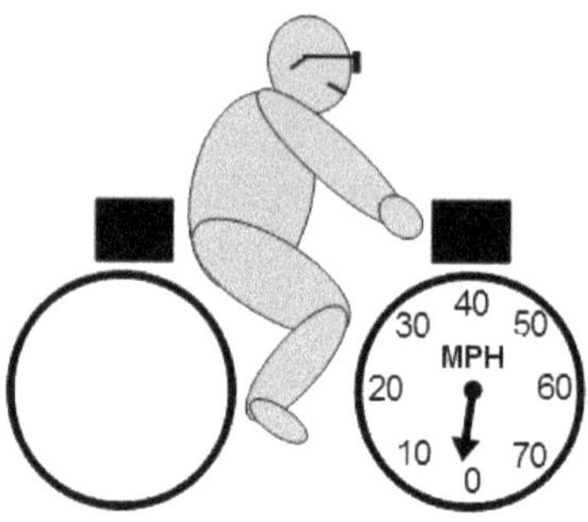

Stage 9: No Better Spot in All England

Trouble House to Seven Springs

It's questionable whether anyone with the epithet 'Great' would ever admit to being bewildered, but if you'd mentioned to Constantine the Great, whose coin had been unearthed the previous day, that his impact on this corner of his empire would be overshadowed by that of a portly engineer from Sheerness, he may at least have been perplexed. That portly engineer was Dr Richard Beeching, he of the cost-saving report whose legacy of disused railways still adorns the English countryside 50 years on and whose axe also fell at the Trouble House, where I resumed my northbound journey under cloudy skies the next morning.

Before setting off I scuttled down the footpath opposite to seek out any remains of Trouble House Halt, a stop on the Kemble-to-Tetbury branch that closed in 1964. I was hardly expecting any, to be honest, since the halt was not a station in the normal sense, not even having a platform and making do with a couple of upturned beer crates to assist passengers. The reason I'd singled out for inspection this particular halt on this particular disused line was its two claims to fame. First, it's believed to have been the only station in England built specifically to serve a pub, which it did, alas, for only five years from 1959. And second, it was from this halt that was despatched, on the very last service in 1964, addressed to 'Dr Beeching, Paddington Station, London', a coffin -- containing nothing but empty whiskey bottles. I imagine the doctor got the message.

Of the line just its alignment and a weedy embankment remained. Of the halt, nothing at all. It's a fair bet, however, that even as you read this, some lucky enthusiast is admiring the name board that hangs in his shed announcing long-lost 'Trouble House Halt'.

*

Beneath low, thick cloud and with no breath of breeze, I pedalled up the lane past Cherington. On a dull weekday morning the Costwolds' back roads were deserted and each isolated stone barn had the air of a forgotten remnant from the Dark Ages. Though cycling across a significant range of hills, I felt hemmed in by the lack of any long-distance views. Everything around me -- hedgerows, fields, barns, trees -- seemed to have absorbed the heavy grey of the sky. Once again, the observant H.J. Massingham, he of the exuberant 1930s prose, had been here before me. Noting the peculiar local relationship between land and sky, he traced the cause to the nature of the Cotswold stone. A change in the cloud cover, he wrote, will see a corresponding change in the stone 'from paleness to a sea-like glaucous and from dullish purple to the bloom of the grape.' (Massingham, H.J. *Cotswold Country.*)

But what *is* this material? Geologically the Cotswold Hills are an escarpment formed from a layer of that tilted Jurassic outcrop I encountered on the first day, the one that dips south-eastwards. Here it forms oolitic limestone, which is to say that it's composed of oolite, a rock made from ooids -- small, spherical grains of calcium carbonate -- laid down some 150 million years ago. These few dry facts have had a number of significant consequences.

The most significant for today's ride was that, since I'd arrived from the south-east along the escarpment's 'dip slope', the terrain's elevation wouldn't become clear till I reached the much steeper 'scarp slope', facing north-west. This westward push of England's watershed has vastly extended the catchment area for the east-flowing streams, thus creating a single mighty river, the Thames, on whose tidal banks has grown up one of the world's mightiest cities.

Back here in the hills, the grainy limestone has been as effective a colander to rainfall as the Dorset chalk, letting the water seep through to leave yet more dry valleys -- or 'bottoms' as they're called in these parts. The rock itself of course has proved a valuable resource, being quarried over the centuries to generate the building material that forms that classic Cotswold village look so favoured by architects and calendar designers.

It was into one such village that I eventually descended from the blandness of the wolds. Frampton Mansell is such a perfectly picturesque place that you don't know whether to snap it or scream at it. Had I chosen the scream, no one would have heard anyway, as the place appeared quite deserted. The scarp slope, or Cotswold Edge to give it its local name, has here been cut back into the hills by the west-flowing River Frome, whose steep valley sides are crowded with tumbling tree tops, between which peeks the roof of a grand house here, the chimney of a tiny cottage there, the squat tower of a sturdy old church over there. It being summer, every back garden was awash with red and yellow fruit trees, pink rose bushes, green and gold vegetable patches or speckled-blue hanging baskets. Even under cloudy skies, it was as if someone had finally turned on the colour switch. Offering a mellow background to all were the walls of that Cotswold stone. And here I have a favour to ask you.

If, like me, you find yourself reading one or two guides to the Cotswolds, each time you come across the phrase 'honey-coloured Cotswold stone', please scream out loud. Go on. At some point someone somewhere compared its colour to honey -- and now it seems all writers just can't help themselves from following suit. Standing here in Frampton Mansell, at last it dawned on me why the description is so irritating: it's not actually true. Massingham realised it. I've realised it. And the next time you're in the Cotswolds it will be your turn to realise the truth: what most Cotswold stone actually looks like is the inside of a banana.

Time for a drink. That morning in Frampton Mansell it was just coffee from the flask, but on another occasion Julie and I had sampled both food and drink at the village's Crown Inn -- or, as it was styled when built in the seventeenth century, the local 'cider house' -- and I can think of no better spot in all England at which to spend a lazy hour or two on a balmy summer evening. Especially as you may well find yourself among locals only, since the website www.british-towns.net boldly declares that in this idyllic village with its idyllic views and an idyllic pub there are no 'visitor attractions' at all. Strange but true.

*

England's canal network is in essence an attempt to connect the natural, navigable lower reaches of various rivers with each other by man-made, navigable waterways crossing the watersheds between them. Where the watersheds cross higher terrain, as here in the Cotswolds, construction costs -- and transit times -- could often be saved by tunnelling through the hills rather than incorporating locks to climb over them. Before the coming of the railways these difficult and dangerous projects produced the longest tunnels the country had ever seen and several of them still pass under the English Watershed today. While the longest of all, the 5-kilometre Standedge Tunnel, burrows under the Pennines some way north of my destination, the first under my own route lay beneath Tetley's tyres as I pedalled between Frampton Mansell and the next village, Sapperton. At nearly 3.5 kilometres, Sapperton Tunnel was the longest tunnel of any kind in England when it opened in the year of the French Revolution, 1789, to connect eastern and western portions of the Thames and Severn Canal. Although disused for over a century now, its western portal (entrance) is still visible part way down the scarp slope near the village of Daneway.

Also between Frampton Mansell and Sapperton, something strange happened to my finger. The same strange thing that apparently happens to everyone's finger hereabouts...

We are what we eat. But, at least in England, we also appear to be what we speak. Having heard a sentence or two, most natives could probably locate another's geographical origin by region: the north-west from the long 'oo' in 'book'; the north-east from the 'ai' sound in 'wine'; the London region from the long 'aa' sound in 'bath'; and so on. Linguists can be more accurate. For example, a qualified linguist who knew nothing about me needed only five minutes' conversation to nail my accent to 'somewhere between Derby and Nottingham'. They're less than 30 kilometres apart, but she was spot on. Much of the knowledge behind such feats comes from a survey undertaken in the 1950s by the University of Leeds and led by Harold Orton. The date is a clue to one of the two key drawbacks of such research: the results tend to hold true only as long as other influences, such as television, have not taken over. The other of course is that the further a speaker has moved from their origins during their lifetime, both geographically and socially, the weaker the hold of their original accent.

None of these caveats, however, had stopped me from consulting a linguistic atlas based on Orton's findings (details of which can be found under 'Selected Sources' at the end of this book) to establish where lies the boundary of south-west England from the point of view of dialect and accent. For no justifiable reason, I picked on the word 'finger', which is traditionally pronounced 'vinger' by rural south-westerners but 'finger' elsewhere in England. The 'vinger/finger' frontier cuts right across

Gloucestershire and intersects the watershed route somewhere between the villages of Frampton Mansell and Sapperton. And if you think I was going to approach a likely-looking inhabitant in each, stick up my digit and ask them to name it... you can think again!

*

With ever more evidence that I was now in the Midlands, I pressed on, keeping to the heights east of the Frome valley. Villages were still more or less empty; the entire moving population of Winstone comprised two black cats, a ragged dog and a tractor driver. Rather more activity was to be seen in the fields, where the harvest had begun. Somewhere near Duntisborne Abbots I pulled up in puzzlement beside a sports field beyond which two four-by-fours were parked. Bigger than a football pitch and with each end featuring a pair of blue-and-white posts too short for rugby, it had me scratching my head -- until a clunk, a shout and a clatter heralded the arrival from the far side of two horses, each bearing a helmeted rider and a swinging mallet. My first-ever sighting of a polo field.

It turns out that this was Jackbarrow, used by Cirencester Park Polo Club, one of eight clubs in the Cotswolds. While nowadays regarded as a classically English pastime, polo originated in ancient Persia, slowly spreading east and west through Asia -- including India, where in the nineteenth century the British picked up the game and ran with it, so to speak, bringing polo back to Blighty, renaming it after the Tibetan word for ball, *pulu* (it had variously been called *chougan*, *tzykanion* and *kanjai-bazee*, amongst other names), codifying the rules and spreading the game around the world. While the UK's governing body, the Hurlingham Polo Association, is based not far from here in Oxfordshire, the other local connection is more widely known, for the only polo player that most people in England could name, although he retired from the game some years ago, lives just down the road, near

Tetbury: Prince Charles.

*

After a noisy stint along the A417, including what, at nearly a kilometre, must be a contender for England's longest lay-by, Tetley and I finally coasted up to a genuine viewpoint on the Cotswold Edge called Barrow Wake.

While the leaden layer of cloud had held station we'd risen to some 300 metres, a height at which my helmet seemed almost to scrape against it. The view down the scarp slope to the Severn Valley was therefore like looking down from the ceiling of a vast chamber whose walls lay somewhere in the mist. Immediately below my feet the treetops tumbled down to some hummocky ground through which the curves of a dual carriageway carried to the vale a constant flow of traffic, whose distant but insistent roar drifted back up the slope. Their immediate destination must have been Gloucester, whose cathedral I could just see disappearing into the mist. Seven travelling days ago at Eggardon Hill I'd wondered if my next view of the sea would be from here on the Cotswold Edge. Well, not today, but in clearer weather? I posed the question to the only other soul taking the air at Barrow Wake that lunchtime. Sporting an old green jumper over well-worn khaki trousers tucked into muddy brown socks, which in turn disappeared into a pair of scuffed but still sturdy brown boots, this was a chap who'd be difficult to spot in a mountain rescue. He was enjoying his packed lunch at a picnic table.

'The sea?' he said, spraying bits of cheese roll over the grass. 'The sea?? No, lad, you're miles from the sea up 'ere.'

'Oh, I mean the Severn Estuary, not the open sea.'

'Not even that. You can see the Severn Bridge -- I mean the old one -- from Wotton Hill, down the other end of the Cotswold Way, but up 'ere, no. Why, I doubt you can even pick out the river. Too narrow by now. No, no, no.'

Keen to nudge the conversation -- my first of a rather solitary day -- in a more positive direction, I asked this walker, who must have been pushing seventy, what you *could* see from here on the right day.

'Ah, grand view,' he said, pulling back the next mouthful of roll just before it went in. 'One o' my favourites. Birdlip's broader maybe, Cleeve... well, 's alright if you like Cheltenham I s'pose... but from the Wake 'ere, well, you've got more to get your teeth into, if you get my meanin''.

Before further interrogation I let the view specialist feast on a little more lunch.

'I can see Gloucester,' I announced eventually, 'but only just. Is there more beyond on a clear day?'

'Oh, is there more? Is there more?? There's Wales for a start. Radnor Forest, that's right in Mid-Wales. There's the Malverns, spot them anywhere, like a baskin' whale. And the other way there's the Forest o' Dean, great walking country that. On that thing over there...' He gestured at an information board. '... they say you can see Birmingham. Pah! Birmingham my granny's bottom. Who'd want to see that place anyway?'

Feeling in no position to suggest anyone, I thanked the old fellow, wandered around a little and then pushed off, my own appetite aroused by the sight of his picnic. An early afternoon pub rendezvous with Julie was not far off and after a bumpy cross-country track or two I emerged at my penultimate checkpoint of the day: another lay-by, but one with an unusual feature.

*

At 'Thames Head', just north of Kemble, near Cirencester, a seasonal spring is marked by a monument that declares it to be 'The Source of the River Thames'. It's not. There's no such thing as *the* source of any river; otherwise the millions of gallons a day that flow, for example, under Westminster Bridge would all have to come from a single small spring. It's not even the source furthest from the river's mouth. That honour lies just upstream from the trickle that passes beneath the lay-by at Seven Springs on the A436.

Having carefully descended the rough steps behind the parked cars, I'd found myself in a small glade in the shade of a huge tree against which I'd propped Tetley. From a small cavity in the moss-covered stone wall that kept the lay-by from tumbling into the hollow gurgled a little stream of water that would have taken a good ten seconds to fill a pint mug. Across the rock-strewn floor of the glade it flowed until disappearing under a neatly formed arch through a similar wall on the opposite, south side. Above the arch a block of stone bore the following inscription:

HIC TUUS
O TAMESINE PATER.
SEPTEMCEMINUS FONS.

(Here, o father Thames, is your sevenfold spring.)

In flowing through the arch and under the road, this stream becomes the River Churn, which passes through Cirencester before joining the Thames near Cricklade. While the other six springs lie in the hills around, even here I stood 22 kilometres further upstream from Westminster Bridge than Thames Head. Dipping my cupped hands into the stream, I slurped up a cool mouthful. Mmm, a certain eye-crinkling Gloucestershire tang, but doubtless better for me than a similar mouthful by the Embankment.

*

Lunch called. Remounting Tetley, I slowly pedalled along the lay-by.

'Gotcha!'

The voice had come from the direction of Suzie's, one of those tempting 'sausage stops' that adorn the luckier lay-bys of

England.

'What?'

'One mile an hour,' said the grinning policewoman I now saw leaning on Suzie's counter, brandishing a speed-gun. 'You're nicked!'

'It's a fair cop,' I admitted to the fair cop as I freewheeled over. 'Caught many motorists today?'

'None actually. Thing is: coming downhill round a bend most drivers actually *over*estimate their speed. They brake when they see me, but don't need to.'

'So it'd be less dangerous if you weren't here.'

'Thought had occurred to me too. So I'm off now I've had my snack. You eating at Suzie's?'

'No, I'm meeting someone across the road at the pub.'

'Oh.' And then again: 'Oh.'

'What do you mean 'Oh'?'

A short silence and then: 'Good luck!'

Even from the car park of The Seven Springs, where Julie was waiting to help me load Tetley into the car, we could both see what 'Oh' meant. It already being late for lunch, we decided to give it a try anyway.

While some English pubs, like The Crown at Frampton Mansell, have managed to survive with their character intact and others, like The Old Inn at Holton, have gone upmarket, others have popped up aiming at the very antithesis of the traditional pub market: families. For families, read children... or, as the Hungry Horse chain calls them, 'kids'. The Seven Springs, which I'd identified as a rendezvous point without due care and attention, is part of that chain.

Well, we were spoilt for choice. I could have dived into a Bucket o' Wings, tackled a 20-ring Stacker or feasted on a Foot-Long Hot Dog. Julie could have munched away at a Leaning Tower of Pizza Burger or the slightly racier Bollywood Bad Boy Burger. And we could have enjoyed any of these delights to some challenging background music whose lyrics were, if I caught them right: 'Uh ug uh ug uh ug uh ug uh ug uh ug yaaaaa'. In the end we were such hungry horses ourselves that we did find something edible and I managed to clear the taste of the Thames with a surprisingly decent pint of Abbot.

Uh ug yaaaaa.

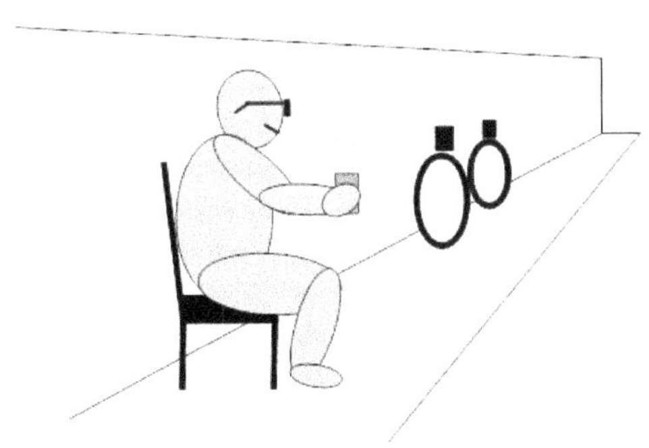

Stage 10: Scent of Provence

Seven Springs to Moreton-in-Marsh

Resuming from Seven Springs lay-by a week or two later, I'd managed to choose yet another morning of heavy skies -- but on this occasion did have time for coffee and a chat at Suzie's. Business was brisk and the smell of fried bacon wafted deliciously into the late summer air and along the line of vans. Suzie herself was on friendly form, multi-tasking as cook, cashier and confidante to the lads taking their morning break.

'Did you get to that drop last week, Geoff?'

'You mean when they was badgerin' me on the mobile while I was 'avin' my bap? Said they could smell the bacon down the phone. Yeah, they got their stuff on time. Always keep a few minutes in my back pocket, I do.'

'S'alright for you, you're freelance. My gaffa's got me as a dot on 'is bleedin' screen, ain't he? Knows exactly where I am. Was bad enough when the tachos came in, but with satnav it's worse 'an ever.'

'Saves you time, though, doesn't it, satnav?'

This last was me being devil's advocate. My own days as a van driver in the 1970s were pre-everything, when contact with the depot was strictly via phone boxes, and only when I wanted. If I said I was in a jam on the A52, that's where I was -- as far as the depot was concerned. While I'd suspected that modern communications would be a bane to the drivers, I felt sure they had their compensations.

I was wrong.

'Bah! The work of the devil. Satnav 'ad me off down a farm track last week. Don't think the farm-'ands wanted the ladies' fashions I'd got on board. No, I still got my OS maps stuffed behind the seat. Can't beat 'em.'

While we were talking Suzie had been lining up a tea and sausage bap on the counter for an apparently invisible customer and now, as she seemed to have a minute to spare, I asked how business was doing.

'Oh, brisk, you know. This is peak time. Where you off to on your bike, then?'

'Moreton-in-Marsh today.'

'Did an event there last weekend. Beer and cider fest... hang on a minute.' A tanker driver had just got down from his cab and approached the hatch.

'Usual, Dave?' said Suzie. 'There it is.'

The invisible customer. Now that's service.

*

While it was completely overcast, at least today's clouds were on the move, hurried along by a keen south-westerly -- England's prevailing wind once again pushing me on my way north-east. From this point the watershed describes a series of giant S's as it swings above the headwaters of the westbound Chelt, the eastbound Coln, westbound Beesmoor Brook, eastbound Windrush and so on, the lanes that follow it revealing glimpses over the Cotswold Edge and beyond. First the 'basking whale' of the Malverns appeared again, blessed with a patch of weak sunshine, and then, as my angle changed, Cheltenham and Gloucester dominated, Churchdown Hill between them, Forest of Dean behind. Now and then stands of beech or ash would swarm up the scarp to engulf the road and block the view, redirecting my attention to the map on my handlebars. In one of these map-gazing moments one name caught my eye: Salt Way. I was pedalling along it.

Salt's success in preserving food put its extraction and distribution at the heart of many civilisations: Chinese, Hebrew, Greek -- and, of more significance to England, Roman. The word 'salary' comes from the Latin '*sal*' (salt) and it's believed that Roman soldiers were sometimes paid in salt (and therefore 'worth their salt') or at least paid in order to buy salt. Across the world many 'salt roads' are still to be found and this particular Salt Way led to the south-coast ports from Droitwich, Worcestershire, the southernmost of England's salt towns mentioned as such in *Domesday Book*. A visit to Droitwich museum leaves you in doubt as to what a gruesome and unhealthy job the town's saltworkers did. Counting myself lucky not to have been among them, as many of my ancestors, I eventually pulled off the Salt Way and down into the small village of Ford for lunch.

*

'Sorry, Desert Orchid's gone. But you can have Red Rum if you like.'

The barman was dealing with a customer on the phone, but there was already no mistaking the overriding theme of the Plough Inn. Not only rooms named after racehorses, but walls covered in photos, paintings and newspaper cuttings that featured all aspects of racing. Cheltenham race course lay barely 15 kilometres distant, while just 15 metres away, that's to say immediately across the road, was to be found one end of the gallops attached to Jackdaw's Castle, the stables run by renowned trainer and former jockey Jonjo O'Neill.

Since the Cotswolds as a whole is known as a 'horsey' area, I'd been surprised to see so few horses over the past two days: a couple at the polo ground, one or two being led through a village street, but that was it. As I left the Plough with their potato and leek soup inside me, this rapidly changed as field after field was alive with sleek-looking horses of all shades: munching grass, galloping around, coming over to see if the blue-helmeted cyclist perhaps had a tasty treat to offer. The common warning sign 'Beware Horses' was here rendered as 'Beware Racehorses', although exactly what extra precautions motorists should be taking was unclear -- checking in the rear-view mirror for one about to overtake?

Horses were not the only animals to put in a sudden appearance, for as the route turned farther inland away from the scarp, countless pheasants and partridges fluttered into my path, only to flap along ahead of me for a few metres before trying to dive through an impenetrable thicket. These birds must have one of the smallest brain-to-body ratios in the natural world. You could walk along these Costwold lanes and literally pick them up by the armful. Quite why some people spend so much time and money trying to shoot them I've no idea.

Such distractions had by now come as a welcome diversion from the endless Cotswold villages. Pretty they may be but, to be honest, after several hours I was getting a bit sick of their cutesy charm. By Snowshill, I was desperate for any normal, brick wall and pedalled straight through -- or rather plodded straight back up to the ridge from which the road had dropped me.

By the time I'd passed Broadway Tower, an impressive eighteenth-century folly conceived by Capability Brown, the landscape was at last beginning to vary. The underlying limestone must have been giving way to neighbouring strata of mudstone or sandstone, as the land use was changing from mostly pastoral to mostly arable. Where there'd been sheep and horses, there were now cabbages, beet and -- quite unexpectedly -- lavender. Stretching away on both sides of the road were huge fields laid out in those parallel rows of lavender familiar in the south of France. This was Snowshill Lavender Farm, begun only in 2000 and now covering over 20 hectares near the Gloucestershire/Worcestershire border. Even in late summer, with the flowers long gone, a hint of their scent remained on the air. Why spend a year in Provence when you can spend an afternoon in the Cotswolds?

As the watershed arced to the east, my occasional views over the scarp slope were also changing. Where there'd been the Severn and the Vale of Gloucester, there was now a northward view over the Vale of Evesham, drained by the lower reaches of the Avon. I paused to take in one of these panoramas, as it showed me a particularly significant point on my route. It's the broad catchment area of the Warwickshire Avon that would now force me way, way over to the East Midlands in order to pass beyond its headwaters before curving back to the same meridian on which I now stood. With the afternoon skies finally lifting, on the far northern horizon I could just pick out a grey line of hills enclosing the plain. These had to be the Lickey Hills at the other end of Worcestershire, lying at a straight-line distance of some 40 kilometres -- but, for me, four more counties and at least seven travelling days away. The watershed at its most wigglesome.

*

Things closer to hand soon demanded my attention, for the 'Five Mile Drive' of the busy A44 requires all the concentration a cyclist can muster, to weave a steady path between the pot holes on his left and the thundering trucks on his right. Fortunately the still-relentless wind had veered in sympathy and quickly blew me up against Bourton-on-the-Hill, where I was able to turn out of the traffic and onto a tranquil lane that skirted the many-shaded browns and greens of Batsford arboretum, before whisking me down an exhilarating descent and into the middle of Moreton-in-Marsh.

Moreton rattled with noise and movement. While the school run filled the roads with agitated drivers, market traders dismantled their stalls and shop-owners flicked their door signs round to 'Closed'. Quickly getting my foot inside Tilly's tea shop, I persuaded the girl behind the counter to pour one last cuppa and sell an emergency caramel slice to a weary cyclist. Nothing much can beat sitting around watching other people work and I happily sipped and munched away opposite the shrinking market.

A notice attached to the town's old 'curfew tower' and dated 1905 lists the market tolls of the day: from 3d (about 1p) for a hand cart up to a shilling (5p) for a 'waggon'. Tolls for the fairs were higher: from 2s 6d (12.5p) for a swing or a 'cocoanut shoot' up to 6 shillings (30p) for a roundabout driven by a pony. Roundabouts driven by steam were prohibited, with no explanation offered. For 5 shillings (25p) a year a resident could put up a stall outside his or her house at any event. For some reason earthenware dealers would be charged per yard of frontage, while 'shows, menageries and 'bazzars' would pay by the square yard. How the stallholder nearest to me had been charged today I knew not, but as he rolled up his awning he was whistling 'Happy Talk'.

'Good day?' I asked.

Shrugging his shoulders, he summed it up in the phrase which to a foreign ear sounds negative, but which to a fellow Englishman communicates positive satisfaction:

'Had worse.'

And so had I. While I'd found few pedestrians in these empty Cotswold villages to engage in conversation, I'd benefitted from a friendly sausage stop, a cosy pub and a changing landscape. While no sunbeam had fallen on me, nor had any raindrop.

Had worse.

Stage 11: Priorities of Middle England

Moreton-in-Marsh to Edge Hill

One summer Sunday 24 years before, I'd turned up with a Leicestershire pub cricket team for a pre-match drink at the inn designated by our Oxfordshire opponents. While the match was forgettable, the inn was certainly not and my 24-year wait to stay there was finally over as Julie and I had checked in for a two-night stay. Though about six kilometres off route, The Falkland Arms easily justified the diversion.

Oak-beamed inside and ivy-covered outside, this quintessentially English pub lies half-hidden on a narrow dead-end lane in the village of Great Tew, just east of Chipping Norton. The village itself has had its ups and downs since its foundation before the Norman invasion. By the seventeenth century, over a hundred years after its inn first opened, it was home to about 450 residents but in 1914 the then owner of the local estate, a descendent of the industrialist Matthew Boulton, died without an heir, heralding an era of public trusteeship in which many of the houses were abandoned and fell derelict. Such a beautiful location -- with thatched cottages all made from local ironstone, an iron-rich limestone that oxidises from its original grey to a colour that *is* rather honey-like -- was, however, always going to attract incomers and by 2001 the population had nudged back up to 153. One of those lucky enough to have been brought up here is journalist and broadcaster John Sergeant, son of the local vicar and whose childhood home was therefore Great Tew's vicarage.

When I'd visited in the 1980s I'd assumed that The Falkland Arms had got its name from the Falkland Islands, but, of course, I'd got things back to front. In the seventeenth century the Horse and Groom Inn was renamed after the then Lord of the Manor, the 2nd Viscount Falkland, while the islands got their name later from the 5th Viscount Falkland, First Lord of the Admiralty.

Whatever its provenance, the inn sign bearing the blue and red Falkland coat of arms creaked in the breeze outside our room; every floorboard creaked at the slightest touch; windows didn't quite close and mysterious doors looked as though they'd never been opened. In other words, The Falkland Arms proved to be everything a quirky old country pub in the middle of England should be. With countless jugs hanging low from the ceilings, with eccentric and mostly unrelated information adorning the walls, with Wadworth's ales having made the journey from Devizes via (I hope) a shorter route than ours and with traditional pub food and chatty staff, this for me was heaven.

*

The morning after Julie had picked me up from Moreton's market place she dropped me off in the same spot but with the muzzy head I deserved after an evening's over-imbibing at Great Tew. Through eyes narrowed against a brightening sky, I noticed a middle-aged man and woman admiring Tetley the bike.

'Far to go today?' he asked.

I filled them in on my short- and long-term plans.

'Ah, Kinder Scout,' she said. 'Up there you'll need your

wellies, not a bike.'

'You've walked Kinder Scout then?'

'On Chernobyl day.'

My brain was slow to process a word I didn't expect to hear.

'You know,' she insisted, 'in the 1980s, that thing in Russia.'

'The nuclear accident?'

'Yes. We didn't know anything about it till we got home, but the radioactive cloud was supposed to be spreading across the Pennines while we were up there.'

'No after-effects I hope?'

'My husband here's always been a bit strange, so it's hard to tell.'

Cheered by the banter and with my head slowly clearing, I pushed off out of town.

Where do the Cotswolds end? For that matter, where do they start? The broadest definition I've come across is that used by *The Rough Guide to the Cotswolds* (2011, Rough Guides), which pulls in Bath, Stratford-on-Avon and Oxford to create a huge swathe across the south Midlands of about 4,500 square kilometres. The Cotswolds Area of Outstanding Natural Beauty covers less than half that. What we have to remember is that the Cotswolds are a range of hills and a relief map suggests Bath as the southern limit and Chipping Camden the northern. While the western boundary has to be the Cotswold Edge, it's in the east that things get a bit hazy. Even Mr Massingham himself becomes a little vague. In comparing the north-eastern extremities of the Cotswolds to a pair of horns, he agrees that the tip of the northern horn is at Chipping Campden, but commits only to the base of the eastern horn being at Chipping Norton. As to its tip, he wanders off into an inconclusive tale about the underlying limestone's continuation into

Northamptonshire -- which is definitely not the Cotswolds.

Be all that as it may, yesterday's eastward descent from Batsford to Moreton felt like the end of the serious hills and certainly today's route east along the A44, under very welcome blue skies, was less of a challenge to Tetley's gears. However, soon after passing the practice tower of the Fire Service College, which occupies another ex-wartime airfield, I was off the bike again and examining a huge stone monument just yards from the road. On its four faces were inscribed 'Gloucestershire', 'Warwickshire', 'Oxfordshire' and 'Worcestershire'. This was the Four Shire Stone, a sixteenth-century construction to mark the spot where the boundaries of four counties used to meet. Used to, because Worcestershire -- unfortunately the most prominent of the inscriptions -- hasn't reached this far south since a boundary change in 1931. This was, however, a definitive goodbye to Gloucestershire, which had borne Tetley and me safely over four travelling days, and an unexpectedly southern hello to that most Midland of counties, Warwickshire.

According to its council's slogan, Warwickshire is 'working together for you'. Only 5 kilometres beyond the Four Shire Stone, it seemed to have worked itself into exhaustion, for it abandoned me once again to Oxfordshire. County boundaries are two a penny round here.

*

Stones of a much older vintage were the feature of my next stop. In approximately the same period that saw the origin of that small stone circle above Portesham way back in Dorset, as well as many other features I'd passed since then, other ancient Britons were raising what we know as the Rollright Stones. More precisely, since there are other Rollright Stones nearby, they were raising the 'King's Men' circle of sixty-two now misshapen and lichen-covered limestone blocks. Or sixty-three. Or seventy. A nearby notice written by the Rollright Trust challenges the visitor to count the stones three times and, should the total be the same each time, to make a wish that would then be granted. After a first count of sixty-three I then made it sixty-two, sparing the Trust the need to bribe enough referees to get Nottingham Forest promotion.

Sipping at my gruesome vacuum-flask coffee, I sat on one of the lower stones and considered the scene. This was the most easterly stone circle in England, on a not particularly prominent hill, and yet once again it was bang on the country's central watershed. Surely the profusion of ancient structures along this route can't be a coincidence. Surely their builders knew the wider significance of this line, in other words knew their geography better than many of us today. Via old-fashioned snail mail I raised this question with Nick Crane, he of *Two Degrees West*. Crane's own experience of travelling along watersheds is surely unsurpassed in the modern era: his astonishing seventeen-month, 10,000-kilometre trek across the backbone of Europe from Cape Finisterre to Istanbul led to the best-selling book *Clear Waters Rising* (1997, Penguin). He was, however, less convinced on the matter than I. While acknowledging that sections of the English Watershed probably had political or symbolic meaning, Nick felt that there was no evidence for the watershed as a whole having any particular significance in prehistoric times.

After staring into space for a while, I concluded that we'll probably never know. What I did know was that I needed something to take away the bitter taste of that coffee and, after rummaging around in my bag, pulled out a cake that Julie had managed to pick up the previous day in Chipping Norton -- or 'Chippy' as she discovered the locals call it. Bearing the name of another local town, this would be the next entrant in my Cake Research Project: it was a Banbury Cake. Now, being a relatively flat piece of pastry with narrow holes on top and flour sprinkled all over, this confection had convinced me it was going to taste like an Eccles Cake. On first bite it did; on second it did not. The ingredients -- and subsequent research tells me they were supposed to be currants and candied peel -- were either dry, small or absent. Peering into the piece left in my hand, I did discern little black things that could have been currants or insects or... well, let's just leave it there. Either way, the bland Banbury Cake sank to second bottom on the chart, just above the devilish Dorset Knob.

*

According to the information boards, these ancient stones probably knew more about food than I did, for, surprisingly, 'The Rollright Stones recommend Wyatt's Tea Room' -- a tip I was happy to follow, not only to get the taste of stale coffee out of my mouth, but now also that of dry cake.

A fair number of national politicians and journalists live around here. Without any clear indication of what they really mean -- admittedly a shortcoming that applies to almost everything they say -- many of them often refer to the priorities of what they call 'middle England'. Well, if they want to mug up on the subject, they could do worse than sitting quietly in the tea room at Wyatt's Garden Centre, Oxfordshire, eavesdropping on the conversations.

'How old are they now?'

'Jonah's fifteen, Rebecca's twelve and little Jimmy's eight next week.'

'Of course, he was born just after our Pauline's twins.'

'Gosh are they eight already?'

'Well, you know Pauline was only eighteen when she had them and she's twenty-six now.'

'And Jeremy?'

'Thirty last month.'

'Oh, how time flies. Another ten years and he'll be forty.'

And Pauline thirty-six, I thought, the twins eighteen, Jonah twenty-five... and these two grandmothers probably still here, still astonished by the passage of time. With my own advancing years, I've found that listening to other people's conversations gets nearer and nearer the top of my favourite pastimes list (just behind watching other people work), but one skill I haven't yet developed is being able to focus consistently on one conversation or another. Here in this busy tea room, snatches of various discussions drifted in and out.

'Why do they stand up to read the news nowadays? Makes my legs ache just watching them.'

'He's got a mobile forge, of course, but I don't think he'd get it on the plane.'

'Ooh, I say, apple and blackcurrant flapjack. Well, you're only young once. Actually it was twice with me and a Tuesday both times.'

'It looms, that's what it does. Looms and blocks the light. Shouldn't be allowed in a place like Chippy.'

'Well, he'll regret it, believe me. She's got two already and a third in the pipeline, though what colour this one'll be heaven knows.'

and, most intriguing of all...

'Oh, the Khyber Pass isn't what it used to be, you know.'

To be honest, I'm not sure middle England's preoccupations are much related to politics.

*

Following the watershed along the ridge above Hook Norton brewery, source of the ale of the same name but lacking a brewery tap, I pulled up again to take in the long views that opened out to both south and north. For once there were no notable features save for fluffy white clouds billowing above and deep green Oxfordshire countryside billowing below. At first the only sound came from trees bowing and rustling in the gentle northerly, but my lowering of Tetley onto the verge prompted a sudden scuttle behind a hedge from a startled horse, followed by the scornful cackle of a crow. With a drop in the wind came that rarity in twenty-first century England -- a silent minute -- before the distant drone of a light aircraft and then the lower tone of a van interrupted it. Though the road was unclassified it seemed popular with white vans, as they passed one after the other: the builder's van, the decorator's van, the butcher's, the carpet layer's and the TV man's. Soon after resuming I found myself waving down the postman's red van to draw his attention to the small black dog that seemed to have adopted me at the last farm and was now wandering dangerously from side to side of the road, a little way behind.

'Oh, don't worry,' he said (the postman, not the dog), 'that's just Tiggy. He's allowed to run between the farms.' Looking at his watch, he added: 'He'll be off to the Grange.'

So this little dog, one black ear vertical, the other flopped down, had daily appointments with the local farmers. By the time I'd waved the postman off Tiggy had run ahead and was looking back, a frown formed by his bristly grey eyebrows, as if to say: 'Well, come on. I can't hang a round all day.' At the Grange, with no backward glance, Tiggy duly scampered off into the farmhouse, where a tasty snack doubtless waited.

*

Like most English people, I'd heard of Edgehill but never been there. What we remember from school is the Battle of Edgehill, the first battle of the Civil War, and those who were paying attention could tell you it took place in 1642. Beyond that most of us (including me) would be blank. Who won? Sorry, Miss Catlow, can't remember.

Edge Hill (two words) is the continuation of the watershed ridge back into Warwickshire at a point where the land falls dramatically away to the north-west, while Edgehill (one word) is a hamlet that sits astride the road along the top of the ridge. Dominating the hamlet is an extraordinary castellated tower, with no castle around it, built in 1742 to commemorate the battle's centenary and now forming The Castle Inn, chosen location for today's rendezvous with Julie. Spotting an information board on the far edge of the pub's terrace, I dumped Tetley and wandered over in hope of some reminder of what Miss Catlow had doubtless told us scatterbrains some 45 years before.

The first news was that the battle didn't take place up here at all, but down on the flatlands below; hence the location of the board. Eagerly I drank in its explanation. War had been declared on August 22nd, since when troops had been manoeuvred around the country. It was now Sunday October 23rd. Control of London, already in Parliamentarian hands, was key to victory and a march on the capital from his temporary headquarters at Shrewsbury had been King Charles's intention before finding himself in close proximity to the Parliamentarians' main army here in the Midlands. It is reputedly right here on the site now occupied by the tower that the king raised his standard on Edge Hill. Meanwhile the Parliamentary troops, under the Earl of Essex, were deployed down on the plain towards Kineton, a village I could just discern through the treetops, about 5 kilometres away.

The king's army descended the ridge, a hard enough task today by the looks of it, but with weapons and horses it must have been a tricky start to the day. The opposing armies, about 30,000 men all told, engaged in battle on open fields between Radway, a village at the foot of the ridge, and Kineton. At first the Royalists, both cavalry and foot soldiers, drove their opposite numbers back towards Kineton, but a resurgence from Essex's foot soldiers then drove the king's men back towards Radway. The day's fierce encounters saw over 1,000 men dead and many more wounded, but by nightfall a combination of depleted ammunition stocks and sheer exhaustion saw an end to the fighting.

The following day the message bearing Charles's offer of a pardon for Essex, should he surrender, is believed not even to have got beyond the enemy troops and eventually the Parliamentarians simply withdrew, returning to their garrison at Warwick, some 16 kilometres to the north.

Now here's the rub. With the Parliamentarians gone the king was theoretically left free to march south-east to London, but what the Royalist troops actually did is advance southwards via Banbury and Oxford to the Thames at Reading. This gave Essex time to regroup and reinforce London's defences to an extent that the Royalists withdrew to Oxford, there to set up their headquarters for the duration of the war. The king had missed his chance.

Partly for this reason, some commentators regard the Battle of Edgehill as having ended not in a Royalist victory but effectively in a draw. The site of a later, more decisive battle in the Civil War is also located on the English Watershed and lay for me a couple of days' travelling to the north.

*

Having arrived early, I popped into The Castle Inn for a pint of Hooky Gold (a relatively recent Hook Norton ale: pale, tasty, with a satisfying bite), a reluctant chat with Chaos the dog in an otherwise empty bar and another, higher scan over the battlefield from the pub's viewing balcony. It was here that Julie joined me after a visit to nearby Upton House, but neither of us could solve a visual mystery. From both guides and maps, it was clear that most of the fields across which the battle was fought have since been built over by the MOD's Temple Herdewyke site, a vast spread of storage facilities and old railway sidings which incorporate a monument to the battle but which are, of course, out of bounds to the public. The mystery is that this MOD complex was nowhere to be seen.

Stage 12: A World Gone Mad

Edge Hill to Kilsby

After a second night at The Falkland Arms, the mystery of the invisible MOD site was solved as I whooshed down Edge Hill on a chilly morning, the brisk air sharp against my ears. From a different angle the depot buildings peeked out from their cover of trees, thousands of which obscured the view from above.

As I screeched the brakes to take a sharp right turn just in front of the armed guards at the entrance, a thought occurred to me. Whooshing and watershed following don't really go together. Having cycled parallel to my pre-marked line on the map, I now found myself in a valley between the ridge I'd just left and another that rose before me. Something was up. Pulling over, I looked more closely at the map perched on Tetley's handlebars.

Just as in Dorset's Blackmore Vale, the watershed briefly struck out across low-lying land to get from one patch of high terrain to another. Here rise the headwaters of the River Dene, which flows north-westwards to join the Avon near Stratford, close to those of a small tributary of the Cherwell, flowing in the opposite direction to Banbury and the Thames. Having sneaked between the two, I now found myself pushing Tetley up the steep slopes of Burton Hills, an outcrop of ironstone overlooking the mudstone vale. So slow was my progress that a middle-aged lady not only overtook me on foot but also passed me again on her way down.

'Shouldn't you be riding that?' she asked, rather too sharply I thought.

'Protecting my knee,' I retorted.

'Worth it for the view from the top anyway.'

She was right. Still catching my breath, I stood hands on hips to take in the huge swathe of the Midlands spread at my feet. Earlier in the year the bright yellow of oil-seed rape would have been speckled here and there, but this chilly September morning it was entirely shades of green and gold that rippled and rolled to the horizon. An information board claimed you could see Coventry from here, but no urban blobs interrupted the rural landscape today. Visitors wanting a taste of the old country could do a lot worse than to wander across this half-forgotten corner of England, from pub to pub, village to village. Avon Dassett, Fenny Compton, Wormleighton, Priors Hardwick -- they're just as picturesque as the more renowned Cotswold or Chiltern villages and, built from ironstone that here is rather toast-coloured, their back-lane cottages, draped in timeless wisteria, are just as likely to take you back a century or two, before the motor car started racing through.

But maybe not up here on the top of Burton Hills for, though they provide a treat for the eyes, the ears are assaulted by the continuous roar from the nearby M40. While the battle against it was lost many years ago, at least the motorway does bring some benefits to the local people, who, on a good day, now find themselves only an hour and a quarter's drive from London's North Circular Road.

The same could not be said of another planned development

about which I was about to learn more than I expected.

*

The information came from a quietly spoken, somewhat frail-looking seventy-something as he waited at the table opposite me in the bar of the sixteenth-century Hollybush Inn at Priors Marston I'd pulled over, out of the stiff north wind, for an early lunch. What he was waiting for was a pack of rolls to take to workers at the nearby church who were busy dismantling a part of the organ surround whose Baroque style, he told me, clashed with the essence of the medieval church. As he'd showed some interest in the map I was perusing, I asked if I was right that the route of the proposed high-speed railway between London and Birmingham, HS2, passed near here.

As he slowly cast his eyes to the rafters, long grey hairs drifted away from his tilted head.

'Proposed, planned, opposed, confirmed,' he said, 'and, if you want my opinion, soon to be quietly dropped.'

Having received my assurance that I did indeed want his opinion, he let me have it smack between the eyes, though never raising his voice above a murmur.

'The whole thing's a complete nonsense. Should never have been conceived. Now, you probably think I'm just a nimby protecting my own patch, but it wouldn't really affect us here in Priors Marston. More Priors Hardwick's problem actually. No, it's the cost-benefit analysis. Shot full of holes. I'm a trained economist, you see. Been helping out with the campaign.'

I'd read about the controversy surrounding the new line, but didn't know many details. 'What are the holes?' I asked.

'Oh, where should we start? The cost? Well, a year ago they said it'd cost twenty-four billion. With the extra cuttings and whatnot that's crept up to thirty-five billion or so. But I had a chat with someone who'd left their team and he reckoned the real total would end up nearer twice that.'

'Seventy billion pounds? Ouch.' The numbers had made me gulp down my hot carrot and coriander soup too quickly. 'It's not as though the country's wallowing in spare cash at the moment.'

'Far from it, my friend. And the benefit side... well, if anything, the numbers are even wilder. The biggest benefits are supposed to come from time saved by the passengers -- and do you know how much it would save the type of passenger they're talking about?'

'Birmingham to London?'

'Yes.'

'Hm. Half an hour?'

'Ten minutes! After taking a local train into Birmingham from the suburbs where these high-earners live, getting to another station, getting on another train, and then, at the other end, diving into the Tube... it'd be ten minutes saved. That's all it's about.

'Madness.'

'You're right, the world's gone madder than ever. But the light at the end of the tunnel -- ha, sorry no joke intended -- is that it didn't make the Queen's Speech, so I think the whole shenanigans will be quietly dropped. Same not true for Tesco, alas.'

'Tesco?' I asked, taken aback by the sudden switch in subject matter.

'Yes, we're lucky to have a pub still open in this little village... I'm not boring you, am I?'

'Not at all.'

'... but they're doing their best to close down all the local shops, the planners. Nearest place people go shopping here is

Southam. Two supermarkets there were, but now they've let Tesco's in, how long will they last?' He didn't wait for me to take a guess at this one. 'I was at the public meeting. What a farce that was. Presented all our research, we did, and then some woman stood up with a theatrical tear in her eye and a claim that her human rights'd be breached if she couldn't shop at her precious Tesco's. And you know what?' I didn't. 'The council took it in. Hook, line and sinker. So now it's done. Has the world gone mad or what?'

I did know the answer to this one. 'Completely mad.'

'Aye,' he said, just as his rolls appeared, 'and so will the workers be if they don't get their lunch. Cheeri-bye.'

And with that he was off, leaving me with more to think about than I'd bargained for.

*

Involvement in local campaigns against the hated planners seemed to be pretty widespread around here, for it was on this stretch of my route that I passed more signs of protest than anywhere else. 'No HS2 Rail Link', 'Shuckburgh Wind Farm -- Just Say No', 'Unite and Fight'. It used to be an estate agent, but now it seems the chair of a planning committee is the most despised professional in England.

It came as something of a relief to get back to the uncontroversial history and geography of the rolling Warwickshire landscape through which I was passing. Wiggling away on my left for some time had been the Oxford Canal, a waterway that clings so closely to the contours that its 240-year-old route between Oxford and Coventry must be nearly double the straight line. And just just over the border into Northamptonshire the eastern horizon gradually filled with another significant hill.

A glance back at the map of watersheds will show that the English Watershed, whose line I'd been following since Morgan's

Hill in Wiltshire, joins up hereabouts with another major one: the East Anglian watershed between those rivers flowing south into the Thames Estuary and those flowing north to the Wash. The actual watershed junction lies on top of Arbury Hill, at 225 metres the highest point in Northamptonshire and whose top is formed by the square embankment of yet another Iron Age fort right on the watershed. Unfortunately, with no public access to the hill itself, I was restricted to the view from the lane between Hellidon and Catesby from which to raise my water bottle to the latest significant milestone on my journey. From now on, all the rivers on my right, including the Nene, which rises just beyond Arbury Hill, would be headed for the 'real' North Sea, that is to say they would enter it either at the Wash or even further north. And this time it's not just me that felt this to be the start of a different territory.

*

An historian named Charles Phythian-Adams, along with his team at Leicester University, has put forward the hypothesis that during medieval times there existed in England a series of what he calls 'cultural provinces' at a scale between local communities and the nation. Through detailed research into historical social traits at some sample locations, he's proposed fourteen 'provinces' in the country's cultural landscape at the time. And here's the rub. In overlaying a map of the boundaries between these provinces and a map of England's main watersheds, there's a remarkable match in most areas. Here along the Warwickshire/Northamptonshire border, for example, I was also straddling the suggested 'border' between the cultural provinces that Phythian-Adams calls 'Severn/Avon' and 'Wash/Ouse'.

From Toller Down in Dorset I'd wandered unknowingly along the border between 'French Channel' (Dorset, Wiltshire and Hampshire) and 'Severn Estuary' (Somerset); and then along that between 'Severn/Avon' (Gloucestershire, Warwickshire, Worcestershire and Shropshire) and 'Thames' (Oxfordshire, London and the Home Counties). The fact that these areas still sounded to me like identifiable English regions suggests that the medieval cultural landscape is still very much embedded in the English psyche... and that the significance of the 'English Watershed', the line I was following, has held steady over the centuries.

Buoyed by this boost to the coherence of what I was doing -- something that, I admit, I'd begun to lose sight of since I'd left the Cotswold Edge -- I pedalled into the first sizeable town en route since Devizes.

*

Depending on their age, Daventry is a town many people know either from signposts or from their radio dial, rather than from actually visiting the place. I fell into both categories. While signpost fame comes from its location just off the A5, its celebrity to the 'radio dial generation' comes from the goings-on at Borough Hill.

It's said that the Danes planted an oak tree on this prominent hill just east of the town to mark what they regarded as the centre of England, and an axeman and an oak tree still appear on Daventry's coat of arms. But it was in 1925 that the BBC chose Borough Hill as the single point in England and Wales from which the greatest number of listeners would receive their radio signals. At first it was long-wave transmissions that were broadcast from here but it was the BBC Empire Service (later BBC World Service) on short wave from 1932 that made 'Daventry Calling' a familiar announcement across the world and ultimately enabled Daventry to take its place on the radio dial next to Luxembourg, Hilversum and the rest of those atmospheric names from the heyday of radio. While a tall mast still stands proudly on the hill and forms an easily recognisable landmark for drivers between junctions 16 and 17 on the M1, the BBC left the site in 1992 and at the time of this ride the mast was owned by a Canadian-Australian telecomms company.

Above the rooftops I caught a glimpse of the latest mast I rode up to Daventry's small town centre, before propping Tetley against the walls of the Moot Hall. This eighteenth-century ironstone building has served variously as a meeting place for the council, a women's prison and an Indian restaurant, but it was its current role as a cafe that attracted me today. 'Moot' is an Old English word for a meeting and also gives us the modern adjective 'moot', meaning debatable. Appropriately, it was a moot point that I inadvertently raised as I placed my order.

'Cup of tea and a cake, please. You don't do Northamptonshire seed cake, do you?'

Aware that my cake research project had generated only four contenders so far, I'd been on the internet in search of more and had come across something of that name. The pleasant woman behind the counter, whose accent was Irish, thought for a moment before reporting:

'No, never heard of it.'

'Oh, never mind, I'll have...'

'... Neither have I, but I know who will.'

This voice had a local accent and was that of a woman behind me, waiting to pay.

'Who's that?' I asked her.

'The WI. If the Women's Institute hasn't heard of a cake, it doesn't exist. I'll just phone my friend. Hang on a minute.'

A little taken aback by this generous offer of help and also a unsure how a portion of Northamptonshire seed cake might be delivered through a phone line, I sat down with my tea. After a few words on her mobile, a pressed button, a short ring and another few words, the local woman approached my table.

'Doesn't exist,' she stated confidently. 'She doesn't know it, her friend doesn't know it, WI doesn't know it, doesn't exist. Where have you heard of it?'

Wondering by now if I'd accidentally used the secret password of an MI5 unit staking out Daventry tea rooms in an undercover operation to nail a gang smuggling drugs into Britain via small items of confectionery, I hesitated before replying.

'Er... well, on the internet actually. I just put "regional cakes" into Google.'

'I see,' she said, and then repeated it. 'I see. If you give me your email address I'll investigate and let you know.'

Having done as she asked, I spent the rest of the day's ride wondering what sinister, cake-based world I'd got myself into.

*

While the road signs *into* Daventry town centre had been crystal-clear, there appeared to be no signs *out of* town at all. Maybe no one ever leaves. However, my uncertainty as to where I was gave me the opportunity to ask the help, one after the other, of three young locals wandering along the pavement. Keen to help though they all were, it's interesting that the first two seemed incapable of giving any clear directions, while all three had no idea where I -- or they -- were on my large-scale Ordnance Survey map. As an ex-geography teacher, I felt compelled to follow this up, but my fears that map-reading might have gone the way of the apostrophe in English lessons were, thankfully, not confirmed, as it turns out that map-reading is still right there in the Department for Education's 'Key Stage 3' curriculum for 11-to-14-year-olds. Perhaps the three Daventry youngsters were just having a bad day.

More by process of elimination than anything alse, I eventually found my way onto the Daventry-Kilsby road. While it has nothing visibly remarkable about it, the A361 does claim one strange attribute of note for, at 314 kilometres, it's the longest three-digit A-road in Britain, having come all the way from Ilfracombe in Devon. Yes, I thought you'd be impressed. What struck me as strange was not so much the fact itself as the disconcerting realisation that someone had bothered to notice. And while collating obscure transport facts, I can't let the motorway the A361 crosses just before Kilsby go without a mention either.

Built in 1959 and therefore one of Britain's earliest motorways, the M45 was initially one of its busiest too, being part of the fastest route from London to Birmingham -- until the new M6 took almost all the traffic, leaving it now as one of the quietest. A glance down from the over-bridge is nowadays rather like watching one of those quaint 1960s film clips featuring four pristine motorway lanes virtually empty of traffic. I almost expected a tiny Triumph Herald or a streamlined Ford Zodiac to come trundling into view.

The village of Kilsby, however, owes its existence to much older journeys, having developed at the junction of two cattle-drovers' routes and prospered as a staging post on the east-west, Coventry-to-Cambridge stagecoach road. And parked outside The George, as scheduled, was my own stagecoach driver in the form of Julie, fresh from a shopping excursion to nearby Leamington Spa (vibrant, she reported) and Rugby (badly rundown apparently).

*

Back home that evening, I nervously logged into my emails. And there it was: a link to the recipe for Northamptonshire seed cake. Daventry's secret cake agent had delivered, but I'd evidently failed to explain that my interest lay not in making cakes but eating them. What a fantastically helpful lady though. As it happened, the fact that the recipe included two tablespoons of caraway seeds saved the need for a taste test. Can't stand seeds between my teeth, nor can I imagine why anyone would. Yes, I suppose the clue was in the name.

Stage 13: International Frontier

Kilsby to Thornby

As the crow flies, it's just 15 kilometres from Kilsby in Northamptonshire to Willey in Warwickshire, but as the watershed wanders it's a staggering 53 kilometres. The discrepancy's cause is the giant bite out of the landscape taken by the west-flowing headwaters of the River Avon and its tributaries, thrusting the watershed further east toward more east-flowing headwaters of the three great rivers that drain into the Wash: the Ouse, Nene and Welland. In being bent eastwards, my route pushed further and further back into the great Jurassic ridge. It also made its only incursion into the East Midlands -- a distinction from the West Midlands that outsiders may think a fine one, but which those native to these parts take very seriously indeed, suggesting again that the psychological inheritance from our medieval forbears may be stronger than we sometimes pretend. More surprisingly perhaps, the route also crosses an international frontier.

*

Now, I have to admit that this stage was ticked off out of sequence... for a good reason. Back in February, not long after we'd set off on that overcast morning from Abbotsbury, the English winter had intensified, with more than half the country suddenly covered in a slender, pristine blanket of snow. After two days and nights of clear skies and low temperatures, the Midland countryside had been transformed into a glistening gallery of views too good to miss. After Julie had dropped me off once again outside The George at Kilsby, I stamped my boots to keep the cold at bay. Before I could reach open country, there were a few major barriers to cross.

The road I stamped onto was the busy A5, thankfully for only a hundred metres or so before turning onto a bridleway to Crick. The track's dirt surface, however, proved just as unyielding as the main road's tarmac, so that only slight smears in the frost would mark the passing of my boots. Beneath here lies Kilsby Tunnel, carrying the main railway from Euston to Birmingham and the north-west, engineered by Robert Stephenson and opened in 1838. Its alignment can be identified by motorists, from the giant, round, castellated towers beside the A5, marking ventilation shafts and now listed buildings. For two years over a thousand men worked on the tunnel and it's reputed that, when the roof collapsed, a good number of them were saved from drowning by a single engineer who swam to a shaft gripping between his teeth a rope attached to a raft that bore his colleagues.

By the time I crossed yet another railway, the 'Northampton loop' from the main line, passing above the path this time, the song of those few birds out and about in the frost had been drowned by the roar of a dragon. As it roared it stamped, the vibration running through the hard ground and right up the trunks of the leafless trees beside it. The name of this dragon was M1 and the path to Crick burrowed beneath it. But I didn't take it. For what had brought me on this short, noisy diversion to the north of the actual watershed line was yet another long-distance route, now squeezed between these intertwining transport arteries but, when laid out some two thousand years before, representing a solitary thread of civilisation across a wild, undeveloped landscape.

I was standing on Watling Street, another of the Romans' major routes across their province of Britannia, linking Portus Dubris, Londinium and Viroconium Cornoviorum (Dover, London and Wroxeter, now in Shropshire). In fact, what the Romans straightened and surfaced was an even older track used by the Ancient Britons -- although the name Watling Street is actually Anglo-Saxon, meaning 'the road of the people of Wæcel'. This might have meant simply foreigners, in this case the Welsh, for, just as with today's A5, that was the ultimate destination of this route to the north-west.

Just here is one of the best spots along its entire length to see Watling Street, where the old alignment doesn't coincide with a modern road, but yet is still discernible. It's a straight, grassy path between parallel rows of trees and bushes, today glistening with frost. Crunching the thick grass underfoot, I set off in the direction of Rome, some 1600 kilometres away, straddling as I did so an international frontier put in place some centuries after the Romans had left: that between the Saxon kingdom of Wessex and the Viking lands of the Danelaw.

After King Alfred's victory in 878 at the Battle of Ethandun, whose memorial I'd passed on the edge of Salisbury Plain, the Treaty of Wedmore specified Watling Street as the boundary between Saxon and Viking territories. One significant legacy of the Danelaw is the pattern of East Midland counties, the Shires, and their county towns, the Five Boroughs: Derby, Nottingham, Lincoln, Leicester and Stamford (Rutland). Though not one of the Five Boroughs, Northampton, whose county I was still in, was also Danish.

Still 1599 kilometres from Rome, I turned off towards Crick.

*

Having rejoined the watershed, I crossed the M1 by Tunnel Farm, above a railway tunnel on the Northampton loop line, and trundled into the village. With its recent by-pass, Crick is now a quiet place as well as an attractive one, still with plenty of ironstone houses and, in The Red Lion, a pub with a good reputation but also, this being midweek in winter, with a firmly closed door. And so, thirst quenched only by my flask of coffee, I headed out on the footpath to West Haddon. An hour later I was heading back again.

It's the pleasure I get from map-reading that keeps me from investing in a GPS device. Occasionally however -- as with that other invention of the devil, the mobile phone -- I have to admit that the ghastly gadget might, for a second or two, have been bathed in the rare glow of usefulness. The path was there. And then the path was not there. I was there. The path was elsewhere. Where was the path? Or, a question of equal significance, where was I?

The context for these questions was a large, hard, frosty field south-east of Crick, which the path and I entered together, but from which the path departed alone. For, scour it as I did, no point of egress could I find. And it's not as though this was a featureless field. It included not only the north portal of another canal tunnel, this one containing the Grand Union Canal as it passed beneath the modest Northamptonshire Uplands, but also an incongruous mound marking the canal's subterranean alignment: features quite clearly marked on my map. But where the map suggested the footpath should breach the eastern hedge I found only hedge and barbed wire. It must have been somewhere else. Thrice I scoured the field. Thrice I cursed it.

(Back home that evening I accessed a website called, suitably enough, www.wheresthepath.com, which shows in side-by-side panels an Ordnance Survey map and an aerial photograph of the same location. As you move the cursor in one, it automatically moves the cursor in the other. Aha! The coppice in the on-screen map and the coppice on which I had been aligning my on-field map were two different coppices. One was still there and the other... the other had been stolen.)

On my reluctant return to Crick, the village seemed to hold no attraction at all. Rather than a leisurely lollop along the footpaths to West Haddon I now faced a 5-kilometre slog along busy main roads and narrow lanes. To distract me from the sharp ridges of frozen soil to which I retreated with each passing vehicle, I regularly gazed southwards, to the right, in search of the physical reason that so many communication lines northbound from London -- road, canal, rail -- converge on this little corner of Northamptonshire. It's a feature of Midland geography so often referred to but so little seen that it's gained almost mythical status. I refer to the Watford Gap. While many Londoners believe the Watford of the Watford Gap and the Watford of 'North of Watford' to be one and the same, this one is at a low point in the Northamptonshire Uplands near the village of Watford, some 4 kilometres south of Crick. It's a characteristic of the gentle landscape of the southern half of England that many topographical features, though they may have gained a name, are barely visible at all and the Watford Gap is a prime example. Its 'fame' derives from the eponymous M1 service area, just south of the village.

Spot it, however, I could not. Perhaps it's clearer from the south. After all, if so many route-builders over so many centuries have been drawn to it like a wasp to jam, it must be visible from somewhere.

One very visible feature was unexpectedly audible as well. At the crossroads north of West Haddon Grange, I heard a faint, deep buzzing. After a hundred yards it had become a loud, deep buzzing. By the time I walked beneath the electricity transmission lines that were evidently its source, it was beginning to be painful. The website www.answers.com explains that cold weather causes a reduction in the 'corona inception voltage' of transmission lines, leading to 'audible noise'. For audible, read deafening.

*

So by the time I stumbled into the small supermarket in West Haddon, I was tired, uncomfortable and annoyed. Moreover I'd just realised that I'd not spoken to a soul in about four hours.

'Just this sausage roll and a can of pop, please.'

'Two pounds ninety, sir.'

'Is there...'

'Yes, next?'

Well, she was busy, I suppose. To take the calorie hit and regather my battered thoughts, I sat on the steps of the village's churchyard. Almost immediately a tall gentleman wearing a trilby, a tie and a smart overcoat descended from the church.

'Sorry,' I said, getting up. 'Am I in your way?'

'No, no, not at all,' Mr Trilby was quick to stress. His accent was East Midlands, probably local, and his breath, like mine, puffed sharp clouds into the cold air as he spoke. 'You 'ave your snack, lad. If you've walked far enough to deserve it, that is.' This was accompanied by a grin that took a good twenty years off his seventy-five or so. I gave him a brief summary of my morning.

'Oh, I've walked those fields. Good few years since the last time, mind. The only problem was the farm dogs. Vicious beasts. They're just wolves really, aren't they? Half-domesticated, but wolves all the same. Why do people keep 'em?'

By now he was leaning on his stick by the handrail and I'd stood up to join him. I carefully wiped away some crumbs from my beard.

'Well,' I said, 'I suppose they have them to keep intruders away.'

'What piffle! I've got more chance of intruders at my little house in the village, but I don't keep a pack of wolves in the front garden, do I? Dogs seem to know I don't care for 'em much. Give me funny looks.'

'Me too.'

'Bet you 'aven't come across many people out and about today.'

'No. None in fact. There wasn't a soul to be seen in Crick.'

'Aye, it's like that in all the villages round 'ere. It's the commuting, you know. Some folks they just sleep here. This time of year I'll bet half of 'em don't see the light of day in their own home from Sunday afternoon to Saturday morning. Like ghost towns in the day, they are. Crick, Naseby, Guilsborough, here. Tried it myself once.'

'Commuting?'

'Yes. Drove from here all the way to Rugby every day.'

Rugby must have been about 15 kilometres away.

'How long did it take you?'

'Ooh, well, you're going back a bit now, but probably twenty minutes in the car. Twenty-five on bad days.'

'I used to commute into London by train and it sometimes took me two hours, door to door. Four hours a day there and back.'

For a few seconds he stared at me as if this was some monstrous lie and then challenged me:

'Four hours?! What on earth did you do all that time?'

'On the train? I practised my Rubik's Cube.'

Another long stare.

'It was the 1980s,' I added, as though this might justify what he clearly regarded as some sort of unnatural activity.

'Well,' said my short-lived friend. 'Time is money and I'm already overdrawn. Enjoy the rest of your walk, son. Oh, and...'

As he started off down the steps, Mr Trilby waved his stick at my face. For a moment I thought he was going to accuse me of gross perversion, but instead he raised both eyebrows and said:

'... Crumb.'

'Mm?'

'One more crumb on your beard.'

'Oh, thanks. Bye.'

Touching his trilby, he was gone. It was to be my only conversation from one end of this day's walk to the other.

*

Cold by name and that day very cold by nature, the small but scenic village of Cold Ashby was reputedly where Oliver Cromwell spent the night before the Battle of Naseby, a feature of the next stage. The sausage roll having revived me, I'd strode up the 6-kilometre lane to Northamptonshire's highest village, in good spirits. At only 200 metres above sea level, Cold Ashby's not exactly perched on an Alpine pass, but its approach did afford broad views all around, with the upper Avon Valley clear to the north and west and the headwaters of the Nene cutting a low, wide landscape out of the slopes to the south and east. At every turn, the bare frosted branches twinkled in the afternoon's bright wintry sun.

From here the watershed turns east once again, as did I, between frosty walls and frozen hedges to the rather smaller village of Thornby, sitting astride the busy A5199 Northampton-to-Leicester main road, where Julie was waiting in the car park of another Red Lion, the umpteenth closed pub of the day. Should any reader be considering following any of these watershed routes across rural England, I would strongly recommend the summer or at least the weekend, rather than winter midweeks when, with public houses no longer obliged to stay open for certain hours of the day, our rich landscape turns into an ale-free desert.

Though just 16 kilometres, plus the odd circuit or two of a field caused by the coppice thieves of Crick, this had seemed one of the toughest stages of the entire journey. The evening's weather report confirmed that East Midland temperatures hadn't risen above minus four all day. My deeply chilled feet are, I think, still recovering.

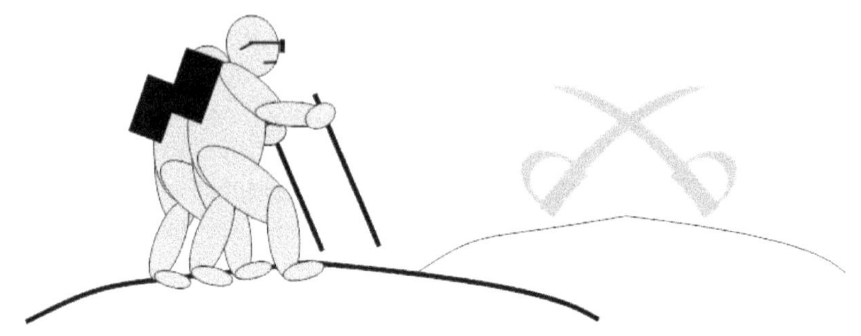

Stage 14: In Cromwell's Footsteps

Thornby to Husbands Bosworth

It was a Saturday in June 1645. Since the indecisive encounter at Edge Hill, England had been at war with itself for almost three years, the map of territory controlled either by King Charles or by Parliament being in a constant state of flux. A misty sun rose over the Royalist forces, lying just south of Market Harborough and under the command of Prince Rupert of the Rhine, many of his men still tired from a recent attack on the Parliamentary garrison at Leicester. The bulk of the Parliamentarians' 'New Model Army', under Sir Thomas Fairfax, lay some 15 kilometres south at Guilsborough and his first command of the day was to march nearly half that distance to a low hill north-east of Naseby, marked by a windmill. From here, Fairfax and his Lieutenant General of Horse, Oliver Cromwell, rode north to establish the location of Rupert's army from a steeper hill overlooking Clipston.

As the sun rose higher, both armies advanced, but significantly Fairfax's troops were for a long time hidden behind Naseby Ridge and by the time Rupert realised quite how near they were, retreat was no longer an option: he had to attack. From the

Sulby Hedges in the west, across Broadmoor to the eastern hills, the armies engaged each other in battle. So close were they that little musket fire was possible before hand-to-hand combat dominated, with swords and the butt-end of muskets being wielded as principal weapons.

Although Rupert's initial attacks on Fairfax's left (west) flank found some success, the numerical supremacy of the Parliamentary troops, the consequently greater width of their front and especially the attacks by Cromwell's cavalry on the Royalists' left (east) flank all proved critical. The remains of Fairfax's men eventually fled, pursued by Parliamentarians, and it's said that the road north was littered with Royalist dead all the way to Leicester, which Fairfax eventually re-took four days later.

King Charles himself, who'd commanded a small reserve force in the battle, survived it but, that Saturday's events having destroyed the heart of his army, lost the war within a year -- and his head within four. Cromwell was to become Lord Protector under the republican Commonwealth, leading a fanatical regime that, while marking the beginnings of parliamentary democracy, also brought misery and death to many, most notably in Ireland.

*

It could have been called the Battle of Broadmoor or Sulby or Sibbertoft, but history records it as the Battle of Naseby and, since the watershed skirts both village and battle site, Julie and I took the opportunity to walk a stage which would otherwise have been better cycled, to get a closer feel for the events of 366 years before.

Our trudge up the hill from Thornby was the same as that undertaken by Fairfax's troops early that June morning -- though, in our case, on a rather brisk September day. On what was to be the last day on earth for many of them, they would have noticed the upper Nene valley emerge as a shallow dip in the rolling green hills to the east. 'Nene' is thought to come from an old Celtic word meaning 'bright one'. Downstream it's pronounced to rhyme with 'mean', but up here in Northamptonshire it rhymes with 'men' and one of its sources is a spring a few metres into the field opposite the large oak tree at the entrance to Oak Farm, from where a muddy tractor emerged as we passed.

Naseby is an attractive village with an open feel to it -- perhaps because, as predicted by Mr Trilby of West Haddon, it was almost deserted. The sole inhabitant appeared to be the friendly assistant at the village store, from whom we bought supplies for an early lunch, but who was unable to guide us to the source of the Avon, supposedly a prominent village feature. It turned out to be less than 100 metres from her counter, opposite the bench where we feasted on her cheese and pickle sandwiches. Behind the low brick wall of the Manor House an unusual metal cone marks what must be a spring, whose location in a small depression suggests that it could at times have risen under pressure to form a fountain on the cone. From here (and, it must be said, from several other sources nearby), the Avon flows through 137 kilometres of the south Midlands, past the Royal Shakespeare Theatre at Stratford and on to Tewkesbury in Gloucestershire, where it joins the Severn.

*

Regaining the route of the Parliamentarians, we walked up the lane towards Clipston, where an obelisk, erected in 1823, marks the site of the windmill where Fairfax's forces assembled. While the spot is quite elevated, bang on the watershed in fact, you can see why Cromwell and Fairfax needed to ride north to get a better view of the enemy position. Interestingly, the inscription, written by 'John and Mary Frances Fitzgerald, Lord and Lady of the Manor of Naseby', who'd had the obelisk erected, comprises an undisguised bias towards the King. Charles's defeat, it thunders, 'led to the subversion of the throne, the altar and the constitution' and British subjects, it exhorts, should never 'swerve from the allegiance due to their legitimate monarch'.

Duly chastised, we walked over to the other lane running north from the village, the route ultimately taken by Fairfax's men, and it proved still true that from this switchback lane the fields of Broadmoor are indeed hidden until you're almost upon them -- as, crucially, an advancing army would be hidden from those fields.

Just beyond the crest of the ridge a short path to the left takes you to the second memorial, sited immediately above the field of battle, which now forms a peaceful patchwork of mostly arable farmland draining west towards the Avon. This pillar, erected in 1906, sported until recently an information board displaying a Parliamentarian prejudice almost as acute as the opposite prejudice on the obelisk. Today's display, however, is politically correct and gives an unbiased and detailed overview of the thrusts and counter-thrusts of the battle itself.

*

Significant headwaters certainly came thick and fast on this stage. From the northern outskirts of the next village, Sibbertoft, a source of the River Welland sets off on yet another route to the North Sea -- much shorter than the Nene's, via Stamford and Spalding. It was here, however, that the watershed exhausted its long eastward thrust and we were at last permitted to turn back towards the west, into the glare of the afternoon sun, past a property intriguingly named 'The Wrongs' and onto a broad plateau.

Being an addictive map-reader, I'd always been fascinated by those labels written in a wiggly old typeface that record the locations of lost villages all over England. The site of one of them, Old Sulby, was marked as being down in the shallow valley to our left. How were they 'lost'? Why were they abandoned? In search of answers, Julie and I had recently attended a talk on the subject at a local Working Men's Club by one Ray Sutton.

Dr Sutton confirmed that, when quizzed on the subject,

people resident close to a lost village almost invariably blamed the Black Death, the fourteenth-century plague that probably cut England's population by about a third. However, at least in the context of Leicestershire, the county we were about to enter, the picture is more varied than that. Much more crucial than the plague were either flooding or the tendency of landowners, especially monastic landowners, to clear inhabitants for the sake of a sheep run. Here at Old Sulby, of which just a few humps and bumps remain, it's thought most likely that the villagers were indeed moved on in the fifteenth century as the local abbot cleared the land for agriculture, still the site's main land use today.

From the lane along the plateau more obvious than medieval remains were windsocks to both north and south. Were we walking along here between 1943 and 1945, we might have found ourselves too close for comfort to the landing gear of a Wellington bomber, for the line of the current road was then the main runway of Husbands Bosworth military airfield, home to 85 Operational Training Unit. The official Air Ministry criteria of a fairly level, well-drained site and unrestricted approaches from the east mean, as I'd already discovered, that many of England's wartime airfields lie on or near the watershed route. While the operations at these airfields were deadly serious, the records for this one note that at Christmas 1944 the station put on a well-received pantomime called *Near White and the Seven Twerps*. The north side of the site remains in use for aircraft as The Gliding Centre, home to Coventry Gliding Club and the East Midlands Air Support Unit.

This explained the regular drone of helicopters that Julie and I had heard as we crossed this open land, soon to be joined by the roar of traffic squeezing past us after we'd rejoined the A5199 and scuttled into the village of Husbands Bosworth, the day's destination, and into the bar of the Bell Inn.

This would be another attractive enough village if it weren't for the main road that cuts it in two. The 'Bosworth' (Old English:

'Bar's farm') came before the 'Husbands' (as in husbandry), which was added in the sixteenth century to distinguish it from another of Bar's farms a few miles away, which became Market Bosworth and after which the battle in the War of the Roses was named. It seems to be unknown when 'Husbands' mislaid its apostrophe. The village has at least two claims to fame.

The first was in 1616 when nine alleged witches were hanged at Leicester Jail for having 'bewitched a young gentleman' of Husbands Bosworth. Examination of the documentation from the time makes it clear that all they were guilty of was having failed to cure a teenager evidently suffering from epilepsy. The boy's father happened to be the local Lord of the Manor. They were the last women in England to be hanged for witchcraft.

The second arose 33 years later and involved a strange coincidence. Though the defeated Charles I had escaped the Battle of Naseby, he was put on trial in 1649, accused of being 'a tyrant, traitor and murderer; and a public and implacable enemy to the Commonwealth of England'. He was found guilty and hanged. The king's chief prosecutor was one John Cooke, first Solicitor General of the new Commonwealth and baptized some 40 years before at All Saints church, Husbands Bosworth, right here on the edge of the battlefield.

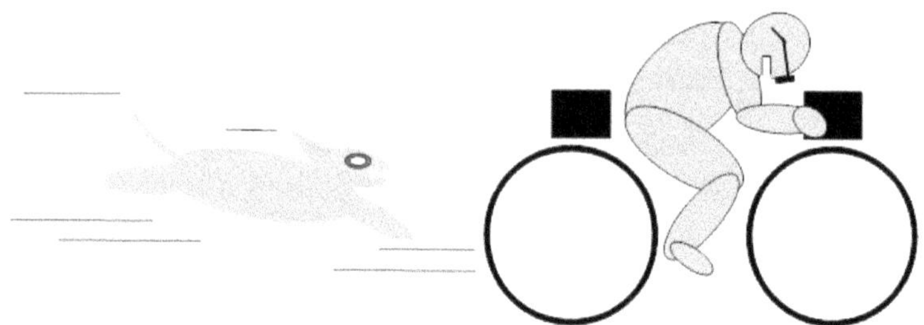

Stage 15: Didn't I Mention the Dog?

Husbands Bosworth to Willey

Home wasn't far away, less than 40 kilometres to the north, and this would be the nearest the watershed got. Time for a lazy breakfast, then, before driving Tetley and myself down to resume the route with a short spin in the saddle around south Leicestershire. So it was probably my half-sleepy nonchalance that let a gust of wind snatch my glove and throw it off the parapet of the disused railway bridge just north of Husbands Bosworth and into the brambles far below.

I couldn't do without it. The cool northerly was due to blow for most of the day, reaching force seven, were the Radio 4 weatherman to be believed. No way down this side, but access under the bridge from the farm opposite. Appearing from the outbuildings came an overwhelmingly polite lady:

'Yes, of course. Sorry about the mud. Would you like me to get it for you? No? Well please help yourself. Through that gate.'

A farmer who apologises for the mud on her land... whatever next? Retrieving the glove was no problem -- a jolly walk along the trackbed of the London and North-Western's old Stamford branch.

Getting back onto the road, on the other hand, was a task fraught with danger for, on clicking open the garden gate, I awoke a sleeping hound that Mrs Polite had somehow failed to mention. What breed it may have been I cannot say, for to me, as to Mr Trilby of West Haddon, all dogs are simply tarted-up wolves.

Now, my antipathy to the canine world having been revealed, I should justify it. While I'm always outwardly friendly -- 'Hello, dog, nice dog' -- the beasts are generally quick to sense my underlying hostility. It's their own fault. One of their brethren had once taken exception to my attempt, as a courier, to deliver a parcel to its owner and had had such a go at me that I was laid off work for a while and eventually gave up the job as being no fun any more. The tale, however, did have its funny side. Since the mad dog's owner, another farmer just up the road from today's ride as it happens, chose to ignore my suggestion that he pay my medical costs, I made use of the Small Claims Service.

This excellent British institution invites claimants and defendants in a disputed case to submit written statements of their respective positions to the county court, where a judge will review them and usually come to a decision without the need for any face-to-face meeting. Mad Dog Farmer's defence was that there was no proof of his docile doggy attacking the dastardly, parcel-wielding courier... despite the fact that his farm hands had dragged the hound away from the bleeding body, prostrate on the floor of his own barn. The system of written responses naturally gives scope for a certain sarcasm. My suggestion was that there could be only three explanations of the situation which the farm hands encountered:

1. While seeking the parcel's consignee, I had wilfully attacked myself with a dog-shaped implement and thrown myself to the floor, or...

2. Having been attacked by another dog at another address, instead of reporting to the nearest hospital I'd chosen to drive to his farm, there to lie bleeding on his barn floor in

anticipation of being discovered by another dog, or...

3. His dog had attacked me.

He paid up within 48 hours.

Mrs Polite's dog eyed me. I eyed it.

'Hello, dog, nice dog.' Steady movement towards the gate onto the road.

'Grrr.' Small movement.

'I'm just leaving now.' Brisk movement.

'Grrr....aaaagh! Aaaaaagh!' Loping movement.

'Here goes.' Leaping movement.

Funny how you can vault a gate that looked unvaultable just a moment before. Hearing the commotion, Mrs Polite emerged again.

'Didn't I mention the dog?'

'No.'

'Oh, she just wants to play.'

All dog-owners say that. By what twist of logic they think the planet's most intelligent species should consider what some small-brained, slavering wild beast may or may not want I have no idea. Not today, Bonzo.

Pedalling smartly away, I reassured myself that the day could only get better.

*

Weaving between another source of the Wash-bound Welland and the Avon-bound Swift, I turned west towards Bruntingthorpe just as the wind defied the BBC and backed 90 degrees to blow straight at me over the handlebars, as it continued to do for the entire outward portion of the day. In planning this whole journey I'd considered setting off from Derbyshire and heading south-west to the coast, but instead chose the opposite direction in the hope of assistance from England's prevailing south-westerlies. Just my luck that this loop against the general trend of the route coincided with the strongest winds.

Well-blustered after half an hour of it, I pulled up for a swig of coffee by the perimeter of Bruntingthorpe Aerodrome. Yet another former World War Two airfield, Bruntingthorpe was still marked on my map as a 'proving ground', the American term for a military test area, having been one of thirteen bases for the USAF Strategic Air Command in the UK during the Cold War -- the only one on this watershed route. At the time I passed by, it had theoretically been demilitarised for years and was home just to two old Lightning F6s and the Lightning Preservation Group. I say 'theoretically' since the barbed-wire fencing, along with a dense stand of obscuring trees around the perimeter, seemed expensively sturdy for a home for old planes. However, it's true that an online glance at the airfield's north-east corner via the 'Earth' view on Google Maps(TM) will probably reward you with an interesting array of aircraft through the ages.

As I pedalled into the small village of Gilmorton, I couldn't help wondering which invention would have impressed most those men who built Gilmorton Castle some nine centuries before: the aeroplane, the internet or the bicycle. The Normans being among history's most enthusiastic data-gatherers, my money was on was the internet. I could imagine King William's local enumerator -- let's call him Jacques le Bon from Leicester -- sitting on a convenient rock in the middle of the village and tapping his laptop into life.

Project: domesday

Username: lebon

Password: jaimeleroi

Date: 10/03/1086, Wednesday

Location: Gilmorton

Lord: (Jacques checks his notes) Godfrey

French Households: 4

Freemen's Households: (Jacques flicks his notepad) 24

Slave's Household: 1

Tax (in geld): 14

Enumerator's Comments: (Jacques taps away enthusiastically) English freemen rather rude about their king. Too attached to their church. Suggest one castle and more French to put English in their place.

With a flourish and a smile, Jacques hits 'Send'.

When the Normans came to build their castle here, they located it -- as in many other settlements across the country -- right next to the church. Nowadays there's nothing but the motte surrounded by a shallow ditch, but climbing to the top of it I could still sense the message that the Normans intended: We're in charge now -- you'd better get used to it and show us some respect.

*

By this point, the streams to my right were flowing not to the Wash but to the Trent and thence the Humber. One of the biggest of Phythian-Adams's 'cultural provinces' of the Middle Ages therefore spread away from the watershed to the north, but the one with the shortest name: 'Trent'. All the rest of this journey would effectively be a tour around the southern and western frontiers of this province.

Cycling west from Gilmorton, it wasn't long before the familiar roar of the M1 once more drowned out first the birdsong, then the wind in the trees and finally all thought. Sited on one side of the motorway bridge, right next to the din, was a traveller's encampment, complete with washing lines, chained dogs and rubbish; on the other, among the trees between the carriageway and the pylons, the parallel line of another disused railway. This, though, was no branch line.

Perhaps more than any other mainline in England, the Great Central Railway arose from the vision of one man. As chairman of the GCR's main constituent company in the north, Edward Watkin drove the project to build a new high-spec, high-speed line to London and then on through a Channel Tunnel to the Continent. While his tunnel was not completed, the mainline to London was and services between Marylebone and Leicester, Nottingham, Sheffield, Leeds and Manchester commenced in 1899. What was remarkable was that the entire 'London extension' was built not only for high-speed use (its arrow-like orientation towards the capital contrasting sharply with the meandering paths of the older mainlines), but also to the continental loading gauge, i.e. to accommodate the standard cross-section of European rolling stock. It was the last mainline railway to be built in Britain until Kent's 'High-Speed 1' opened in 2003, finally realising Watkin's dreeam of a purpose-built line direct to the Continent.

It was also the first to close, in the late 1960s, and its trackbed is now partly built over. Don't blame Dr Beeching himself. A physicist and engineer, he did exactly what the government asked of him: advised which line closures would most effectively make the short-term cost savings they wanted. The lack of vision -- such a sharp contrast with Watkin's outlook -- lay, as it so often has, with the country's politicians, whose horizons rarely extend beyond their five-year term. Still benefitting from the GCR's smooth alignment across south Leicestershire is the parallel motorway. In danger of suffering even now from the politicians' short-sightedness are those large tracts of the south Midlands through which the 'High-Speed 2' line is proposed, when the old GCR route might have saved them all the trouble.

*

Grumpy as the sight of these abandoned railways tends to make me, I'm easily cheered up by a snack and the Ashby Parva Plant Centre fitted the bill perfectly. Veering away from most centres of population and therefore from most cafes, the watershed route scores highly on garden centres, whose own tea rooms tend to show off English cuisine -- at least the version I appreciate -- at its best. By this I do not mean miserable portions of fancy food placed tastefully in the middle of enormous plates, but huge portions of plain food squeezed onto any old plate. Hitting the spot at Ashby Parva were a giant bacon roll and a steaming hot pot of tea.

While replenishing my depleted calorie stock, I kept my ears open. Having crossed the M1 and being within sight of Warwickshire, I should have been somewhere near the east/west accent boundary: where 'Leicestoh' once again becomes plain 'Leicester', where 'rain' becomes 'rine' and 'five' becomes 'foive'. Satisfyingly, those present seemed to be half and half. Gruesome though the West Midlands accent sounds to many, I was particularly delighted to hear one lady announce the price of their purchases to her partner:

'It cooms to ite nointy-noin, Jiff.'

Pedalling further west I wondered whether it was something in the West Midland air that intervened between brain and mouth to corrupt the vowel sounds in such a bizarre way. But who am I to talk? Many East Midlanders, including me, are so crude that we still pronounce the 'g' in 'finger' and don't even bother to add a 'y' before the 'u' in 'student'. However, it turns out that I'm not alone in my opinion of the accent in the region I was entering. A 2005 survey of 5,000 people found 'Birmingham' to be the 'least pleasant' regional accent in Britain, followed by 'Glasgow' and

'Liverpool'.

Is there any other country where pronunciation, intonation and dialect make such sharp twists and turns in such a small area? I sometimes wonder if motorists crossing England need any navigation system at all. Just wind down the window and listen to the locals nattering to know exactly where you are: a kind of ChatNav.

*

The end of my day's battle with the strong south-westerly came near the village of Willey, at the corner of Magna Park, a huge complex of modern warehouses at the very end of Leicestershire and once again on the line of Watling Street, here coincident with the A5. Built on the former Bitteswell Airfield, a satellite to Bruntingthorpe in the war, Magna Park was at the time I passed by the largest dedicated distribution park in Europe, with over 600,000 square metres of storage space -- or, in the more traditional unit, 84 football pitches' worth.

Why here? Why so big?

Well, in the days when most computers were the size of Dr Who's phone box and their programs took hours to run, I used to work for a software company that was one of the few in the country to possess on its whirring tapes a database of the UK road network. For a small fee (actually, more like a small fortune), we'd load the locations of all a company's customers into the Big Beast and ask it where the company should build its distribution centre if it wanted to minimise transport costs. Unless Scotland were included, the magic answer that eventually popped out on something akin to a teleprinter would, more often than not, be Lutterworth. Or Crick. Or Daventry. At any rate, somewhere in this 'sweet spot' where the M1 and M6 diverge. (Include Scotland and it'd be Warrington.)

The same's probably still true -- and no doubt an app on your mobile phone will tell you so in seconds. Anyway, it's for this reason that the area I'd been wandering through for the past few travelling days is positively awash with huge warehouses for such household names as Asda, Argos, John Lewis, BT, DHL, TNT and so on.

I turned one of the corners of Magna Park and, with some relief, let the wind blow me eastwards past the main entrance. From this side I noticed that the designers of this particular development had made some attempt to ease its inevitable impact on the local landscape: graded shades of blue for some warehouse walls, plenty of planting on bunds around the perimeter and the whole sited on top of a ridge (hence its occurrence on the watershed) so that, from most viewpoints, only a vertical silhouette rather than its vast horizontal expanse would be seen.

Now off the watershed route and breezing through the outskirts of Lutterworth back towards the car at Husbands Bosworth, I reflected on a mostly jolly, if rather solitary, day that had taken me from the eleventh century to the nineteenth and twentieth and provided ample occasions to grumble at some of the current century's annoyances -- a harmless pastime enjoyed across all sections of English society, not just by greying, middle-aged white men like me.

And then a final opportunity for grumpiness presented itself, as a short convoy of blue-and-red Argos trucks overtook me on their way from Magna Park. All companies nowadays seem to require corporate 'straplines': from the catchy 'Every little helps' (Tesco), via the clever 'No FT, no comment' (Financial Times) to the eye-wateringly naff 'Because we're worth it' (L'Oréal). I wonder how many hours were spent in committee meetings at Argos HQ before they finally came up with the utterly meaningless message now emblazoned across the sides of its vehicle fleet: 'Delivering value'?

The most effective one I've seen, however, may well have been accidental: on the back of a McVitie's truck the biscuit-lover will find a stark warning: 'No biscuits left in lorry overnight'.

Stage 16: Barnacle Brad and the Ferret

Willey to Corley

... or 'willow wood' to 'heron wood'. The suffix '-ley' is Old English either for a wood (or, strangely, for a clearing in a wood) and dominates the place names on this stage, confirming a shifct back into land settled by the Anglo-Saxons and away from that once dominated by the Danes, with their '-by' (-'settlement') villages such as Ashby, Thornby and Naseby.

Having let the windy spell run its course, I was also cycling once again through a landscape where humans actually ventured abroad, a phenomenon helped by the fact that an Indian summer seemed to be in the air and it was a Saturday. Apart from those that work weekends, what do the English do on a sunny Saturday? Well, from the evidence of today's ride through north Warwickshire, they seem to spend it driving and walking; tending their gardens, painting their houses, flying their model planes; fishing, playing football and rugby; and, of course, cycling.

At Cloudesley Bush, where my route once again crossed the Fosse Way, a whole peloton of racing cyclists had to pull up at a 'Give Way sign', causing a frantic squealing of brakes.

'Destroys your rhythm, doesn't it?' I called, as I'd pulled up opposite.

'You get used to it,' said the young lad bringing up the rear.

'Where are you going?'

'Dunno. I just follow the rest.'

'What if you get a puncture?'

'Somebody'll... uh, ooooh, here we go.'

And they were off. A moving image suddenly swam into my head from two thousand years before, in which a column of Roman legionaries was steadily marching north along this very route. At the crossroads their leader quickly raises his hand and calls a halt, but one slacker is not paying attention, walks into the stationary soldier ahead and half the column clatters to the ground, spears and all.

'Get up, you rabble!' shouts Furious Maximus. They struggle to their feet, helmets still askew. 'Who didn't halt when I called halt?'

Silence.

'We can stay here all day...'

'It was Brainius Minimus, sir.'

'Minimus, you cloth-eared goat! Fall out!'

Clatter.

'Out, not down, you wretched rodent!'

Perhaps I've watched *Monty Python's Life of Brian* one time too many. To be honest, with little in the landscape to distract me, my own mind had wandered. In order to bring some focus to the day, I resolved to establish the reason for the very odd name of a village I encountered just after crossing the M69, one that didn't end in '-ley', by interrogating some of its residents as they went about their Saturday business. They lived in Barnacle.

First up was a middle-aged woman pruning her somewhat vicious rose bushes.

'Barnacle? No, no idea. Nowhere near the sea, are we? Can't have been any barnacle-scraping businesses based here.'

True enough. Next I interrupted a rather younger woman cleaning her car.

'Ah, now...' she started encouragingly, laying her sponge on the bonnet. 'That's exactly what I asked when we moved here a few years ago.'

'And what did you find out?'

'I found out that when they dug the M69, they uncovered a secret tunnel between two farms that had been safe houses for the Parliamentarians in the Civil War and that Oliver Cromwell himself stayed in one of them.'

'Gosh. And the name Barnacle?'

'Nope. No idea.'

By this point a group of three children aged from about eight to twelve had scuttled by and, thanking the car-washer for her information, I decided to try my luck with them, catching the group up as they approached a stile into a field.

'Excuse me,' I called, 'Do you know why this village is called Barnacle?'

'No, give up, why?' asked the eldest, a boy, as he hovered mid-stile.

'Oh, I don't know myself. I was trying to find out.'

It was evident from their shared glances that this was probably the most pointless project they'd ever heard of, and yet they still didn't cross the stile.

'We've got a question for *you*, mister,' stated the middle one, a girl. 'You've gorra map. Tell us 'ow far it is to Bulkington.'

'Where's Bulkington?'

Such a question clearly reduced my standing, already hovering at dunce level, one further notch to complete idiot.

'It's where we're goin'. Over there,' she explained, nodding northwards.

Glancing at my map, I told her: 'Two kilometres.'

'How far's that?'

How despondent would her teacher have been on hearing that?

'About a mile and a half.'

'Phew, it'll take us all day,' she estimated and, nudging their younger companion, who'd been staring at me intently while wiping his nose on his sleeve, added: 'Come on, Brad.'

Brad, however, had a question of his own.

'Where you goin', mister?'

'Derbyshire,' I said truthfully, if a little prematurely.

'Where's your tent?'

'I haven't got one.'

'Where'd you sleep then?'

'Pubs, hotels, sometimes at home. I go home every night at the moment.'

His logistical curiosity satisfied, Brad abruptly changed the subject again.

'Is that yours?' He was pointing at a rectangular box in the grass verge, about the length of a grown man, with wire mesh on one side. How he thought I might have carried it on my bike I didn't ask.

'No. Why?'

'Just the job for Freddie.'

'Who's Freddie?'

'My ferret. Look, it's got like a door an' all. 'Oo do you think it belongs to?'

'Well, my guess is it's been dumped here and doesn't belong to anybody.'

''Ow d'ya think I can get it 'ome?'

'Has your dad got a car?'

'Yeah, 'course.'

'Well, if I were you, when you get home I'd describe this to him and ask him if he'd drive you over and pick it up.'

'Please.'

'Please what?'

'No, I'll ask him please can he do it. Blimey, you're not very polite, are you, mister? Bye!'

*

Though its residents seemed to be making the best of the fine weather, I have to report that Bedworth (or 'Bed'uth, as it's called locally) is not the most enchanting town in the Midlands. With its traditional weaving industry having disappeared long ago, its town centre redeveloped in an uninspiring postwar 'box' style, its coal-mining on a steady decline until the last pit closed in the 1990s and now the recession seeing a number of premises freshly boarded up, it's been played a poor hand. Bedworth is, however, a town on the watershed and dutifully I pedalled into, through and out of Bedworth as hastily as I decently could.

The countryside to the north-west of town, though, opened up into a rolling scene of small farms, tree-lined lanes, bright green meadows and thick, mixed woodland that was to last, for the most part, until I left Warwickshire over three travelling days later. Beyond one of the woods to the north, and at one point just visible through a gap in the trees, lay South Farm, part of the Arbury Park estate. Here in 1819 was born one Mary Anne Evans, daughter to the estate's land agent and a perceptive and creative woman who went on to write novels about social and political life in small-town England, to considerable literary acclaim. She's better know by her pen name, George Eliot.

I happily admit that I've never knowingly read a single word written by George Eliot. Having been put off any such Victorian novels by the tiresome tomes we were forced to digest at school -- Dickens, Brontë and so on -- I've never been tempted to return. My partner and support driver Julie, however, is a voracious consumer of novels and, with more grit than I, had recently tackled Eliot's *Middlemarch*. I therefore defer to her for an opinion. Wincing at the memory, she tried to sum up her reaction in one sentence.

'They should have got out more.'

In a recent *Desert Island Discs*, actor and presenter Tony Robinson chose *Middlemarch* as his book for the desert island, as he too had never managed to read it. Good luck, Tone.

*

Weighty literature apart, though, I'm always drawn to a bookshop and was therefore surprised as well as delighted to find myself turning off the lane near Astley at a sign I couldn't resist:

'Astley Book Farm. Cafe Open.'

If there's anything better than a bookshop, it's a bookshop with a cafe. If there's anything better than a bookshop with a cafe, it's a huge, cheap bookshop with a cafe. Astley Book Farm claims to be the largest second-hand bookshop in the Midlands -- out here in the middle of, well, nowhere -- and who can doubt them? After a deliciously squishy carrot cake washed down by proper coffee, and a tour of the labyrinthine main shop, during which I successfully resisted any purchase that would add to the weight on the bike, I paid a visit to their 'Ten Bob Barn' and knew immediately that here my resistance would fail.

Younger readers need to know that a 'bob' was a shilling, i.e. twelve old pence, i.e. five new pence and that therefore a 'ten bob book' is as cheap as chips. I strongly recommend any book-lover to seek out this barn, but in case you can't, you may get a flavour of the kaleidoscopic choice you're missing for your fifty pence investment from the selection piled on a spare shelf by the barn's only other customer that afternoon, an elderly gentleman with reading glasses perched on the end of his nose. His chosen titles read:

Court Jesting
The Menacing Rise of Japan
Alcoholism, Love and Birth Control
Striptease in East London
Baby Oil and Ice

'Good prices, aren't they?' I said as he carried them out to the till.

'Absolutely,' he confirmed. 'And who needs fiction when real life is so fascinating?'

Absolutely. However, with Tetley already carrying a heavy load (i.e. me), I settled for a small anthology of essays in praise of British places of particular appeal to the authors. Bedworth, I noticed, was absent.

*

Duly sated, I pedalled north through Astley ('east wood') to Ansley ('hermitage wood'), and then south through Arley ('eagle wood') and past Fillongley (not so simple: 'the wood of Fygla's people') to Corley. At the time of *Domesday Book* much of the land around here was owned by Countess Godiva, while other parts of Warwickshire were in the hands of her husband Leofric, Earl of Mercia. We can infer that they differed in their treatment of tenants, since it was allegedly to draw attention to the repressive taxes imposed by Leofric that the countess -- also allegedly -- rode naked through the streets of Coventry, about ten kilometres from here.

You may think that cycling south is an odd way to reach the north, which was, after all, my objective, but this counter-intuitive southward lurch of some 25 kilometres was occasioned by the need to keep the tributaries of the Trent-bound River Tame (as in Tamworth) to the north, coincidentally also keeping my route well to the outskirts of England's second city, Birmingham, which is itself drained by the Tame.

After passing a storage depot for Chinese double-decker buses (strange what crops up in the English countryside), the route finished at another Red Lion with another pint of Old Hooky and an update with Julie.

'This is a surprise,' she commented as we supped our drinks in the pub's garden, the only other sound being birdsong and children's laughter. 'I've just got off the M6. You wouldn't think it was only a few hundred yards away. The motorway planners seemed to pick idyllic villages to name their service areas after. Shame really. To most people, Corley probably just means noise and exhaust fumes.'

'Like the Watford in Watford Gap. Have you been?'

'No.'

'It's a peaceful little village. Even Newport Pagnell's got a bit of charm. Actually, it looks like there are some more service area villages to come on the watershed route. We'll see what they're like.'

'A guide to villages just off the motorway?'

'Been done.'

'That's saved a lot of schlepping around then.'

*

For the benefit of the residents of Barnacle, according to the *Oxford Dictionary of British Place Names*, their village name turns out to be a corruption of 'Bernhangre', Old English for 'wooded slope by a barn'.

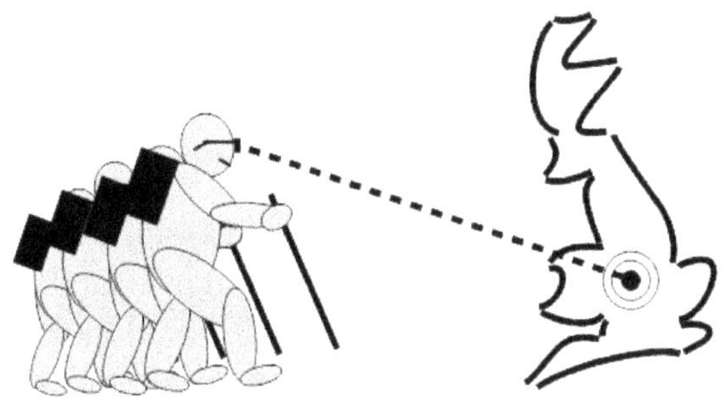

Stage 17: Central Question

Corley to Meriden

The sign was uncompromising. Prominently placed among the outdoor tables of the Bull's Head and casting a shadow over our roast beef and Yorkshires, it declared 'CENTRE OF ENGLAND'. The village of Meriden seems confident of its traditional claim. I'm less sure. Before addressing the day's central issue though, the four of us had needed to justify Sunday lunch by a little exercise.

After the hard slog of the Naseby stage and with the promise of softer country paths this time, Julie had donned her walking boots again. We were joined for what turned out to be the shortest stage of the entire journey, by an old school friend -- another Richard -- and his wife Wendy. Freshly retired from a career persuading the country's movers and shakers of the wonders of aluminium, Richard once spent his days in what was, for a Beatles fan, one of the best jobs in the world: persuading starry-eyed visitors to Liverpool of the wonders of the Fab Four. He'd been Deputy PR Manager for Liverpool City Council.

My old friend's wanderings around the country suddenly prompted a question I was surprised I hadn't asked him before:

'Are people really different in different parts of the country?'

Richard cast his eyes to the leafy tree tops. Setting off from Corley Moor down Windmill Lane, we were already embraced in a blanket of green and gold. After his many years in the public relations game, I felt sure he was giving careful consideration to a professionally diplomatic reply. I was wrong.

'Southerners are elitist snobs,' he started, 'Northerners are a friendly bunch -- if you're lucky enough to pick the right ones -- and Brummies, well, now and then...' We all looked at him. Wendy hails from not far away -- surely a compliment was coming. '... they're quite stroppy actually.'

'What about Sutton Coldfield?' I asked.

'Lots of 'em are snobs, just like round here in Solihull. Full of snobs.'

So there you have it: a solid vote for regional stereotypes.

'You haven't lived in the south-west, have you, Richard?' Julie asked him.

'No.'

'Don't bother. Suspicious folk. Don't take to strangers.'

'Aren't you from the south-west yourself?'

'Yes.'

*

Our route took us through patches of mixed woodland, pitted with badger setts among the patches of late flowers, across sloping green pasture and through fields of uneven stubble left after the harvest. Though the air was still balmy, this Sunday morning had dawned with tumbling, lead-grey clouds carried on a south-westerly and soon we felt those 'spits and spots' of rain so beloved of the weather forecasters.

Having taken another sharp lurch to the left to avoid the headwaters of the River Blythe, destined ultimately for the Trent, the watershed had us walking north to south again. While the actual line of the watershed followed the busy B4102, I'd chosen a parallel route about a kilometre to the east which followed the Heart of England Way, a wandering 160-kilometre / 100-mile route from Staffordshire to Gloucestershire. Though its green-and-white waymarkers probably looked attractive in a PowerPoint slide, against a real background of woods and clouds, they're not what most walkers would call fit for purpose.

The signs directed us, however, out of the showers, through more cosy woods where birdsong once again drowned the background traffic noise for a while.

'Starlings,' said Julie.

'How do you know?' I asked.

'Oh, summer days in Wookey as a child, walks to the allotment with my grandfather.'

'The one who taught you to turn a match round in your mouth?'

'That's him.'

'My own granddad took me for walks around the streets of town. I'm quite good at the height of factory chimneys and the manufacturers of manhole covers.'

'Not quite the same.'

We'd spilled out onto a narrow lane in the hamlet of Eaves Green and something caught Wendy's attention.

'Ah, I know what that is,' she said. 'It's been on the news.'

Spread over what looked like an otherwise ordinary driveway was a temporary shelter housing a couple of old armchairs, some tables, a huge, smoking stove and a board that read

'Day 367'. The '7' had clearly recently been a '6'. Reading a newspaper in one of the chairs was a middle-aged man. I approached him.

'My friend here says you're famous,' I said. 'What's it all about?'

'Don't know about famous, but I'll gladly tell you the tale.' He was softly spoken with the accent of a well-educated man. 'It's all about that field opposite.'

Across the road, behind locked gates, was an unassuming field with a couple of cars and a few caravans. Unsurprisingly it turned out that this was another unwelcome gypsy site -- but this time with several differences. For a start the travellers were not actually travelling any more; some time ago, apparently, they'd started building permanent pitches, but without planning permission. The predictable protest by local residents had been a particularly well-organised and fiercely determined one: this was clear enough from their 'camp' which, by the time we passed, had notched up over a year's continuous vigil. And finally, this individual case had generated not only widespread press coverage but also some actual support in Westminster for a tidying-up of the planning laws, in which travellers had been treated as an exception to the general rules on development in the Green Belt.

This latter must be counted as a rare and welcome breakthrough in the weird world of planning policy. It's odd. England, supposedly the home of parliamentary democracy, seems to have lost the link between representatives and represented. Anyone living anywhere but the country's remotest corners can see that there are far too many people here. So many that our most precious natural resource -- the landscape -- is being irretrievably eaten away by development. But what's self-evident out here seems so often to be invisible in the corridors of Whitehall. It'd make more sense for government targets for new housing should not be minima, but maxima. And in some places that maximum should be zero. Here in the narrowing gap between Birmingham and Coventry is one of those places.

I wished the quietly spoken protester good luck.

*

An irony of the development issue is that this particular corner of the Midlands is not exactly a rural idyll in any case, for, as we walked past the field in question, our conversation was drowned by the roar of the A45 dual carriageway above. This trunk road -- until the opening of the M6, the main route from the industrial West Midlands to the east coast ports -- itself found fame of a sort, being mentioned in the lyrics of Madness's 1982 top-ten hit 'Driving My Car' (and, in an odd pop-music coincidence, passing right by the English home of ELO front man and Traveling Wilbury, Jeff Lynne.)

By the time we settled down to our roasts in the courtyard of the Bull's Head, a seventeenth-century coaching inn cited in a Warwickshire county history as the handsomest in England, things had quietened down enough for more conversation. When the other Richard and I left school, he'd gone on to study History and Politics, while I'd done a course on Economics and Pedantry. No, actually I couldn't find a course on Pedantry and so had to make do with the next best thing: Geography. He seemed to know what was coming.

'I expect you're going to tell us this isn't the centre of England,' he said to me as we sat beneath the sign proclaiming it.

'This isn't the centre of England,' I obliged.

'I knew it. OK, who says?'

'Well, the Ordnance Survey and me, but we say different things.'

'Let's start with the Ordnance Survey.'

'Right. Well, it turns out that 'centre' is a pretty vague concept and so what they've identified is the 'centroid' of England.'

'What's a centroid?'

I glanced down at my notebook.

'You're using a crib sheet, Guise!' declared my former classmate.

'What if I am? The centroid of a two-dimensional shape is the intersection of all straight lines that divide it into two parts of equal moment about the line.'

'What's a 'moment'?'

'Er, dunno. But anyway, the OS says the centroid's near Fenny Drayton in Leicestershire.'

'Maybe your version is simpler.'

I think it is and tried to explain it by drawing on my napkin. What Meriden may actually be claiming is that it's the furthest place in England from the sea. What 'the sea' may mean is open to question, but to me it means the *open* sea rather some narrow tidal backwater. If you look at a map of England, the three bits of open sea anywhere near the Midlands are the Wash, the Bristol Channel (which I reckon starts at Sand Point in Somerset) and the Irish Sea where it washes the Wirral. The place that's furthest from any of these has as its nearest sea the shore at Mockbeggar Wharf on the Wirral, 142 kilometres (88 miles) away.

'And where exactly is this place?' asked Wendy, pointing at the untidy dot in the middle of the napkin.

'Exactly? It's the tee of the 12th hole at the Gay Hill Golf Course, a few miles west of here in Solihull.' (At grid reference SP0877, in fact.)

'And what method have you used to be so precise?' asked Richard.

'Ah, my method's top secret.'

'I.e. probably flawed.'

'No comment.'

Stage 18: Cyclists Everywhere

Meriden to Lapworth

Meriden village green was deserted. But when I'd been here just over a year before I'd been surrounded by other cyclists.

*

Dark clouds, I remembered, had rolled overhead while at ground level an important event in the cycling calendar was taking place. Once a year cyclists from many parts of the country, but especially of course from the Midlands, gather here to remember those fellow cyclists who died in action during the two world wars.

Until I came across a memorial in Arras, France, whose purpose was similar to that in Meriden, I hadn't been aware that cycling had had any role at all in military operations. However, in a number of conflicts and especially on both sides in World War One, the speed and flexibility of a cyclist was particularly appreciated as scout, messenger, ambulance carrier and even as an infantryman. In the British Army several cyclist companies existed and even, eventually, an entire Cyclist Division.

Organised by the Cyclists' Touring Club, this was the

ninetieth such annual meeting and well over a hundred cyclists were gathered on the green. It being a religious ceremony, I stood well to the back and it's fairer to say that I was surrounded by parked bikes than by their riders. However, I wasn't the only one steering clear of the hymns and hallelujahs and, after the scrupulously observed minute's silence, we started chatting.

'Not as many as there used to be.' Speaking was a short woman with grey hair but muscular calves. Her taller partner, almost identically dressed but somewhat chubbier, responded:

'Oh, it's just the weather. Not everyone's like us, dear. Some people have got a lot more sense.'

'Have you come far?' I asked.

'Only about twenty k this morning. We're staying with friends in Coventry. But we used to come up from Oxfordshire every year.'

'Would now,' added Mrs Muscles, tapping him on the midriff rather more sharply than necessary, 'if it wasn't for your stomach.'

'You underestimate me. I'm still up for it. What about you?' he said to me. 'Haven't seen you here before.'

'No,' I admitted. 'Hadn't even heard of it till this year actually. And before you ask, I've only cycled from just round the corner, where I was dropped off.'

'Fair play to you,' said Chubby. 'How far do you usually do each day?'

'Oh, it's not the distance, it's the pleasure, the views, the people I meet.' I was blathering.

'How far?'

'Cycling? About twenty miles I suppose.'

He slapped me on my back.

'Good for you! An honest cyclist. Whatever next?'

*

Once again on Meriden Green the day after the short walk to the Bull's Head, I looked up at a sky that once again threatened rain. While England's total rainfall isn't excessive in global terms, the average number of rainy days here is unusually high. According to the Met Office, over the last 30 years some parts of the country have experienced rain of over 2mm on as much as 260 days in an average year. These, admittedly, are in the Lake District. In the Midlands it's more like 160-200 days. Even so, that's more or less every other day. One reason for this journey's non-continuous nature is that I'd tried to avoid those days with particularly poor forecasts. The knowledge that I was attempting to dodge some 200 hundred days of rain made me feel a little better about those days where I failed.

Pedalling south, I smiled at the sharp contrast between the genteel annual scene on Meriden Green and the village's remaining claim to fame. For there's an unexpected connection between this Warwickshire village and late Hollywood 'mean man', Marlon Brando -- in particular with his portrayal of gang leader Johnny Strabler in *The Wild One*. Picture the iconic film poster. Apart from Brando, the key ingredient was made in Meriden: the Triumph Bonneville motor bike. The same marque featured with Steve McQueen aboard in *The Great Escape*, with Evel Knievel aboard in some of his stunt jumps and with Bob Dylan alas no longer aboard in his serious motor bike accident of 1967. While the Meriden factory was closed in 1974 and demolished ten years later, Triumphs are still manufactured not far away in Hinckley.

Within ten minutes the threatened downpour had begun and, luckily, I was able to stable Tetley at short notice beside Berryfields Farm Shop, where a sandwich board bearing the magic words 'Cafe Open' rattled in the wind. On entering I must have looked a little like the wild one myself, but twenty minutes, two coffees and one 'squidgy lemon and ginger cake' later, the rain had stopped and the sun come out again, as indeed had I, once more almost human and in greater need of exercise than ever. And exercise is what I got, for while the clouds had melted away the wind had not. Along one lane after another, as nettles, grass and saplings bowed towards me, I bowed towards them in a continuous windy joust that was to last almost all afternoon.

*

Outside Berkswell Grange the driver struggled to keep the horses calm, the rain lashing against the carriage as Droylesden held a flapping brolly over Lady Berkswell's first guests. Inside, however, all was calm, for Lady Berkswell had already retired at an early hour, a habit to which she'd already become accustomed since her late husband's sudden departure from this world. What, she would say to the servants, is the point of staying awake without dear Henry? Sleep was now her only comfort and the sleeping draft prescribed by Dr Matravers her only pleasure. Though she felt sure her guests would not object to her absence until breakfast, she did wonder, as blessed sleep began to welcome her again, what that nice Dr Watson and his mysterious friend Mr Holmes would make of the strange tale she would then recount...

Standing astride Tetley, I surveyed Berkswell Grange and there was no denying that, apart from its age, it was indeed the sort of house that could have hosted a weekend party put onto the page by Conan Doyle: wide gravel drive leading to elegant frontage half-drowning under rampant wisteria. The only half-truth in the above fantasy, however, is Sherlock Holmes himself, for it was here in November 1933 that Peter Jeremy William Huggins was born, son of a Lord Lieutenant of Warwickshire. By the time the first episode of Granada Television's adaptation of the Sherlock Holmes stories was first broadcast in 1984, Peter was already a successful actor, but it will always be by his definitive performance as the edgy, inspired detective that most people will remember him -- under his stage name, Jeremy Brett.

Barely a kilometre beyond Berkswell Grange, at Catchems Corner, I crossed once more the proposed HS2 route -- the new high-speed railway line between London and Birmingham. As stated on the placards in front of a house that, if it survived at all, would have the 'up' line just feet from its window: 'No business case. No environmental case.'

With completely disparate points of roadside interest coming thick and fast, 3 kilometres later I passed a pub with a strange, possibly unique, connection. While there are plenty of inns named after monarchs, a good many after coats of arms and a fair few after animals, is there any other named after a song? As usual, though, it's not a simple tale...

In 1904 Harry Williams moved to the then-named Plough Inn at Meer End when his father became its licensee. Harry was a musician, penning a few songs with his friend Jack Judge. In 1909 Jack, evidently a cocksure young man but often short of a few bob, shook hands on a bet that he could write an entirely new song and perform it in public by the following evening. Now it gets complicated. Jack won his bet and, what's more, the song began to take off. Moreover, even though his friend Harry apparently had no input to it, Jack was a man of honour and fulfilled an old promise to Harry that, should he ever write a successful song, he'd add Harry's name to the credits, whether he'd helped or not. With his share of the royalties, Harry Williams earned enough money to buy the pub for his parents and, to acknowledge the source of his wealth, renamed it after the song. Jack's grandparents were from Ireland and the song he'd written, referring to their home town, gained much of its poularity as marching song in World War One: 'It's a Long Way to Tipperary'. The pub is now called The Tipperary.

*

Benefitting from the tune's gay 2/4 rhythm, I whistled my

way along as Tetley and I continued to battle against the persistent wind. Everything around me was still in motion. Near the shores of the Mediterranean there are winds that blow for so long they have a reputed tendency to drive the locals slowly bonkers. By the time I'd bounced over a rough field and into Hay Wood, I was beginning to expect the sign to Bonkersville just around the corner.

Instead, the wood enveloped me in its calm, dark cloak and, dropping Tetley on the grass, I pulled off my helmet and simply sat for a while with my back against a tree, staring at nothing in particular but the stillness. Bit by bit, small movements in the forest caught my attention. High above, the tops of the trees were still waving, further down leaves and twigs rustled with the flutter of the odd, unseen bird and nearer to hand a white butterfly skipped from log to log. Eventually, I'd been motionless long enough for a rabbit to venture out and try his luck around Tetley's tyres.

This was a remnant of the ancient Forest of Arden, whose name itself reveals its age, for the 'Ard' is the same Celtic root, meaning 'high land', as in Ardrossan, Ardnamurchan and many other place names in Scotland. Formerly covering a huge swathe of the Midlands from the Avon to the Tame (which is why it's crossed by the watershed) and encompassing the sites of the future Birmingham and Coventry, the Forest of Arden was theoretically the location for Shakespeare's *As You Like It*, where it's the destination of Rosalind's flight. Indeed, Shakespeare himself was an Arden, on his mother's side, the family being descended, it's thought, from one of the ruling families of Mercia.

Nowadays Hay Wood forms a precious breathing space between the various conurbations of the West Midlands and is popular for an afternoon's outing -- as I was to discover when two horse-riders disturbed my reverie, prompting me to saddle up again myself. The further west I cycled in the wood, the more walkers I encountered. This was probably down to the proximity of Baddelsey Clinton, a moated manor house owned by the staunchly

Catholic Ferrers family for over 400 years -- and therefore a safe hiding place for Catholic priests for many of those years -- and now owned by the National Trust.

This meant it would have been a prime target for Julie, who'd dropped me at Meriden and whose National Trust membership gave her plenty of scope for visits parallel to my cycling and walking routes. Remembering this prompted a quick glance at my watch and a final surge against the resolute westerly towards our rendezvous point in Kingswood... or Kingswood Brook... or Lapworth...

Here was another unexpected mismatch between map and reality. The OS map was unequivocal: the pub car park was in a small community by the canal called Kingswood Brook, not far from a slightly less small community called Kingswood. No one, however, seemed to have explained this to the locals, who had proudly placed a sign on the main road into the village announcing it as Lapworth -- the name of a completely different village that lay, according to my map, a good three kilometres away.

'There's a mystery here,' said Julie as she wound down the window.

'Yes, The Mysterious Case of the Displaced Village,' I suggested.

'Sherlock Holmes?'

'I think I've read it. Dr Matravers poisoned Lady Berkswell to stop Droylesden inheriting the estate.'

'What? Have you gone bonkers?'

'Probably.'

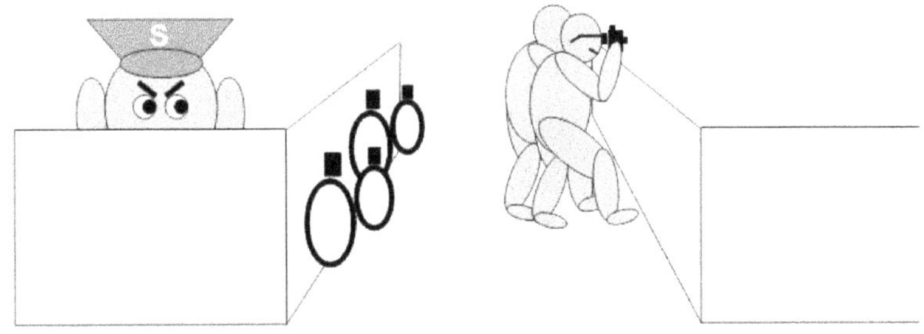

Stage 19: Offending St Modwen

Lapworth to Lickey

If you're not already naturally given to patience, which you probably would be to take it up in the first place, narrow-boating surely teaches you its value. At the lowest lock of seven in a line, a sturdy woman of middle age was winding open the last gate, puffing out her cheeks as she did so.

'Have you done them all today?' I asked.

'We have indeed.'

'How long's it taken?' asked Pete, my cycling buddy for the day.

'Well, I'm not timing it, but we were up before dawn.' It was now 10.30. 'Mind you...'

'Kccchhhh!' suddenly squawked the machine in her hand. 'Ready to come through. Kccchhhh.'

The words came in stereo, since they were uttered into his own machine by her companion, a round man in a striped tee-shirt and floppy white hat, standing at the tiller and therefore only about fifteen metres away.

'Kccchhh. OK.' she said into her walkie-talkie, not looking at him. 'Mind you, after five weeks on the canals, time seems to pass in a different way.'

'Where've you been?' I asked.

'Llangollen in North Wales.'

'Oh, you've been over the famous aqueduct.'

'Yes, the Pontcywhatsit. But actually the one at Chirk is better, even more impressive.'

'Kccchhh. Coming through. Pay attention. Kccchhh.'

Pete and I were looking down over the advancing bows of the narrow boat from a small bridge in the middle of which was a gap of about an inch.

'Sorry,' said Pete quickly. 'We're distracting you.'

'Oh, don't mind him.'

'You're not going to raise this bridge and have us in the water, are you?'

'Don't worry. It's just the gap they used to pass the horse's rope through.'

'Kccchhh. Kccchhh.'

'OK.'

'We'll leave you to it,' I said. 'Bye.' And then, waving at the tiller man, added: 'Kccchhh. Bye, skipper. Kccchhh.' I don't think he appreciated it.

*

'Just as well you weren't on the boat,' said Pete, as we pedalled along the leafily shaded towpath of the Stratford Canal just west of the Lapworth's flight of fourteen locks. 'Some skippers don't take kindly to sarcasm from the crew, especially in the middle of a tricky manoeuvre.'

He knew what he was talking about. Pete is a Yachtmaster, qualified to hire himself out as master of an ocean-going yacht, and had been paying close attention to the rather different manoeuvres being negotiated on the canal. But now his attention had been drawn to something on a vessel moored on the far bank.

'See that blue ensign?' he said, pulling up and pointing at a blue flag with the Union Jack in the corner. 'It's probably illegal.'

'How can a flag be illegal?'

'It can only be flown by certain people, like ex-officers of the Royal Navy or members of a royal yacht club.'

'Says who?'

'Says maritime law.'

'Mar: sea. Maritime: related to the sea. This isn't the sea.'

'Smart arses don't go down well at sea either.'

'Fair comment.'

Pete then filled me in on odd pieces of flag etiquette of which I, being a self-confessed landlubber, had been totally unaware. Ensigns are apparently ‘worn’ by vessels, whereas other flags (not Union Jacks) are ‘flown’. Ensigns used ashore, however, are flown, not worn. A Union Jack (or Union flag) can never be flown at sea by a private citizen. Only Her Majesty’s armed forces have that privilege and it's a criminal offence to break this rule. Argument continues about the right of an Englishman to fly the St George's cross whilst afloat, because it is also the flag of an admiral. It's said that this will only be resolved if taken to court.

'Actually,' he continued, 'we had an odd experience with the St George's cross in Greece the other week.' Pete and his wife Margaret regularly sail the Greek islands and were just back from their latest adventure. While we were cycling under a warm

Warwickshire sun, Margaret and Julie were swanning around the air-conditioned shops of Birmingham's Bull Ring, just 15 kilometres away. This idyllic stretch of England's waterways felt much more remote than that.

'What happened?'

'Well, we were anchored in a bay off Alonnisos when a flash yacht trailing a huge stars-and-stripes pulled alongside. The man at the helm, almost as huge as his flag, was pointing at my illegally flown flag at the crosstrees and called out: "Yo! Is thayat the crahss of Saint Andrew?" Must have had some Scottish ancestors, but still couldn't recognise their flag. "No, sir" I called back. "This is the cross of St George, St George for England!" At this he just stared at me, opened the throttle and put his helm over to sea.'

'Didn't he say anything?'

'Not a word. And...' Pete interrupted himself with a 'Hm.'

'What?'

'Now that *does* annoy me.' He was gesticulating at another flag of St George draped in the window of an approaching boat.

'Don't tell me that one's against the law too.'

'More against common sense. You see these flags draped by idiots during the World Cup.'

'But I thought you approved of the flag.'

'Not with the word "ENGLAND" printed across the middle! If you need reminding whose flag it is, you've got no right to fly it in the first place, if you ask me.'

*

The watershed had been following, more or less, the line of the canal itself -- a phenomenon I'd inferred from the map but one which it took me a while to get my head around until I remembered there's no systematic relationship between the canal network and the natural drainage system. A canal has as much 'right' to follow a watershed as a road or railway.

After about 4 kilometres, however, at Hockley Heath, the watershed veers west to cross the junction of the M40 and M42 before heading south between the Spring Brook, flowing towards the River Blythe and the Trent, and the River Alne flowing towards the Avon and the Severn. It was during the 1950s, deep in this well-heeled corner of Warwickshire with its grand mansions hidden among the trees, that a mother encouraged her young son to learn the piano.

Nicholas proved to be not only a talented musician, later taking up clarinet and saxophone as well, but also a gifted singer-songwriter. By the time he enrolled at Cambridge in the late 1960s, he'd got together an impressive enough repertoire of gentle folk-rock songs to land a recording contract. Unfortunately, while travelling abroad, he'd also picked up a drugs habit. As his musical reputation strengthened, his own grasp on life weakened and in the middle of a November night in 1974, back at the home in Tanworth-in-Arden where he'd first learnt to play the piano, Nicholas died from a drugs overdose.

Barely known outside folk circles during his lifetime, Nick Drake has gained posthumous fame for an eerily atmospheric style of music that's become more and more widely appreciated. While few could name any of his songs, almost everyone in Britain will have heard his tunes as the background to either a commercial or a television documentary. Birmingham Town Hall has seen a concert of various artists performing Drake songs; the BBC has broadcast not one, but two documentaries of his life; and his grave in the churchyard at Tanworth-in-Arden receives a steady stream of fans coming to pay their respects. These included me, as I'd persuaded Pete to allow a small diversion from the watershed.

In this very small Warwickshire village lies a very small

headstone commemorating a very big talent. Even the sign attached to the nearby oak tree, asking visitors not to leave tributes, is more imposing than the humble memorial to Nick Drake and his late parents. An inscription on the reverse contains words taken from the lyrics of the final song on his final album: 'Now we rise and we are everywhere'.

(Oddly enough, my route had earlier passed within a couple of miles of the idyllic rural home, at Byfield, Northamptonshire, of another English balladeer who died tragically young less than four years after Nick Drake: the classic singer-songwriter Sandy Denny.)

*

At Branson's Cross, my long tour of Warwickshire, the county that is 'working together for you', came to an end and, checking in as county number nine on my wiggly way through England, came Worcestershire -- apparently and happily a shire free from slogans.

Almost immediately the landscape began to change. Fewer trees, more farmland, longer views, steeper hills. Somewhere near Weatheroak Hill we caught a westward glimpse of the day's destination, the Lickey Hills and, duly encouraged, pulled over for a picnic lunch. Under a broad oak tree, I extracted from my big blue bag what I'd promised Pete would be a 'light snack for boys'. The idea had been to assemble something akin to the type of 'snap' I'd take on my cycling adventures as a teenager. Out of the steamy bike bag came two sweaty packets of crisps, two rather bendy Rice Crispie cakes, two half-melted bars of Caramac and two bottles of ginger beer.

'My hiking mate Briggsy,' said Pete, 'says you shouldn't drink fizzy pop when you're exercising',

'Why not?'

'Don't know. Never asked.'

So down the hatch went the lukewarm ginger nectar... along with everything else, melted or not. As we pedalled away, I noticed that Pete, at the front, was wavering from side to side just a little.

'Briggsy was right,' he called.

'What?'

'Wind.'

'Me too.'

'Which end?'

'Both.'

*

Before resuming its general westward direction, our route briefly followed the straight north-south alignment of yet another Roman road: Ryknild Street, running here south from Letocetum (Wall, near Lichfield) to join the Fosse Way in Gloucestershire. Like many of England's Roman roads, the name we know it by isn't actually Roman at all. It was in the Middle Ages that this one picked up the name Icknield Way, only to be later amended to Ryknild Street to distinguish it from the other Icknield Way, an iron-age track across southern England.

While the watershed itself runs across the top of Wast Hills, the path that follows it was definitely uncyclable and so the two ginger-beer-fuelled cyclists blew sharply downhill before turning right to tackle the up-slope. As we approached an isolated cottage, an odd sign caught our attention. Bearing an arrow and the symbol for a telephone, it pointed to us, out on the lane, from within a dense green thicket. Dropping our bikes we entered the trees, there to spot a similar sign way down at the bottom of a slippery green slope. Descending a rather incongruously sited flight of steps, Pete and I found ourselves in a dank, dark, green-and-brown world in which weak sunlight played rather half-heartedly on the deathly still undergrowth and from which the gaping mouth of a tunnel led to another, utterly black world. At our feet, leading into the blackness lay the motionless brown surface of another canal. Quite different in character from the busy Stratford Canal, this, my map told us, was the Worcester and Birmingham Canal, still in use but today quite deserted. A board above the entrance further told us that we were standing beside the southern portal of the 2.5-kilometre Wast Hill Tunnel -- and now we were into the top ten of canal tunnels still in use, at number six.

Apart from the eerie atmosphere, three unusual features were immediately apparent. First, its wide mouth revealed this as a two-way tunnel, a characteristic that probably contributes to the second feature, made clear by another sign to one side: 'Unpowered craft prohibited'. The last thing you want to see swimming into the short pool cast by your narrow-boat's light is a wobbly little rowing boat. And third, the source of the canal's water supply -- often a complete mystery to me -- was very evident in this case, for from the top of the opposite embankment to the edge of the canal itself fell a steeply angled, man-made channel, no doubt draining the surrounding hills but currently without any flowing water.

It was with some relief that we re-emerged into the fresh air and sunshine to push the bikes back up to the watershed and suddenly -- in as sharp a change in land use as you're likely to encounter -- to leave rural Worcestershire and enter the urban landscape of the West Midlands conurbation, spreading over about 600 square kilometres and home to well over two million people. This was West Heath, virtually its southernmost extremity. Where there'd been hedgerows and rabbits now stood pavements and children. From farmyards and cottages to car ports and council houses. After following a mile or two of its busy streets, we climbed up one side of a railway bridge and on the other seemed to have landed on the Moon.

*

Its surface was alternately red and grey, unnaturally smooth and broken only by the occasional scraggy-looking weed. While today not a living soul was to be seen, a century ago the site would have been a maelstrom of activity. This was Longbridge.

In 1905, Herbert Austin rented land here to start work on his young company's new car, an enterprise so successful that within a year he'd bought the site for £7,500. Over the next hundred years it was not only Austins that rolled off the production line but also vehicles bearing the marques of Morris, BMC, British Leyland, MG and Rover. In 1965 came the plant's millionth Mini, but just around the corner lay troubled times. The 1970s, thanks in large part to the efforts of local union convenor Derek 'Red Robbo' Robinson, Longbridge became synonymous in the eyes of the British public with strikes and the Government took the helm as the dominant shareholder. The 1990s saw the German company BMW take over but in 2005 MG Rover, as it was then called, collapsed and soon much of the site had been demolished. Research before this ride had suggested that the site was now under the ownership of the Shanghai Automotive Industry Corporation, but I was about to discover that I'd been misinformed.

'Now, with the greatest of respect,' said a heavy West Midlands accent behind us, making us jump as we were surveying the barren scene, 'you gentlemen may well have permission to be doing this.'

Turning, we faced a tall, gangly man of about forty with an 'S' (presumably for Security) on his cap and a fine pair of ears protruding beneath it.

'Doing what?' I said.

'Taking photographs of property belonging to Saint Modwen,' said Johnny Jobsworth.

'No, we have no permission,' stated Pete categorically, before I'd had time to consider whether this was the best response.

JJ turned to me, the photographer.

'No, we don't,' I confirmed. 'But why would I need permission?'

'Because this whole site, including not only the buildings but the land underground,' he stated mysteriously, 'belongs to Saint Modwen.'

'Who's Saint Modwen?'

'Not who, what,' said Pete, who knew about these things. 'It's a property development company. I've dealt with them.'

'Well,' I said, turning back to JJ and retrieving my camera from its bag. 'You can look at my photos if you like. I shouldn't think any saint, Modwen or otherwise, would find anything suspicious in them.' I showed him a few photographs of old signs, rusty lamps and concrete.

'What are they for?' he demanded.

'It's art,' I said, with more conviction than I felt.

This seemed to be just about the most suspicious thing I could have suggested.

'Art?!' he exclaimed, his raised brow causing the cap to rise an inch above his ears. 'Well, I wouldn't know about that. But all this land, these buildings...' (He indicated some rubble that once may have been a building) '... everything above and below it belongs to Saint Modwen.'

It was a statement that none of us standing there by the barbed wire felt in a position to deny and so, after a short pause, I offered: 'They're not very good photos actually. I'll delete them if you want.'

'That won't be necessary, sir,' said JJ, suddenly all smiles. 'Have a nice day and take care on these roads. Can get quite busy round here, you know.'

Pedalling away towards the hills that now rose sharply before us, I called back a question to Pete: 'It's not illegal to take a picture of any property from a public place, is it?'

'Oh, I think it can be nowadays. Anti-terrorist laws, you know.'

'What would a terrorist be doing around here?'

'Well, for all the security guard knew, you could be making careful plans to blow up a building that's already been demolished.'

Stage 20: Classic Stretch

Lickey to Frankley Green

With the girls it was probably down to the young princess. But with the boys, was it because of Peter Pan or Peter Sellers? Or even Peter Lorre? In the Britain of the 1950s, Margaret was a regular in the top three names for a baby girl -- although by the time of this journey it fallen so far out of favour that it was below Freya. For a baby boy, Peter wasn't quite so popular but nevertheless often appeared in the top ten, from which it has now sunk beneath Muhammed. So, given our ages, perhaps it wasn't so surprising that a day spent with Peter and Margaret was followed by a day spent with Peter and Margaret, an entirely different couple. They'll have to be Peter I and II and Margaret I and II.

Beacon Hill car park, where Julie and Margaret I had picked up Peter I and me, was also our rendezvous point with Peter II and Margaret II. Thankfully, from this point circumstances began to diverge. Bikes had been replaced by walking boots; the watershed party comprised four, not two; and overnight another ominous, overcast sky had crept in from the west.

But what a relief to be in the hills again. To stand on a

hilltop, look down on a broad landscape from above, follow the curvature of the earth with my finger and, crucially, see the weather approaching. After eight days labouring through the low country, striving to pick out England's watershed amongst the rolling meadows and wandering suburbs of the Midlands, I was raised up by the sudden might of the Lickey Hills, which place a dramatic full stop between the West Midlands conurbation to the north and the magnificent Worcestershire countryside to the south. And it's thanks to a number of far-sighted organisations, including the Cadbury family of chocolate fame, who purchased and protected this precious land over a century ago, that the public can enjoy these views to this day.

From Beacon Hill, at nearly 300 metres one of the Lickeys' highest points, a vast panorama stretches to the northern horizon. The bulk of the conurbation spreads out like a multi-coloured blanket from the red roofs of Rubery at your feet to the grey blobs of Birmingham's central business district, some 15 kilometres away. Nearer to hand lie the ugly white scars left by the Longbridge demolitions. Turn 180 degrees and the green fields of Worcestershire roll up beyond the Severn to the misty grey Malverns and, further north-west, lies the even fainter grey outline of Shropshire's Clee Hills, with a hint of the Welsh borders beyond. It's an intoxicating scene, best viewed perhaps from the castellated structure right on top of the hill, donated by the Cadburys in 1904 and containing a informative toposcope to satisfy the most inquisitive observer.

*

With the promise of heavy rain moving in, however, and with a few miles between us and our pub lunch, we weren't in the mood for hanging around and set off on foot to the neighbouring Waseley Hills. For me, it was also a relief finally to be heading north again. The last five travelling days had left me still more or less on a level with Naseby, but now at last I was rid of the huge influence on the watershed exerted by the Avon and its tributaries.

Peter II and Margaret II (actually, if it's all right with you, I think I'll drop their regnal numbers from now on) were two old friends from university days, nowadays living just down the road at Alcester. Though resident here in the West Midlands for a good many years, thankfully neither had succumbed to the local drawl, Peter retaining his lively Merseyside tones and his wife Margaret her soft Sussex English. The first hour, across bright green fields, then through the undergrowth of mixed woodland, still damp from recent showers, was largely spent getting up to date with each other's lives. It was Peter who had the most surprising news.

Like me he'd studied geography. Unlike me, however, he'd spent almost all his subsequent working life -- 36 years of it, he reminded me -- in the same career: what used to be called personnel management before we workers were rebranded as 'human resources'. It had been a challenging few decades with one recurring theme across all the organisations he'd worked in: restructuring. For restructuring, read redundancies. For redundancies, read difficult meetings where, more often than not, Peter took much of the flak.

'Sounds pretty stressful,' I commented.

'You're not kidding,' said Peter. 'Eventually I couldn't even switch off on holidays. Then one day we were walking along a local high street when a small card in a window caught my eye. It read "Sales assistant required. Enquire within."'

'And did you?'

'I did.'

'What was it?'

'A shoe shop.'

Pause for effect, during which I tried to picture a besuited

HR manager kneeling at a besocked foot. And couldn't.

'Ladies as well as gents?' asked Julie eventually.

'Yep.'

'Fab.'

'Staff discount?'

'Of course. And even better -- now I'm sleeping properly too. The thing is: when I lock up the shop at night, I leave the job locked up with it. And there's another, even bigger difference between this job and the old one. People actually leave the room with a smile on their faces. That's something I can't remember happening before. Ever.'

*

Between the Lickeys and the Waseley Hills, the waymarks for the North Worcestershire Path, which we'd been following, were joined by a familiar logo: the ship, crown and oak tree of the Monarch's Way. And yet we were some 30 kilometres *north* of Worcester, the scene of the battle from which the future Charles II was escaping to France. Had he been lost? The reality is that in the first days after the defeat the initial objective of the Royalist escapees had been Wales -- beyond the reach of Cromwell, so they hoped. As we'll see later, however, this was not to be and, when Charles passed through these hills on horseback in 1651, disguised as a servant to one Jane Lane, he was making for Bristol.

Where the path hugged the upper east slopes of Windmill Hill, I couldn't resist leaping up onto the ridge itself to stand to wave my rolled umbrella at the landscape around.

'It's a classic!' I shouted back down to my friends.

'A classic what?' asked Margaret.

'A classic stretch of watershed. Look.' I grabbed the water bottle from my pack and poured a few drops onto the grass at my feet.

'He's cracked up at last,' I heard Peter mumble.

'These drops will find their way to the River Rea, the Trent and eventually the North Sea, while these...' I ran over the ridge top, almost out of sight, before repeating the exercise '... will end up in the Salwarpe, the Severn and the Atlantic!'

'No,' Julie clarified, 'He just thinks he's Nick Crane from "Coast".'

'I heard that!' I called.

'Can you hear this?' she asked.

'What?'

'My stomach rumbling. Where's the cafe?'

'Just there,' I said, slowly descending.

'Some drops of coffee, rather than water, would be welcome,' said Margaret.

Well, it *was* a classic stretch of the watershed route anyway. Just as in the Downs and the Cotswolds, the higher parts of the Lickey and Waseley Hills are largely made up of a permeable rock, in this case broken mineral fragments called breccia, through which the rainfall passes until it reaches the clay beneath, where it emerges in a line of springs around the base of the hills.

Following coffee and carrot cake at the excellent Waseley Country Park cafe (no sign of locally named cakes alas), we set off along the nearest paths to what had once again become a less distinguishable watershed, dodging between fields of late wheat and oats on the one hand and the outer reaches of the conurbation, in the form of Rubery, on the other.

Though it's pronounced 'Roo-bury', when I'd regularly passed this way on Sunday mornings as a child in the 1950s I couldn't help but call it 'Rubbery'. We'd be chugging along the A38 from Derbyshire to Droitwich (a hot spot for Guises, then as now), my father at the wheel of FDB 932, our prized Morris Minor, my mother trying to keep us children entertained. Gazing out at the signs floating past, I'd invariably found my own entertainment by this point.

'Look, mam. There's a rubbery newsagent, a rubbery school -- and look, a rubbery church. Yes, it says so. Do you think they've got a rubbery cross on a rubbery altar?'

'I doubt it.'

'And Lickey village!' I'd giggle. 'Can I get a lickey ice cream there?'

By the time my father had reminded us that our grandparents had done their courting down a byway with the almost unbelievable name of Crutch Lane, I was a gonner.

*

As we approached a footbridge over the abandoned Halesowen Railway, which used to carry workers to the Longbridge plants, a strange sight greeted us. A sad sight. The twenty-first century English ritual in which the location of a fatal accident is marked with flowers, often for months on end, is usually played out on roadsides. What event had occurred here among the trees between a housing estate and the M5 motorway none of us knew, but it had evidently moved many to leave tributes to the victim, clearly an Aston Villa supporter. From their condition, the claret and blue shirts had only recently been draped over the parapet.

Our sombre mood was soon lifted by another stretch with impressive views as we passed through Frankley, the little hamlet after which the nearby M5 service area is named. Eventually passed through, I should say. With two geography graduates perusing the map beneath furrowed brows, it's no surprise that we took several wrong turns. After all, nothing short of a fully-fledged emergency is likely to persuade a geographer, especially a male geographer, to ask for directions.

'The map has to be right,' I stated categorically.

More head scratching.

'I tell you one thing,' averred my erstwhile fellow student, 'we are where we are.'

No one felt they could disagree with this, but it was Julie who asked the key question:

'But where are we?'

'Not sure,' said Peter, but that looks like Seattle.

'Oh, he's completely lost it now,' said Margaret.

'No, look,' he insisted, pointing to the Birmingham skyline beyond Bartley Reservoir.

'Well, maybe,' she conceded, 'but that doesn't really help us, does it?'

Actually this latest problem lay with the farmer's failure to clear a line across his crops to indicate the public footpath, together with our reluctance to damage any of them. This year's harvest had already been poor enough without any more problems.

Luckily the first spots of the forecast showers fell just as we were pulling off our boots outside The Black Horse at Illey, a slight diversion from the watershed for the sake of a decent lunch. More than decent, as it turned out: faggots and mash, in my case, washed down by a mellow, honey-coloured, bitter from Slater's of Stafford, called Queen Bee. The lunchtime chat turned briefly once again to the subject of regional characteristics.

'Well,' opined Peter, 'we've come to learn a bit about Yorkshire people in recent years.' Uh-oh, I thought, this is a

Lancastrian speaking. But, contrary to my expectations, Peter was full of praise.

'They really are hardier than southerners,' he said, to nodded agreement from Margaret. 'Come rain, hail, snow, they just carry on. Stoic is what I'd call Yorkshire folk.'

'What about around here?' I asked. 'What about Worcestershire people?'

'Ah.' Husband and wife exchanged glances. 'Mixed. A mixed bunch, I mean.'

Diplomatic or what?

Finally, as the conversation turned to places to stay around the country, Julie and I learned of an experience that just about trumped any of our own in dodgy B & Bs.

'It was in the eighties when the children were little,' said Peter. 'We were in Bournemouth in one of those old-fashioned places where the guests shared bathroom facilities at the end of the corridor. It was breakfast time and we were just finishing our bacon and sausages when the landlady stormed into the breakfast room waving above her head a toilet seat. "All right," she shouted. "Which one of you has broken this seat?" Silence. "No one leaves till the culprit owns up." At this point our daughter piped up: "Ooh, daddy, naughty daddy, what have you done?" All eyes turned to me.'

'Was it you?' I asked.

'Of course not!'

'No, of course not.'

Stage 21: Beyond the Sunbeams

Frankley Green to Billy Wright's Statue

In Spain the sharp juxtaposition of country and town -- vineyard here, tower block there -- comes as something of a shock to an Englishman. The same thing happens in the West Midlands, as already seen at West Heath and now again at Woodgate: empty field here, drives full of Transit vans there. The boundary of the conurbation, in this case Birmingham Metropolitan District, holds the built-up area tightly in place, like a giant fitted sheet, to prevent it spilling out into the Worcestershire countryside. This time, though, I was to be tucked inside for the rest of the day.

Having left the car once again at The Black Horse in Illey, I was now back in the saddle and cycling solo through Woodgate, Lapal and Quinton at about 8.30 a.m. on a weekday -- which in urban England means the school rush. Flapping parents shepherded their little, red-uniformed charges, a fair few wailing into the cool morning air, away from the traffic and into the school-bound flow. While about a quarter of the children were Asian, all the wailers were white. Slightly older pupils wandered in maroon-blazered independence in and out of the newsagent's, a Twix or a Daim bar already eating away at their teeth and their lunch money. The older you are hereabouts, the darker your kit, for black uniforms seemed to signify senior pupils, waiting at bus stops alongside the tattooed and titivated workers, for the Number 202 that would take them to a more distant place of learning.

Sixty years before, one schoolboy trundling along to one local school was setting off on a journey he surely didn't anticipate. It took him first to Cambridge University, then to the Edinburgh Festival Fringe, onto two phenomenally successful series for the BBC and even into the pop charts, before delivering him to a position as a respected expert in natural history. He's that former stalwart of radio's *I'm Sorry, I'll Read That Again* and TV's *The Goodies*, Bill Oddie. (In an odd coincidence, I'd later be passing through the birthplace of another of the three 'Goodies'.)

I wonder if he knew that the back garden of the neat semi near the end of a neat cul-de-sac in Quinton, where he developed his early bird-watching skills, lay just metres from the English Watershed as it swings up to Blackheath and Rowley Regis? Exactly where it swings had at times been fiendishly difficult to identify from my maps, so regularly does the built-up area obscure the contours. On the ground, however, it was blindingly obvious. Indeed, motorists travelling along the raised section of the M5 around Junction 2 at Oldbury get a clear view of the watershed to the west as it forms the ridge between Turner's Hill and Darby's Hill, both topped with prominent masts. The hilly land I was entering was the Black Country.

*

It's a slippery concept. Although the term Black Country is known to have come into popular use around the 1840s, whether it arose from a ubiquitous covering of soot or from former surface outcrops of coal -- or from something else -- seems to be uncertain. Another source of local debate is the Black Country's extent: while Dudley is certainly in, West Bromwich is only probably in and what about Wolverhampton: in or out? These things matter. Those who are in are fiercely proud of the Black Country, with its own flag (mostly black), its own tartan (almost entirely black) and its own dialect. Birmingham people are 'Brumajums', while the latter refer to Black Country folk as 'Yam-Yams', from 'yow am', i.e. 'you are' in the local lingo.

The character of the area derives, of course, from its key role in the industrial revolution, when its location on the South Staffordshire coalfield (for we have slipped from former Worcestershire into former Staffordshire) and near to limestone supplies made it a centre for heavy industry. As early as 1712 the world's first recorded use of a practical steam engine, that invented by Thomas Newcomen, pumped water from Dudley's Conygree coal mine. But by 1852 it was one of the unhealthiest places in England, the average age of death being an incredible sixteen years, compared to twenty-nine nationwide.

Sitting astride the watershed, the Black Country found itself a natural focus for canal building, since there was every incentive to link the country's east- and westbound navigations through one of the areas most in need of easier transport for bulk materials, both in and out. For 'through', read 'under'. That morning I'd already pedalled unknowingly above Lapal Tunnel, built in 1798 by the happily named William Underhill and third longest in the country (though now disused); and above Netherton Tunnel, in 1858 the last to be built in England for over a hundred years and nowadays notable for one of its towpaths being usable by the public for the tunnel's entire 2.8 kilometres. It was, however, towards the entrance to a third tunnel that I eagerly pedalled on a short diversion off the watershed route, the second-longest canal tunnel still in use on the UK canal network today. At nearly 3 kilometres, this was the Dudley Tunnel.

*

'See that big 'ole in the wall, Trev? That's what yer aimin' at, son.'

The voice was that of the volunteer casting us off.

'And when ya gerinsoide, don't forget to turn left, not roight loike you did yesterdie. We don't want yo losin' any more customers, do we?'

With a tolerant smile Trev cast his eyes to the tops of the trees on the high ridge above the tunnel entrance, to the left of which something caught my own eye.

'Are they coffins?' I asked, with what I hoped was an air of nonchalance.

'Oh yeah,' said Trev into the microphone hooked around his head. 'We use 'em on 'Allowe'en.'

Even though I was the only passenger and sat barely three metres away from him, skipper Trev still used the mike throughout. William, the boat, could have taken some fifty passengers and was therefore somewhat over spec for the job, but a 10.30 departure was scheduled and a 10.30 departure there would be.

As soon as we slipped into the darkness I knew I was embarking on one the highlights of this whole journey. The tunnel fitted the boat like a glove and the slimy brick wall slid by just inches from my face. The 'slime', Trev's booming commentary told me, was not slime at all but calcium carbonate seeping from the limestone above and eventually forming the same features, like stalactites, as in any natural limestone cave. The first surprise came after just a few minutes when we emerged into the daylight of Castle Hill Basin, a roofless cavern from which tunnels led off in one direction to old coal mines, in another to old limestone quarries and in another to the main Dudley Canal. Just before the next tunnel engulfed us I caught a glimpse up on a weedy shelf of several black crosses marked 'R.I.P.'

'Hallowe'en?' I asked.

'Roight,' came the echoed reply. 'Now we're leaving the Dudley Canal and heading for the so-called Singing Cavern.'

A little perturbed that we were leaving the canal I thought we were supposed to be visiting, I kept such concerns to myself and focused instead on how Trev was going to turn this very long vessel around in a very narrow tunnel, since I couldn't help noticing there'd been only the one entrance to the subterranean network from the outside world.

Now I know you're as eager as I was to discover why the 'so-called Singing Cavern' is so called. Trev knew too and as soon as we floated into the vast hall of that name he revealed via his now almost deafening amplification that the wind used to pass through here in a way that sounded very much like, well, like someone singing. In truth, the life of a quarryman down here before electric lighting must have been unnerving as well as dangerous and I'd guess the sound of someone singing would have been among the more pleasant sensations of his working day. For one thing, the cavern's roof didn't look too stable to me, comprising as it did a series of vast brick arches encased in what looked a very flimsy piece of netting.

My mind having temporarily wandered away from Trev's spiel, I physically jumped in my seat when an orchestra suddenly struck up the familiar 'Bom-di-diddle-diddle-diddle-dee-daa-day' of Tchaikovsky's '1812 Overture'. By the time the cavern's coloured lights had started to flash to the rhythm of the cannon I'd settled down again and at the end was able to make a semi-sensible remark to Trev:

'Well, that was...'

Boom!

'... unexpected.'

I'd forgotten the final one.

'Lots of groups used to come down here to listen to live music,' he informed me. 'In fact scientists also gathered in this very cavern to observe the limestone formations. Geological scientists. And we'll see some other features they observed later.'

Couldn't wait. Seriously, the trip would have been fascinating enough in a group but as it was all being put on for my benefit alone, I was genuinely overwhelmed. The next astonishing news was that the tunnel we'd now reversed into (ah, William has a reverse gear, that's how Trev's going to do it) dated only from the 1980s and was the first canal tunnel to be built in England since the Netherton Tunnel, 125 years before. Then yet more amplified revelations boomed around my head: that, since the Dudley Tunnel was only one barge wide, northbound and southbound vessels had to work alternate days; that some of those who legged boats through while lying on their backs and 'walking' along the roof, were professional leggers who walked back after one legging to bring yet another boat or even a whole convoy through; that, until the canal owner spotted them, some bargees used to push themselves along with boat hooks that were gradually destroying the walls; and so on.

Having popped back through the portal into twenty-first century daylight and offered probably over-effusive thanks to Trev and the gang, I pedalled off a most impressed, better-informed and, if only temporarily, slightly deafer cyclist than I'd been an hour before.

*

After a 2002 earthquake whose epicentre was in the outskirts of Dudley, one wag suggested it had caused millions of pounds' worth of improvements. A bit harsh perhaps, but on the High Street, which more or less sits astride the watershed, you can see what he meant. Despite impressive statues at each end (to the Earl of Dudley and local-born footballer Duncan Edwards), it's one of many in England redeveloped after the war where, to be honest, the best thing would be to knock it all down and start again.

After a few more dreary miles through Gornal and Sedgley, however, I came across a jewel. Several times in this journey I'd experienced the effects on the traditional English pub of the recession and of changing tastes. But in the Beacon Hotel on Bilston Street, Sedgley, you have a pub that has clearly just shrugged its shoulders, kept calm and carried on. Wood-panelled walls, cast-iron fireplaces, low hatches to the bar; the only obvious food a pile of cheese-and-onion rolls in cling film, defying you to ask for a different filling; an impromptu debate on trades unions in one room, a lone book-reader in another, a knot of serious drinkers in a third; a blissful absence of music; and certainly no television (God forbid). Out in the back yard stands its own brewery: like the pub, Victorian in origin, but taken over in 1921 by one Sarah Hughes and run to this day with the same recipes by her grandson. Having sat for a calm quarter of an hour with my regulation roll and glass of a smooth, hay-coloured ale called Amber, I was on my way to pick up Tetley from the yard when a chap leaning on the old brick wall of the brewery called me over.

'Oy, yo a football supporter?'

I was wearing my FC Barcelona shirt.

'I am, yes, but not of Barça. The shirt's just comfortable on the bike.'

'Cos my cousin likes football but 'e supports the Villa -- 'ow do yer work that out?'

As this chap was evidently a local I asked his directions to the beacon after which the pub was named.

'Mind yo,' he added after directing me, 'yo wanna watch out. Thi's bin trouble up there. Out 'o sight o' coppers, y'see.'

He was right. After a short push through brambles and past the caged-in beacon tower, I emerged in an unkempt area of littered bushes and ragged paths called Cinder Hill. It was the same atmosphere as at Darby's Hill where I'd called earlier: great view, shame about the surroundings. Here, a sign banning the consumption of alcohol confirmed the kind of trouble they'd had. I wondered if anyone had considered tidying the place up, installing a toposcope, building a cafe -- somewhere to celebrate alcohol rather than banning it. If they can do it on the Lickey Hills, why not here?

While the views were a little hazy today, to the east you could still see an endless urban carpet as the conurbation stretched through Wednesbury and Walsall to the horizon, and to the west the contrast offered by the rolling landscape of Staffordshire and Shropshire, with its yellow fields, dark-green woodlands and spiky-black church spires. Hiding behind a second hill to the north was my next destination, the end of today's ride and, as home to over 200,000 people, the biggest city on the entire English Watershed.

*

While I didn't notice any sign welcoming me to Wolverhampton, what no newcomer can fail to notice is that you've suddenly arrived on the other side of the world. Culturally at least. More than half the faces I pedalled past were Asian; brightly-coloured sarees graced the streets; and pairs of turban-topped men discussed the day's hot topics...

'Did you see that save?' said one, as I pulled up at one junction.

'The number of times he's rescued the Wolves this season.'

Some interests cut across cultures.

Turning left towards my first objective, I couldn't help but be impressed by the shiny white domes of the Sikh temple, expressing the same sort of confidence in its builders' beliefs that drove Christians 150 years earlier to raise the spire of St Luke's church just along the street. Sweeping past both, however, I was in search of a less esoteric shrine.

In the seventeenth century a certain style of furniture lacquering became fashionable throughout Europe and in England, where it was called 'japanning' after its Asiatic origins, and one of the most important centres for this trade was Wolverhampton. By the nineteenth century, either here or in nearby Bilston, japanning employed some two thousand workers, including young John Marston. John's plans, however, lay elsewhere and in 1877 he set up a cycle factory, eleven years later registered the marque 'Sunbeam' for his bikes and around the turn of the century watched the first production motor car of the same name roll out of his Wolverhampton factory. Famous for their revolutionary streamlined designs, Sunbeams soon started to excel in the new sport of motor racing and in 1927 the sensational Sunbeam 1000HP (affectionately known as the 'Slug', after its shape) became the first car to hold the world land-speed record at over 200 mph. Slug by name, not by nature.

By this time, alas, John Marston had died, although not before becoming Mayor of Wolverhampton. The site of his Sunbeam Motor Works lies off the suitably named Marston Road and it was to see if anything remained that I'd taken a short diversion. While most of the old site was taken up by modern industrial units, I was delighted to see that the a long facade of what must have been the Sunbeam offices remained, a simple sunbeam motif picked out above the top window. Over the door an inscription announced the building's current use: another Sikh centre. As I stood opposite admiring the building, a saree-clad lady bowed at the entrance as she walked past. It's just possible she was a fan of the Slug -- but probably not.

*

With a train soon due to whisk me back to the car at Illey, I decided to leave Wolverhampton city centre to the next day but couldn't leave without paying tribute to the man probably regarded as the city's most famous son.

The chap leaning on the brewery wall at Sedgley hadn't been the only one to comment on my football shirt today. While most of England happily ignored it (and why shouldn't they?), six or seven people on this stage had shouted out some remark or other. It's perhaps understandable why Wolverhampton should be football mad. When the English Football League was founded in 1888 a quarter of its member clubs were from the West Midlands, including Wolverhampton Wanderers FC, whose tenure of Molineux Stadium started the following season and has continued ever since. During that time Wolves' finest period was the 1950s when, as English league champions before official European club competitions had begun, they defeated Hungarian side Honved, considered by many to be the best team in the world, to become 'Unofficial World Champions'.

Captain of the side through almost all those golden days and also, on a record ninety occasions, captain of England, was Billy Wright. Though born in Shropshire, Wright will always be associated with Wolverhampton and his all-action statue, in front of the Billy Wright Stand, shone out that grey afternoon like a beacon to another time.

Not only is Molyneux the nearest Football League ground to the English Watershed, but Wolverhampton's railway station -- formerly Wolverhampton High Level -- is probably the nearest mainline station as well. A dash from one to the other got me aboard in the nick of time.

Stage 22: Careless and the King

Billy Wright's Statue to Man-Monkey Bridge

In 1978 I found myself in a mini-bus with several other like-minded persons heading for Peterborough to admire England's first mini-roundabout. (Yes, we'd been let out for the day.) While 'the pimple' is no longer there, that jolly little outing came to mind as I stood on the corner of Princes Square, Wolverhampton, admiring England's first automatic traffic lights. Or rather the successors to them, as the 1927 originals have long since been replaced; but in honour of the significance of those now taking charge of this complex junction, their poles are still painted in the traditional black and white hoops.

In a city centre positively awash with historic landmarks I then nipped down Lichfield Street to glance up at the Grand Theatre where Lloyd George made his 'Land fit for heroes' speech in 1918; pushed Tetley past the 'MOTH', as the locals apparently refer to the statue of Prince Albert in Queen Square (it stands for the Man On The Horse), whose unveiling prompted Victoria's first public outing after five years of mourning for her beloved; and finally cycled once more past Billy Wright before heading out west.

The watershed, which here sneaks between the eastbound River Penk and the westbound Smestow Brook, led me past the impressive red-brick pile of Wolverhampton Grammar School, *alma mater* of early rocket designer Sir William Congreve and Governor of the Bank of England Sir Mervyn King, alongside formerly elegant terraces and eventually among currently elegant homes that benefit from broad views over the rolling Shropshire countryside. In leaving Wolverhampton I was also finally escaping the West Midlands conurbation, bringing the city's motto to mind: 'Out of darkness cometh light'. Just as I swung over its last rise, I was tempted into a conversation that added a new insight into one of the previous day's themes.

*

Temptation took the form of a calorie boost at the aptly-named 'Scrumptious' sausage stop. With me as his only customer, Mr Scrumptious was free to chat about his life as the proprietor of a snack bar in a Staffordshire lay-by.

'Should have done it years ago', he revealed.

'Why's that?'

'Oh, I used to have a proper job, running a cleaning company. Paid all right but, you know, the wife said I always came home grumpy. Sold the company, bought this van -- and now she says I come home smiling.'

'From working outdoors?'

'Partly that, partly from living just over there, but mostly it's 'cause the people I talk to all day -- like you, for example -- seem happy to see me.'

'Certainly am,' I confirmed, munching my sarnie.

'They leave smiling... and so I leave smiling.'

I told him the story of my friend Peter II's reincarnation as a happy shoe shop assistant.

'There you are,' said Mr Scrumptious. 'Same thing. Miserable job, miserable bloke. Happy job, happy bloke.'

Not that I wanted to stress the misery side of things, but I did raise the question of Wolves and their current form. Surprisingly my host's already broad smile couldn't have widened any further.

'Yeah, shame about that, but then I'm a Baggies supporter myself.'

'The Baggies' being arch-rivals West Bromwich Albion, I felt an explanation was needed.

'Ah, it's like this,' he went on. 'Me and my two brothers were born near the West Brom ground before the family moved over 'ere to Wolverhampton. Now, they were only little and both started to follow the Wolves, but I was already an established West Brom supporter. It was too late for me to change. Once a Baggy, always a Baggy.'

'How old were you?'

'Six.'

So there you have it. Football's not only engrained in the life of many West Midlanders, but the engraining takes place at a remarkably tender age. Having found that we both regarded as the lowest of the low those who abandon support for one club just to switch to a more successful one -- a Manchester United or a Chelsea -- we went our separate ways: Mr Scrumptious back to his hot plate and I to my hot saddle.

*

Even though it was by now October, it was certainly a warmer day than recently and, after sweating my way up and down a few more lanes, I was soon pulling over for another refreshment break, this time at a pub sitting a few yards inside Shropshire, the eleventh of the traditional counties on my route. While the watershed itself lay along the top of the slope about 400 metres to the east, the county boundary (with Staffordshire) here faithfully followed a south-north lane called County Lane for a good 4 kilometres. According to the barman, if something positive was afoot both county councils would claim local jurisdiction over the lane, while if some work were needed -- the more usual case, he added -- both would try and avoid it.

English county boundaries are weird and wonderful things, each reflecting a unique cocktail of local and national history, current and former geography... and fierce, half-forgotten rivalries that read like pages from *Lord of the Rings*.

In pre-Roman times the limits of a tribal area were pretty fluid but this area seems to have been solidly inside the land controlled by a Celtic people called the Cornovii, whose capital is thought to have been a hill fort on The Wrekin, a landmark just over 20 kilometres west of County Lane. Wisely the Roman invaders based most of their own administrative divisions on existing tribal territories and thus two thousand years ago I would have been cycling well within the land that came under the *civitas capital* of Viroconium Cornoviorum (Wroxeter), just beyond The Wrekin.

It was in Anglo-Saxon times that a significant frontier began to appear in these parts, though one that wandered to and fro as the strengths of two kingdoms waxed and waned. In the east, a fourth-generation descendent of the Angle invaders, Creoda, had become the first monarch of Mercia, a kingdom whose capital was at Tamworth but which at one point extended as far west as the physical boundary that still bears the name of the later Mercian king who created it: Offa's Dyke. In the west lay the Welsh kingdom of Powys -- or the 'Paradise of Powys' as Welsh literature has called it -- which at one time extended way east of here to include the land on which Birmingham now stands.

As County Lane rose on a low promontory, I peered across the sunny fields in search of the paradise that is still Powys, but while The Wrekin and Wenlock Edge -- both in Shropshire -- were clear, the hills of mid-Wales were lost in the afternoon haze. After the hubbub of the conurbation, though, this quiet country lane that had prompted my latest dip into history felt like a paradise of sorts.

For the Mercians, the ninth century proved to be a disastrous time. While its eastern part, essentially the modern East Midlands, was lost to the invading Danes, the western rump was taken over by King Alfred's West Saxons. The significance of this to County Lane was the imposition of Wessex's system of shires, a shire being an area under the control of a 'shire-reeve', or sheriff, for it was not long after that Stafford-shire emerged.

'Stafford' comes from the Old English *stæth*, meaning a landing place. The 'ford by the landing place' grew up at a convenient spot for crossing the marshy valley of the River Stow about 7 kilometres before it flows into the Trent. With the Danes still a potential threat, King Alfred's eldest daughter Æthelflæd had become ruler of Mercia and she chose Stafford not only as a new *burh*, a fortified town, but also as her Mercian capital instead of Tamworth.

In a parallel development in the west, an Anglo-Saxon town had grown up on the Severn known as 'Scrobbesbyrig' (now Shrewsbury) or 'fortified place in the scrubland', which became the centre of the Saxons' administrative district of 'Scrobbesbyrigscïr', or Shropshire. As smartly as the Romans, in most places the invading Normans simply took over the existing structure, reclassifying shires as 'counties', being areas under the control of a count or earl. At the time of the Domesday survey the boundary hereabouts between Staffordshire and Shropshire must have already been more or less as it is today, since Albrighton, the parish to the west of County Lane was recorded as being in Shropshire; and

Codsall, the parish to the east, in Staffordshire. The survey recorded them as home to nineteen and six households respectively.

And thus has the situation remained. While legislation in the nineteenth and twentieth centuries played havoc with local government boundaries elsewhere in England, the imaginary dotted line along the centre of County Lane has stayed in place. Not too far away, for example, Halesowen was shifted from Shropshire to Worcestershire; Dudley sat as a weird exclave of Worcestershire surrounded by Staffordshire; and most significantly in 1974 a brand new 'metropolitan' county called 'West Midlands' gobbled up whole lumps of Staffordshire, Worcestershire and Warwickshire.

Caught up in the middle of it with his job in public relations was my old school friend Richard, who'd accompanied me along the watershed near Meriden.

"It was a bad time," he says, "Nobody I knew wanted it. There were desperate campaigns, for example by the horrified residents of Sutton Coldfield and Solihull, to stay in upmarket Warwickshire and out of the a county that would include the industrial Black Country. But all in vain. The government claimed it was in the name of efficiency but the strong feeling was that it was all political, Labour being in power and the recalcitrant districts being largely Conservative. But then even Birmingham City Council resented becoming subservient to the West Midlands. In the end Mrs Thatcher abolished the new county in 1986, although the old shires didn't regain their territories as the power was effectively distributed among the seven boroughs that made up the West Midlands. Unfortunetly it put me out of a job as well!"

"But why is the West Midlands still there on the map?" I askd him.

"It still exists as a geographical county, but its council, i.e. its power, disappeared in 1986."

The western claws of the short-lived county council area

stopped just 3 kilometres short of County Lane and the only effect of the 1970s mayhem out here was a strange one. The west side of the lane was in a county known for hundreds of years as Shropshire, but the government in Westminster suddenly decreed it should be called 'Salop', an old abbreviation from the Anglo-French '*Salopesberia*' and often used in addresses. It took a local campaign six years to get the name of their home county changed back to Shropshire. Goodness knows how much these two changes cost in terms letter-heads alone.

And, coming back to the reason for this diversion into county history, why has this short stretch of county boundary remained so stable? Well, with Stafford 23 kilometres away to Shewsbury's 36, it's not equidistant from the county towns. My own suggestion, for what it's worth, is that the boundary runs close and parallel to the watershed between the Trent catchment and the Severn catchment, the two great Midland rivers being at their closest here: a mere 35 kilometres apart.

*

Soon after County Lane finally petered out at the bridge over the M54, the watershed and I passed two old friends of a different sort.

The first was the Monarch's Way, following the future Charles II's sixteenth-century escape route, which we'd last met near Lickey Hills. It was here on the Staffordshire/Shropshire border that Charles -- en route, he hoped, to safety in Wales -- had his most renowned, and possibly narrowest, escape.

It was early on the morning of 4 September 1651 that Charles and his depleted entourage arrived at White Ladies Priory on the Boscobel Estate, home to the five Pendrell brothers, all Catholics. Parliamentary troops, however, were in the area and Richard Pendrell quickly whisked Charles off into Spring Coppice, which I'd just passed as a small area of dense, mixed woodland still straddling the watershed. Although the soldiers arrived shortly afterwards, they searched only the priory, not bothering with the nearby woods because of the rain. It was under cover of darkness that a wet and hungry Charles eventually emerged after an uncomfortable day. His problems were by no means over though, for further west Catholic scouts had discovered that the River Severn was too well guarded to risk a crossing and so the Wales plan was abandoned in favour of a dash to the south coast.

It must have been a near-exhausted Charles that returned to Boscobel less than two days after he'd left. This time the parliamentary troops were searching the woodland as well as the houses and so the would-be king was pushed into a large oak tree standing clear of the woods, along with a surviving comrade from the Battle of Worcester with the almost comically inappropriate name -- given the extreme precariousness of the king's situation -- of William Careless. A descendent of this oak still stands on the same spot, surrounded by a small fence and, from my viewpoint on the nearby lane, looking very obvious indeed -- especially if it had had a man-sized hole in its trunk.

At all events, Careless and the king went undetected, Charles left Boscobel again the next day -- this time headed definitively southwards -- and 'The Royal Oak' became one of the most popular pub names in England, including, as it happens, my own local in Leicestershire. I couldn't help but wonder in what way England's history would have altered if a group of Roundhead militiamen slightly less averse to a little Shropshire drizzle had searched Spring Coppice on that first day.

*

The second old friend was Watling Street, which had come a mere 77 kilometres on the more or less straight Roman route, while I'd been wiggling my way along the watershed for more than twice that distance in order to stay west of the headwaters of various tributaries of the Trent. While Watling Street (the A5) shot off to

Shrewsbury and North Wales, I trundled on my pre-ordained path northwards, the next stop being Gnossall Heath in Staffordshire and more particularly the bar of the Navigation Inn.

Here was another pub, rather like the Beacon in Sedgley, sticking like a limpet to the traditional fare of soft rolls stacked in cling film, in a traditionally unfashionable bar, with pool table, dart board and poor-quality snaps of regulars pinned above the bar, complete with pencilled-in moustaches -- just on the women, naturally. Magic.

Taking my cheese-and-onion cob and coffee to the rear terrace, I pored over the map in search of a cyclable route for the day's last few kilometres that most closely followed the watershed. Oddly enough it seemed once again to be a canal towpath -- odd because I still struggled to convince myself that a canal is not part of a landscape's drainage system, at least not directly. Since the towpath was right there at my feet, I supped up smartly and left straight from the pub yard.

The canal in question was the Shropshire Union (formerly the Birmingham and Liverpool Junction), a particularly interesting waterway for three reasons. First, it was the last major canal to be built in England, not just because it completed the network by linking the West Midland canals (for example the Dudley Canal I'd sampled) with the Mersey, but also because of its date. Completed in 1835, its opening coincided with first shoots of a railway system that would eventually grow to eclipse the canals as the country's primary means of freight transport.

The second oddity was clear to see as soon as I started pedalling along the strangely deserted towpath. One minute I'd be in a shady cutting, the next exposed on top of a huge embankment. So, with the canal cutting a steady line through a wildly swooping landscape, not only couldn't it be following the exact route of the watershed but also its construction must have involved tremendous engineering challenges. The man who'd taken it on with the same gusto as all his works was that colossus of the canal age, Thomas Telford. Gusto yes, but health no, for it was while waiting for these very embankments to settle that Telford died in August 1834. The third feature of note therefore is that this canal was to be the great engineer's last project.

In a way it's the peculiar topography of the Birmingham and Liverpool Canal that may partly explain why the bridge where I left the towpath -- and ended today's ride -- is known by some as 'Man-Monkey Bridge'. Since it'd be the following morning when I'd cross over it, however, the tale is best left until then.

Stage 23: The Staffordshire Iconoclast

Man-Monkey Bridge to Keele

The unfortunate deflation in the shock value of swear words caused by their overuse is a well-known trend in twenty-first-century England, but until breakfast the following morning I'd assumed the villains who nowadays treat cursing so lightly all to be youngsters.

My overnight stay -- without Julie on this occasion -- had been at The Swan in Forton, a hamlet on the outskirts of Newport and just a few miles off route. So tasty was their Three Sheets Ale, from Ringwood Brewery, that my head was veering towards the foggy side of clarity as I sat down to the inn's excellent cooked breakfast. So at first I didn't notice the strange conversation at the next table. Its occupants were three middle-aged men, all with London accents, and their subject, when I eventually focussed on it, was an absent colleague called Mikey.

'Mikey never f***in' washes, you know.'

'What, never?'

'F***in' never. 'E sweats 'is a**e off all day, like the rest of us, but 'e goes to 'is bed still smellin' like a f***in' pig.'

'An' in the mornin'?'

'Smells like a f***in' pig in s**t.'

'What a b*****d! My f***in' brother, now 'e never stops f***in' washin'. Smells like a b****in' p**f. An' e's a tight b***er too. Uses that soap till there's nothin' left but the f***in' Lifebuoy label.'

Silently chewing my bacon and looking the other way, I realised that the most remarkable aspect of the conversation was that none of the three was in any way angry; indeed they were all in good spirits. I began to wonder what they used as swear words if they actually *were* angry. It couldn't have been the F word, as that was evidently just a piece of punctuation.

'Was your breakfast OK?' one asked his neighbour, as they pushed back their chairs.

'Specf***intacular!' he replied.

Couldn't agree more.

*

The single-carriageway A-road back to the watershed heaved with traffic and it was with some relief that I pulled over to lean Tetley against the parapet of Bridge 39 -- or Man-Monkey Bridge, as it's known.

The story goes that one dark winter's night in 1879 a carter was wending his weary way back from a delivery near Newport, along this very road, when he approached the bridge over the canal. Without warning a 'creature', entirely black but for two huge white eyes, leapt from the trees onto his horse's back. Though the man tried to knock it off, his whip -- so he reported -- went straight through the creature and so it was with the creature still aboard that the frightened horse galloped off. Now horseless, the man stumbled into the next village, Woodseaves, to tell his tale, putting such fear into the locals that for years to come they too would report various sightings of the 'man-monkey'.

Now, I've endeavoured to keep the tales in this book within the bounds of fact; and the facts of this case do include the record of the reports themselves, both that of the unnerved carter of 1879 and subsequent ones. Indeed they include the unlikely but true fact that over 100 years later someone claims to have been so intrigued by this story that he was eventually inspired to write a whole book on the subject of the mysterious 'man-monkeys' of Britain. It takes, however, only a short reflection to realise that the only mysterious aspect of the original account is the claim that the whip passed through the body of the beast. After all, there could be any number of rational explanations of what animal it was and from where it came. Peering over the parapet into the deep cutting torn from the landscape by the Telford's canal-builders, I could easily accept that this locale would engender a certain nervousness at any time, let alone when an animal jumped out of the trees in the middle of the night. To imagine therefore that a movement as rapid as the flick of a whip passed through, rather than simply past, a black body seen against a black background, seems an easy mental leap to have made.

I rest my case... and leave any further tales of the would-be supernatural where they belong: beyond the remit of a travelogue.

*

Passing through Woodseaves in a rather more relaxed state than the carter, I finally turned off the busy road and followed the watershed north-westwards as it sneaked between Lonco Brook, flowing west towards the Severn, and the River Sow, whose waters would pass through Stafford to the east before emptying into the Trent. The blue skies of yesterday had clouded over but the lack of a haze meant that the grey hills of Wales now bubbled up on a distant western horizon. Not only the air, but also my head was becoming clearer and it was with keen anticipation that I pulled up at a gate where my map showed both the red dashes of a bridleway and the pencil line I'd added for the watershed disappearing into the huge and mysterious acreage of Bishop's Wood. Mysterious, because before the ride I'd not been able to find the slightest snippet of information about what was clearly the largest area of woodland for miles around. Surely there'd be a noticeboard where the main track entered the trees. Well, there wasn't and there was.

What there wasn't, as I leaned over the gate and peered into the dark green shadows of the wood, was any sign to confirm that any public path at all entered Bishop's Wood just here. What there also wasn't was any noticeboard that even suggested that this might actually be Bishop's Wood, let alone what was to be found within it. More significantly, what there *was* was a rather dilapidated board that stated:

'Caution - Shooting in Progress'

Shooting? Of what by whom? Of ramblers by deranged farmers? Long-distance cyclists by bike-hating vigilantes?

Though I pedalled up and down the lane like a frustrated badger barred from its sett, no other entrance was to be found and so it was with head drooping low over the handlebars that I retraced my wheel marks back to the last crossroads to take a parallel road, which -- contrary to watershed 'rules' -- wandered to and fro across the River Sow. With my chosen route blocked and visibility once again restricted by an unexpected shower blowing in from the Cheshire Plain to the north, I hunched my shoulders and reflected for a while on matters other than the land around me.

*

The matter that came most immediately to mind was the effort needed to keep my steed and myself actually moving forward against the freshening wind. Just a week or two before, I'd paid visits to two cycling friends -- or rather two friends who cycled, for

I'd never accompanied them on their two-wheeled endeavours, nor was ever likely to -- and was granted access to their respective bike sheds. Both raced bikes rather than simply rode them. One was a current world champion and many of the machines in her shed were free gifts from her sponsors. Randomly I lifted one from its rack and was astonished to find that I could raise it from the ground with just one finger. Amazingly the modern carbon-fibre frame of a typical racing bike can weigh less than one kilogram; that's less than a bag of sugar. The rules of most cycle racing specify a *minimum* weight of 7 kgs for the whole bike. The other friend, a champion in the making if ever there was one, also let me pick up one of his bikes and it was barely heavier: two fingers maybe. By comparison, Tetley, my faithful six-year-old touring bike, weighs in at 15.5 kgs and on this stage was carrying luggage of about 6.5 kgs as well. Even with both hands, I can lift it for only long enough to get it in and out of the car.

As I struggled up the windy road that links Stafford and Market Drayton, I knew that there must be reasons other than weight of equipment to explain the discrepancy in speed between me and the racers. There is, of course, the question of the rider's weight. While I know my weight (only too well), I can merely estimate that of my two lighter friends, but I would put the difference between either and me at somewhere between 25 and 30 kgs. So the total weight I had to shift was probably over 40 kgs more than they did. That's the equivalent of their towing behind them a petrol lawn mower -- with its tank full. That'd slow them down a bit.

And then there's the matter of age. I was the wrong side of their youthfulness by some 30 years in one case and 45 years in the other. Oh, and must we mention relative fitness? To give an idea of the level of fitness the world champion had reached, on one day I was there, she'd risen at 5.30 in the morning, driven her bike to the base of a 3,000-metre mountain (this was not in Britain), ridden up the mountain, whizzed down the mountain, ridden up the mountain *again*, whizzed down again and driven home. When she breezed in, I'd not long been up. In the prospective champion's case, an idea of the speeds he reaches in the velodrome where I went to watch him perform is shown by the fact that a few drops of water falling onto the track from a leaking roof -- so little it could be wiped away once a lap by the single pass of a cloth -- was deemed to render the track too dangerous and his race was cancelled.

*

By the time I'd pulled off the road onto a dirt track where the watershed took a sharp right turn -- in fact, where the English Watershed reached its westernmost point south of Hadrian's Wall -- I felt a little more at ease with my humble 30-kilometre days. The rain had stopped too.

I found myself passing between the homes of the seriously wealthy in a village called Ashley Heath. A woman in an apron was clipping a garden hedge that hardly needed clipping. A man in smart corduroys pulled his wheelie bin, which bore the name Newcastle-Under-Lyme Borough Council, noisily along his gravel drive. Both smiled politely as I waved my way by. Near the mast that marked the top of the lane, I saw a sight that I hadn't seen before and certainly hoped was not a sign of things to come. It was a wooden plaque attached to one house's front gate that read:

'Seattle House - Michael - Lydia - John - Caroline'

(The names are changed from the actual ones.)

A house name with the names of its residents permanently included? Surely, like many other naff novelties, this must be an idea imported from the United States. What happens when Caroline leaves home? Or if Michael leaves Lydia? Will they commission a new plaque for each shift in the household's roll call? Mystified, I ploughed on.

Today I'd acquired a small packed lunch and knew the exact seat on which I planned to eat it.

*

As it turned out, the seat of choice was already taken, but taken by someone who was to prove a most entertaining lunch companion.

Turning off the A51 opposite another Iron Age site at Berth Hill onto a short, sunlit lane to the small village of Maer, I'd already passed confirmation that I was in the right place. It was a roadside painting and featured, in the foreground, a balding but heavily bearded gentleman and, in the background, a couple emerging from a small, sturdy church. The man leaving the church and the man in the foreground appeared to be one and the same and the title on a book he held left no doubt as to his identity: it read 'The Origin of Species'. Its full title was, of course, *On the Origin of Species by Means of Natural Selection, or the Preservation of Favoured Races in the Struggle for Life* and the gentleman was Charles Darwin.

The months following Darwin's return from the *Beagle* expedition in October 1836 were filled for the young naturalist with a hectic whirl of presentations, writing and yet more research. By September of the next year his doctors had advised a period of rest and it was to here at Maer Hall, the home of his uncle, pottery manufacturer Josiah Wedgwood, that Darwin withdrew. The peaceful surroundings, however, were perhaps not the main attraction since the choice also guaranteed him the company of his cousin Emma. Less than 18 months later, they married at Maer's St Peter's church, the one in the painting and the one in whose churchyard I'd spotted, on Google Earth(TM), a suitable bench.

The church being raised some way above the lane, I was puffing as I pushed Tetley up the path.

'You could've left your bike down there.'

Looking up, I saw a short lady, some years older than me, sporting a padded blue jacket, tweed skirt and sensible brown shoes. She was eating a packed lunch and she was doing it on 'my' bench.

'What?' I gasped.

'There's nowhere to go up here but the graveyard. No one'll pinch it down by the road. There's no one around anyway.'

The latter point wasn't lost on me, since I realised that these words were probably the first I'd heard since leaving my overnight digs some four hours before.

'Oh, OK. Mind if I lean my bike against the bench?'

'No, lean yourself on it too if you like.'

As we sat side by side, munching our lunches (hers rather better prepared than mine, I noticed) I learnt a fair few snippets from Mrs Tweed -- some worth knowing, some perhaps not. It turned out that this wasn't her first visit to Maer. Once or twice a year for several years, she'd used her 'pensioner's pass', as she called it, to take the bus out here from her home in a nearby town.

'I like to see how the other half live,' she explained. 'Look at that house.' She waved her sandwich at the elegant, three-storeyed Maer Hall opposite, with its lawns, stables and attractive lake beyond. 'It wasn't the original Wedgwood who bought it, you know. It was his son. The old man had worked his way up, but young Josiah, he had it all handed to him on a plate, didn't he?'

'Ha, plate!' I said. 'I get it.'

'What? It's no laughing matter.' Duly reprimanded, I looked down at my cake. 'While he was swanning around out here, his employees were working their guts out in the filth of The Potteries.'

'I thought I'd read he was a bit of a reformer.'

'Aye, well, they all say that, don't they? Have you ever

worked in a factory?'

'Only for a few weeks.'

'Yes, well, my late husband worked all his life in the mills and then dropped dead less than a month after he retired. So I come and sit here with my back to Wedgwood Junior and enjoy the life my Ernest never had.'

'Your back to him?'

'Yes, he's buried here.'

'Where?'

'Somewhere up there. I've never looked. I quite like coming out all this way just to turn my back on him.'

'What about Darwin?' I asked, hoping to nudge the conversation towards the positive. 'Didn't he work out some of his evolution theory here?'

'So they say -- and a fat lot of good it's done us. It's only a theory, you know.'

It seemed that, in trying to knock one of the chips off her shoulder, I'd only succeeded in revealing another.

'Don't you believe it then?' I asked.

'It's not that I believe in all that God nonsense,' she explained. 'Funny thing is that Darwin still did, you know, even though his ideas pulled the rug from under religion. No, it's just that it's all about the past -- how this fish turned into that one, how some animal's eye developed. I mean, who cares? It's all millions of years ago. Whatever happened, it's all gone. The only thing we can change is the future.'

Not feeling I could respond to this in any adequate way, I let her go on. Over the next few minutes, this Staffordshire iconoclast dismissed Capability Brown's work on the gardens we were looking at as 'not a patch on nature'; all visual art -- including that in Wedgwood's designs -- as 'just squiggles and stripes'; and most of human history as 'just too many people scrabbling to get up the same ladder' -- a process Darwin might have recognised, as it happens.

Having had most of my preconceptions on human endeavour merrily swept away, I left Mrs Tweed still surveying her favourite scene (or least favourite -- I still wasn't sure) and pedalled back up the lane, strangely refreshed.

*

Mrs Tweed's accent had included the flat vowels of the North Midlands, reminding me that I'd now entered North Staffordshire. That it is very distinct from South Staffordshire was brought home to me by a friend who I'd hoped might at last make an appearance in this book, after having threatened but failed to in previous jaunts. He's referred to by many, including himself, as 'the Wanderer'.

Since the Wanderer hails from Stoke, I'd invited him to join me in walking a stage not far from his childhood home. In as much as anything is ever actually agreed in the Wanderer's hazy plans, a date had been agreed. And, miracle of miracles, as the date appeared so did he. What didn't appear, however, were the Wanderer's walking shoes. What appeared on the wandering feet was what always appeared on them, so far as I could recall: a pair of soft, rather expensive, lounge shoes. While the Wanderer did appear at our home, he had, it seemed, forgotten why he was appearing. With uncertain weather forecast and a five-size discrepancy between the wandering feet and my own spare footwear, the walk was cancelled.

However, when I suggested that this stage would have been one of the last in the West Midlands, he was shocked.

'The West Midlands?!' he spluttered. 'The Potteries aren't in the West Midlands, lad! The West Midlands is Birmingham.'

'But Staffordshire's surely in the West Midlands.'

'South Staffordshire may be, but they were never anything to do with us', he retorted, as though speaking of some black sheep in the family. 'North Staffs is quite different. Different countryside, different feel, different accent, different people.'

'Well, it's not in the East Midlands.'

'No, no, you're right. That's you lot. The East Midlands starts at Derby. No, I think we all regarded ourselves as being the North Midlanders, more orientated to Manchester than Birmingham.'

'North Midlands hadn't occurred to me.'

'Well, I'm pleased to have given you something to think about at least.'

And so as I pedalled up towards Baldwin's Gate, Wandererless alas, I did think about it. And what I thought was that this business of English regions is pretty complex. The boundaries wander to and fro not only with time but also with the context (government-defined regions versus TV regions, for example) and most certainly with the person you're asking. It was a pertinent moment to consider all this, for as I turned left at Baldwin's Gate I was approaching another watershed junction -- and therefore another 'cultural province'.

*

The Welsh Watershed, marked on the map at the beginning of this book, is a west-east line dividing the catchment area of the Severn from the various rivers of that flow into the Irish Sea, notably the Dee. Extending into England, it divides the waters of the Tern to the south from those of the Weaver to the north and forms a junction with the English Watershed at Camp Hill, part of the heavily wooded Maer Hills that rise north of the A53.

Reminding me of the stretches of watershed back in Dorset, the map showed several tumuli on the hillside, but such was the density of the forest that none of them -- nor indeed much else -- was visible as I pushed Tetley up the narrow, dark lane towards the summit. What was just visible were the roofs of a grand house, set in an even grander natural bowl cut into the side of Camp Hill: another outpost of the nineteenth-century Wedgwood empire in fact. Just beyond here the lane reached its peak and, opening up to the right, the north, was a wide view over deep green fields and deeper green hedgerows, all draining not to the Bristol Channel now but, via the River Weaver and the Cheshire Plain, to the Mersey and the Irish Sea. 'Irish Sea' is also the name given by Phythian-Adams to the 'cultural province' that stretches north from here, encompassing most of Cheshire and Lancashire and focussing on Liverpool.

Satisfied that this was as near as I was going to get to the actual watershed junction which lay, I assessed, a few hundred metres behind me on the hill itself but inaccessible to the public, I turned Tetley east again and freewheeled back to the main road.

*

When Jimmy Perry and David Croft were developing the characters for Dad's Army, it was a stroke of genius to name the platoon leader Mainwaring. The historical tendency among upper-class English families to settle on an unlikely pronunciation of their surnames gave ample opportunity for the lower middle-class Captain Mainwaring to underline his credentials for a rise up the social scale.

'It's not "Main-waring" but "Mannering", he'd stress.

Whether Perry and Croft were aware of the real-life toffs named Mainwaring I don't know, but if so they would surely have used the comic potential of their full title: the Mainwarings of Over-Peover. While the fabulously named village of Over-Peover lies in deepest Cheshire, from the sixteenth century the Mainwaring family estate was at Whitmore Hall in Staffordshire and it was at the Mainwaring Arms in Whitmore that I stopped for an afternoon break.

This was a another proper pub, with proper fireplaces in each room, proper real ale and in this case proper food served by a proper barmaid, with the deepest brown eyes you could imagine. It was only after a proper home-made soup, which I hadn't realised I'd needed, that I noticed the Mainwaring family motto on the pub sign: *Devant si je puis* (In front if I can). An ambition that Captain Mainwaring certainly shared.

*

So far as I can judge, the watershed crosses the M6, as I did, at the over-bridge just west of the Keele service area, and so if the Highways Agency were to follow up my suggestion made with respect to the M4 in Wiltshire (and at the time of writing there's still no indication they will), the service area itself would be an ideal location for a watershed information board. I dare say a number of the long-distance motorists taking a tea break here feel intuitively that they're finally entering (or leaving) the north-west of England.

Although Keele is very a small village, it's not just the service area for which it's name is known. The other reason would form the backdrop to the beginning of the next day's ride.

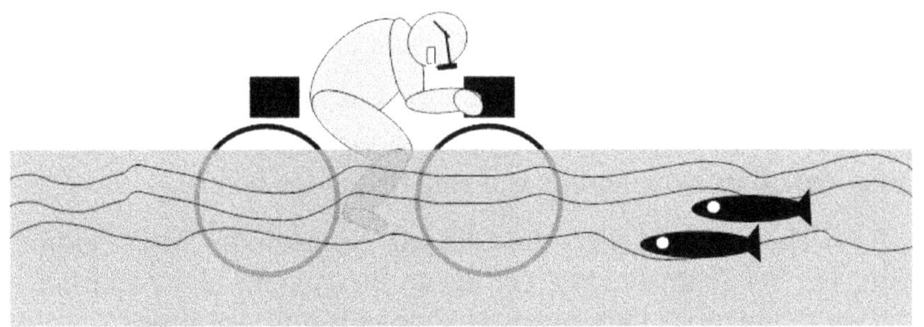

Stage 24: Disaster at Dingle Brook

Keele to Biddulph Moor

More overnight storms had left surface water flowing noisily down the streets, along gutters and through ditches. The golden leaves of autumn had been torn from the trees and cast like surplus treasures by a careless king into every tangled corner, from where the short-lived streams picked them off a handful at a time, rustling them downhill to block the drains and send the water even further afield.

If I couldn't identify the line of the watershed here, this morning, I couldn't do it anywhere. It clearly lay up there among the buildings on the hill, to which several lines of students were doggedly climbing, against the tide. This was Keele University campus.

Pushing Tetley in the same direction, and recognising that sense of a new beginning that always comes with autumn terms, I realised that for many of the undergraduates around me this autumn would be a watershed in their own lives. By the time I'd got beyond the top of the hill and sat down outside the Student's Union sipping a coffee, I was lucky enough to fall into conversation with two of them.

'Are there still nine o'clock lectures?' I asked the young woman sitting opposite. It was quarter to nine and I'd been surprised to see so many students out and about so early.

'Oh, you'd better ask her. She's like my carer?'

The woman who'd spoken was a waif-like figure sitting with her feet on the bench, gloved hands clasped around her knees and long, dark hair blowing this way and that in the breeze.

'Ha!' snorted her short-haired companion. 'She's kidding you. I'm her flatmate. Just get her to the campus and point her in the right direction? Otherwise she'd be in bed till tea-time?'

Like many of their generation, they both spoke in questions. Resisting the temptation to assure them I knew the meaning of both 'direction' and 'tea-time', I instead repeated my question.

'Oh yeah,' said Long Hair. 'Nine o'clock tutorials some days too. My tutor says if he can get there from twenty miles away, I should be able to make it from two?'

'He's right,' said her sensible friend. 'Also says he's they're for our benefit, not his?'

'Oh, you're always on their side?'

I briefly wondered how a tutorial would go with no statements, only questions...

How does quantitative easing work?

The Bank of England feeds money into the economy?

Well, does it or doesn't it?

I just said it does?

It does?

Does it?

It took me a moment to realise that Short Hair had asked me a genuine question: where was I cycling to? Only a few words into my explanation, it was -- somewhat surprisingly -- Long Hair who interrupted to say she knew all about watersheds.

'Oh yeah, yeah. We did watersheds at A-Level. I'm doing Earth Sciences? I'm going to be a surveyor? Well, want to be.

'You never told me that,' interrupted Short Hair.

'Well, you don't know everything, do you? You mean this big watershed crosses the campus? Wow. Where?'

In fact I'd contacted Keele's Geography Department to ask if anyone would like to help me trace the watershed across their campus, but couldn't raise any interest. So I'd only the vague idea of its route that the 1:50,000 map suggested.

'Um, over there, I think.' I pointed at the rise that separated us from the William Smith Building, home to the fairly renowned geography department and named after the creator of the first geological map of England.

'Hey, gotta go,' said the newly enlivened Long Hair, jumping up. As they both hurried off through the metal-post sculpture that dominates the little campus square, Long Hair called back:

'Which side of the watershed are we?'

A genuine question.

'Work it out!' I shouted.

I wonder whether she did.

*

Actually, the little permanent stream draining the south-east side of the campus meant, if I'd got it right, that the Union lay just on the east side of the watershed. After having a second cup of coffee to help me recover from an early-morning ride from Stoke railway station, I set off again myself. It's quite a big campus, in fact the largest single-campus university in the UK, with over 10,000 students altogether. A popular one too, it seems, since in a recent student survey on course quality, Keele came out top among all English universities north of Oxford and Cambridge.

The village that gives Keele University its name gets its own name from the Old English *'cȳ hyll'*, meaning 'cow hill' and even today I was soon out among the fields once again. My conversation at the Union having taken me back forty years to my own student days, I was suddenly shifted back even further when the only way to get drily through some standing water was to pedal hard and freewheel, legs akimbo, as every child does with glee on their first bike.

And then, to complete the hat-trick of youthful evocations, an oddly familiar sound drifted across from a nearby street as if from a nearby lifetime.

'Ay-ow-aye! Ayyyy-ow-aye!!'

The call translates down the years as 'Any old iron?' Rising metal prices have prompted a recent return of rag-and-bone men to the streets of England, after these collectors of unwanted household goods had all but disappeared by the 1980s. As I turned a corner, the 21st-century version came into view: driving a small van rather than leading a horse and calling through a megaphone rather than simply at the top of his voice, but nonetheless identifiably a modern-day Harold Steptoe.

The streets in question were those of Silverdale, formerly a busy corner of the North Staffordshire Coalfield, which prior to World War One boasted more than fifty pits, employing over 20,000 men. By the time Silverdale Colliery closed on Christmas Eve 1998, coal had been mined here for over 700 years. The closure left North Staffordshire with no deep mines at all. The landscape through which I was cycling would be familiar to anyone from equivalent areas in England's recently abandoned coalfields. The empty black windows of long-forgotten brick buildings stared out of scraggy scraps of woodland; strangely smooth hillsides rose above stands of freshly planted conifers; and bright new business parks rubbed shoulders with rusty old gates bearing the initials NCB, but led to nothing but weeds and rubble.

It was a relief to climb up the steep rise to Alsager's Bank, where the morning sun, still low but dazzlingly bright, reflected off neat rows of parlour windows in the east-facing terraces. As I'd climbed, a broad view had opened up to the left, a more dramatic panorama of the Cheshire Plain than the one from the Maer Hills. Several towns shimmered in the middle distance: Crewe, Nantwich and perhaps that was Northwich even further out. Thin grey lines on a distant horizon could have been North Wales. Another corner revealed a quite unexpected object that must have lay some 25 kilometres to the north: a huge, vertical block that rose from the green fields like an alien spacecraft manned by beings that specialised in neat landings. It was a while before it dawned on me that this was the giant telescope at Jodrell Bank, at 90 metres high one of several features destined to be visible for much of the day as I traversed the elevated landscape of North Staffordshire. First though, a short diversion meant a rapid descent halfway to the lowlands again.

Firedamp doesn't sound like the name of a chemical. In fact it's a generic term that can refer to several gases, but most notably methane. What unites them, and prompts the group name, is flammability. Accumulating in pockets within various rock strata, firedamp can explode on release. One of these strata is coal. During the nineteenth century many lives were lost to explosions of firedamp in British coal mines before the Davy safety lamp restricted the flame within a mesh screen. So it came as something of a surprise when I read the date on the memorial to the Minnie Pit disaster.

The pit lay just outside the village of Halmer End and was named after Minnie Craig, daughter of one of the owners. Today it's a small area of woodland, in a clearing of which stands a single pit wheel, painted an incongruous sky-blue, and bearing the inscription: 'In memory of the 155 miners and 1 rescuer who lost their lives in the Minnie Pit Disaster January 12th 1918'.

Behind these bald facts lie countless individual tragedies. Forty-four of the 155 were boys. The one rescuer was Hugh Doorbar, who died searching for survivors two days later. The date in 1918 tells us that the war would already have taken many of the bread-winners from local families, now left to live on even less, a situation that prompted a special relief fund among all Britain's miners. And the cause of such a violent explosion so many years after safety precautions against firedamp had been implemented? Such was the devastation below ground that the official inquiry admitted it simply had no idea.

Offering silent acknowledgement that I'd been born into that lucky generation required to risk our lives neither down the pits nor on the battlefield, I stood for a while beside the memorial before pushing Tetley back up to the ridge. We sometimes forget how lucky we are.

*

The watershed was taking me across the north-western tip of the Potteries, those six towns -- Tunstall, Burslem, Hanley, Stoke, Fenton and Longton -- stretching away to the south-west along the beginnings of the Trent valley. Six? I'd always thought it was the five towns, but, while Arnold Bennett did refer to the Potteries as such in his novels, albeit under fictional names, it's said that he missed out Fenton simply because 'the five towns' had a better ring to it.

Actually, the map on Tetley's handlebars suggested a more obvious number might be seven, the extra town at the north of the line being Kidsgrove. The reason I'd pulled over was to make an umpteenth attempt to track the line of the watershed hereabouts. Kidsgrove marked my first re-entry into England's urban landscape since Wolverhampton and spotting the thin blue lines that mark watercourses among the brown, black and white used by the Ordnance Survey for built-up areas was no easy task. Looking up at reality (always a last resort for geographers) didn't help a great deal. While my mid-term target was clear enough -- Mow Cop's hilltop folly must make it one of the most recognisable silhouettes in the Midlands -- the short-term route among the houses was less so. Opposite me, however, a tempting unadopted road named Clough Hall Drive pointed in a vaguely northern direction and I gave in.

It turned out to be an idyllic track about a kilometre long. Bouncing over unadopted bumps, swishing along unadopted verges and doing more legs-akimbo freewheels through unadopted puddles, I didn't give a second thought to the evident fact that I was heading downhill. One lesson that should have come to mind was a rule for life offered to the Wanderer and his fellow pupils at a nearby Christian Brothers' school in the 1950s. The context was a lesson in sex education (in fact the only such lesson, if I understand it correctly) and the advice was this: 'Two minutes of pleasure are not worth a lifetime of misery'. Should any boy have been less than clear on this, a sharp application of the belt apparently helped his focus. Beyond Kidsgrove's busy main street, the error of my own ways was forcefully brought home by a calf-straining push up the town's hilly northern suburbs. If Kidsgrove was on the watershed, I was the Queen of Sheba. A glance back during one of many pauses for breath revealed a curved, wooded ridge to the south in which the watershed must be hidden and along which a gradient-free route would have delivered me to the same spot. Hey ho.

With 'Mow Cop' coming from the Old English for 'Hill Top', it's no surprise that more serious climbs take place here. Every year brave folk race on foot up to Mow Cop Castle (the folly on the hill) from the railway about 1500 metres away and some 170 metres below. It may not sound particularly serious but the current record, set in 1991, is a very serious 6 minutes 12 seconds. It's called the Killer Mile.

Heading from Kidsgrove through Mow Cop and on for another 50 kilometres to Stockport is the Gritstone Trail, a long-distance path celebrating one of the rock types that mark this out as the start of northern England, and at first I thought the ridge it follows would be the watershed route. But a closer look at the map showed the streams that flow east to Biddulph eventually turning north to join the River Dane and thence the Mersey. My correct route across the southern edge of Biddulph had been confirmed by a rare occurrence.

The author of the website for this town of 17,000 people not only acknowledged the existence of the English Watershed (with Keele's Long Hair, that meant two people on the same wavelength on the same day), but even told me which street it follows. So it was with some excitement that I pedalled along Newpool Road, assured as I was that the rainfall from one side ends up in the Irish Sea while the gutters on the other lead eventually to the North Sea. Thank you, thank you. I finally felt that my long meandering through the lowlands of middle England, with their wiggly streams wandering indecisively hither and thither, was definitively over. From here to Kinder Scout promised to be, navigationally at least, a doddle.

On a day of confirmations, the next checkpoint offered yet another, this time with a personal connection.

*

Ever since my first bike rides, as a child along the banks of the Trent in Derbyshire, I knew -- just as all my cycling chums knew -- that the great river whose flood defences we pedalled along and whose pebbles we skimmed so expertly, started life on a remote, barren heathland called Biddulph Moor in Staffordshire. To an eight-year-old in the 1950s, however, Staffordshire might as well have been halfway to the Moon; none of us had ever been there. Fifty-plus years later, it came as something as a surprise to find that Biddulph Moor was not a moor at all, but a village. With less dispute than the Thames equivalent I'd seen earlier in this journey, the source of the Trent, the second longest river entirely in England, definitely lies behind a cottage off a narrow lane on the outskirts of the village. I could hear it gurgling in the trees, but as it's on private land couldn't see it. Observing me standing on tiptoe atop a grassy knoll, peering in the direction of the cottage's back garden, the postman who'd just made his delivery there called over.

'Lookin' for the source of the Trent?'

'Yes. Thought there might be a plaque or something.'

'There is.'

'Where?'

'Shift yer bike an' you'll see it, mate,' he explained before climbing into his van.

I'd leaned Tetley against an apparently blank piece of wood. Postie was right. With asterisks representing mould, the inscription read: '**** ** *** ****** ** *** **ver Trent'. That was good enough for me. Cracking open a bottle of spring water, I raised a toast to the River Trent and all who sail on her. Or cycle by her. Or him. Do English rivers have genders?

*

Pedalling ever upward, I reached a windy ridge from where my first view of the bleak, purple-grey moorland of the Peak District opened up to the right. As this effectively represented my ultimate goal -- somewhere beyond these outlying moors lay Kinder Scout -- I suppose I should have stopped and surveyed the scene for a while, but to be honest this October afternoon was turning distinctly chilly. Blowing in from North Wales had come a stiff breeze that up here at over a thousand feet found its way through several layers of cycling gear. What's more, I'd soon have to decide when to call it a day and turn back to the nearest railway station. As it happened this decision was about to be made for me.

Now, when coming across a flooded road in a car it's always wise, if possible, to wait until another vehicle with bigger wheels and a higher chassis drives through, to give you an idea of the depth. I knew that. I'd even done it. So why I didn't do it on my bike I can't tell you. All I can tell you is that, when I rounded a bend to be confronted by standing water (subsequently discovered to be the flooded headwaters of the Dingle Brook), I just pedalled on. The only explanation I can offer for this frankly stupid course of action is the pleasure with which I'd freewheeled through puddles earlier in the day. This, however, was no puddle.

My entry was marked by a pleasant swooshing sound. This was followed, in sequence, by a lower gurgling sound, an ominously deeper washing sound, a sharp intake of breath, urgent heavy panting and finally an unrestrained and elongated 'Aaaaauuuurgh!!' as I urged my legs, despite their sodden state and the freezing water, to just keep on pedalling. Eventually, after what seemed like several minutes but what was probably about 15 seconds, the water became shallower and Tetley and I emerged on the far side of the deluge, trailing from our lower reaches miscellaneous parts of Staffordshire.

'A disaster hath befallen me!' I thought, as I dismounted against a farmyard wall. Quiet why I thought it in biblical English I can't say. I believe I may have actually shouted it out loud.

It was only after a few weed-disentangling, sock-wringing minutes, when the driver of a passing car smiled at my evident discomfort, that the rueful smile I managed in return jolted me out of a foul humour and into an overdue sense of perspective. So my leggings were drenched up to the knees; so I'd got no spare socks and would have to pedal on with bare feet in cycling sandals; so my toes would get cold; so this day on the watershed was over. So what? I'd learnt of enough real disaster today to see this little inconvenience in context.

Sometimes we really do forget how lucky we are.

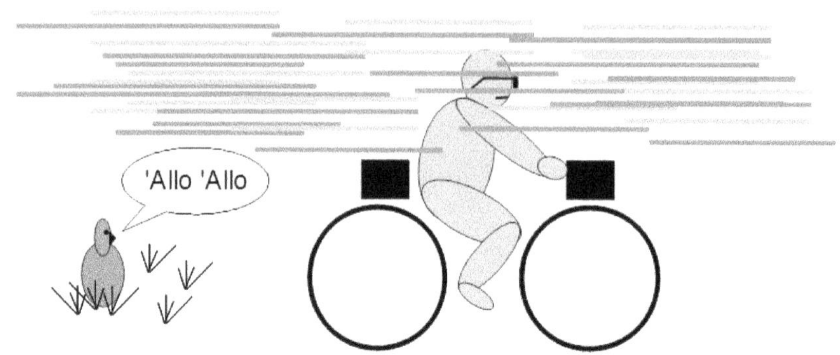

Stage 25: Pikelets, Puddings and Oatcakes

Biddulph Moor to Rushup Edge

One thing you can never accuse the British weather of being is short of ideas. In its efforts to inconvenience my progress, the next day's twin selection from its armoury was fog and cold.

As Julie dropped me off round the corner from the flood, the car's thermometer had read just 4 degrees and now, as I pedalled past the Bridestones -- huge vertical stones marking yet another neolithic tomb on the watershed -- the bracing morning air whistled sharply past my ears. An overnight temperature inversion had left pockets of fog in the hollows and the switchback ride into the Pennine foothills had me popping in and out of the soupy mist like a spoon being dipped in and out of a bowl of broth.

At one point where I temporarily emerged into the daylight, a large hoarding stood beside the road bearing a picture of a mysterious silver globe below the inscription 'SphereMania(R)'. Another identical hoarding followed. And then another. Since no further explanation was offered, I made a mental note to solve this mystery later and it turns out that on a farm near the village of Rushton Spencer strange events occur. Young men and women (at least I imagine they must be young) pay money to have themselves strapped inside a large ball and hurled downhill. Others pay a little more to do it with a few gallons of water swishing around inside the ball with them. Yes, you read that right: they pay people to *do* these things to them. Having looked at the price, I can assure you that I'd pay that to *stop* anyone doing it to me. We're led to believe that the participants are technically sane.

The same is claimed for willing participants in other, similarly alarming activities that bring much-needed income to farmers all over Britain: being chased, being put through military-style obstacle courses, being shot at with paint, being attacked with who-knows-what. Many are supposedly team-building exercises sponsored by the victims' -- I mean, the team-members' -- employers and as such, of course, are by no means a new phenomenon.

Since a company I worked for in the French Alps in the 1990s was especially keen on them, I found myself one winter obliged to join a party heading for the hills, intent on throwing themselves around in the snow: on narrow planks, on wide planks, aboard motorised planks and even with tennis racquets strapped to their feet. I opted for the relative safety of *les racquettes*, but almost all my colleagues hoped to impress the boss, who had a new team leader to choose, by their Gallic bravery on the steepest of ski slopes. All except one.

Neither gifted in winter sports nor, it has to be said, possessing the right shape for them, Jean-Luc flatly refused all involvement and spent the entire two days propping up the hotel bar. It came as something of a surprise on our return to the factory, therefore, to find the identity of the new team leader revealed as Jean-Luc. Mind you, there'd been two other snow-dodgers at the bar: our boss and our boss's boss. A good lesson here, I feel. Among Jean-Luc's new responsibilities was the organisation of future departmental 'offsites', as these jollies were known, and, to my eternal relief, they were henceforth re-directed to the more leisurely attractions available in the vineyards of Provence.

Suffice to say I was not to be tempted by a maniac and a sphere. The watershed route continued to throw up enough items of interest along the way without the need for any diversionary torture, spherical or otherwise.

*

It's also near Rushton Spencer that in 1745 a young drummer was shot, the hillock where he allegedly fell still being called Drummer's Knob. This wasn't just any drummer, but a Jacobite drummer and his drumbeats had given rhythm to Bonnie Prince Charlie's '45-ers as they marched back northward, having given up hope of advancing on London by the time they'd reached Derby, some 60 kilometres south-west of here.

Rather more obvious, perhaps, is an association with the name of the next feature, which would normally have sparkled in the morning sunlight just off my route. That morning, though, Rudyard Lake lay hidden in the fog that was hanging around longer than forecast. Was the lake named after Rudyard Kipling or the writer named after the lake? The dates are the clue. While the author of *The Jungle Book*, *Kim* and many other favourites published his first book in 1886, the reservoir, built by the Trent and Mersey Canal Company to supply their waterways, had been completed at the end of the previous century. It was in 1863 that a courting couple wandered hand-in-hand beside Rudyard Lake, their happy time here to be remembered in the name of their first child, born two years later in distant Bombay.

For a reservoir covering less than a square kilometre, Rudyard Lake seems to have been awash with incident during its two hundred years. Jean Blondin, the nineteenth-century daredevil who walked a tightrope above Niagara Falls, repeated his feat over the less threatening waters of Rudyard; Victorian hero Captain

Webb, the first man to swim the English Channel, entertained the crowds here; and, themselves idolised in their own, rather less heroic way, TV's *Top Gear* team chose Rudyard more recently to test three unlikely amphibious cars -- James May's Triumph Herald emerging triumphant.

*

The morning's initial target was a junction of lanes and tracks called Roach End and the narrow, semi-rough lane that leads up to it leaves civilisation at Swythamley Hall. Now split into private homes, this solid and sensible eighteenth-century house had a brief brush with the loucher strata of English society. Mahesh Prasad Varma, from the Central Provinces of India, was already about fifty and had toured the world at least five times as a guru of transcendental meditation, when he met The Beatles in London during the 'summer of love' in 1967. Five years into Beatlemania, the boys were evidently ripe for some meditation themselves and it was in taking them on as students that Mahesh shot to worldwide fame as the Maharishi Mahesh Yogi. Lennon even wrote a song about him: 'Sexy Sadie' on the White Album. Evidently more worldly wise than his public persona suggested, the Maharishi invested some of his vast earnings in a number of grand houses around England, one of which was Swythamley Hall. By the time it was used as a centre for transcendental meditation in the 1980s, the summer of love was long past.

It was a far from transcendental young man in the grounds of the hall who told me which of the many diverging tracks would lead me to Roach End. The Roaches, at one end of which it lies, is a huge gritstone ridge popular with walkers for its dramatic westerly views. As I'd approached, the rocks (*les roches*) from which the ridge gets its name had floated in and out of view as the fog swirled over North Staffordshire, now preferring the ups to the downs. At Roach End, it finally closed in completely, but oddly enough I didn't care...

*

Knowing the track over The Roaches to be competely uncyclable by normal human beings, I'd already planned a separate traverse on foot as a foursome with Julie and our old friends John and Lindsay, who live not far away in a small cottage on the Cheshire side of the Peak District. John and I have a history of event-planning that borders on the obsessive. Several years ago, fancying a day out to watch county cricket at Lord's, we'd pored for hours, weeks before the match, over a plan of the ground's seating arrangements before finally settling on two seats seven rows back in the Tavern Stand. On arrival we found that, with county attendances having fallen a tad since Dennis Compton had peppered the boundary, we had an on-the-spot choice of not only any seat at all in that stand, but of virtually any position in the entire ground -- including, if we'd brought our whites, maybe first and second slip. On another occasion our thorough preparations for a day's voyage on the Manchester Ship Canal included knapsacks stuffed to bursting point with pork pies, cheese rolls, bottles of beer and enough crisps to feed a salt-starved navy -- only to find the vessel boasted a fully stocked bar.

This time the planning for 'The Roaches Project' had generated several customized maps, encompassed at least three different date windows, roped in two support vehicles and involved several dozen emails over at least six months -- for a walk of barely two kilometres. As R-Day dawned, half the party dropped out of the walk through illness and unexpected commitments and, as Julie (valiantly staggering from her sick bed to support the cause) dropped off just John and me at Roach End, the clouds that had been circling all morning descended to take the hilltops once more into their sodden grasp.

At the end of an unexpectedly smooth upward path that took us up to the ridge, the track rapidly degenerated into an uncomfortable mix of boulders smoothed thousands of years ago by the passage of glaciers and cloying patches of mud that soon covered our waterproofs. Eyes fixed on the treacherous surface, both of us had failed to notice the mist lifting.

Emerging gradually, the panorama revealed first a prominent hill opposite called, John told me, the Cloud, then the edge of Macclesfield and then, further to the right, the grey-white spread of Manchester, with a thin line of Lancashire hills beyond.

As John spoke, a ragged row of youngsters straggled into view before forming a group in front of their leader, his back to the view. The leader spoke.

'OK. Who knows what millstone grit is?'

Silence.

'What about millstones?'

A girl in a yellow hat raised her hand. 'My dad says I'm a millstone round his neck.'

'Why doesn't that surprise me, Nicola? Well, your father seems to know the key attributes of this rock: hard and difficult to wear down.'

And so, waving a piece of rock above his head, the teacher launched into the tale of the millstone grit we were clambering over, of windmills and of the huge circular stones that mark the entrances to the Peak District National Park. Itmay well be the impermeability of millstone grit that accounted for the widespread surface water even right up on top of the ridge and made the landscape such a contrast to the chalk downs of Dorset, the limestone hills of Gloucestershire and most of the other high land I'd already crossed on this journey. While short in distance, this Roaches walk crossed the roughest terrain I'd encountered so far. Up here the day had also turned into one of the coldest, although we'd recently heard of an even colder one from the waitress at a cafe in Leek. If we're to believe the tale, in her youth she and her friends had come up here one winter afternoon when their fringes had become so frozen that they could melt them only by applying lit cigarettes to their hair. (Do not try this at home.)

As John and I scrambled back down to the relative warmth of the road, at least a dozen more walkers and one more group passed us even on a poor day like this. It's easy to see why the Roaches path, like so many in the Peak, is gradually being eroded by the passage of feet.

*

Back on the other misty day, as I approached Roach End on the lane up from Swythamley Hall, a sudden sound made me jump:

"Allo.'

Looking round for the source of the shrill, unexpected voice, I saw no one.

"Allo.'

'Hello?' I responded, dismounting to walk Tetley over to the heather, where the voice seemed to be coming from. Maybe someone was in trouble. Just as the wheels brushed the heather, a red head popped out of it barely three metres away. It was followed by a brown, feathery body and stood about as high as my calf. A grouse, I was fairly sure. A red grouse.

"Allo 'allo,' said the talking grouse.

'Ah, hello,' I said gravely. 'You'd better get back in the heather or you'll get us both shot.' I'd heard odd bursts of gunfire on the way up.

"Allo,' he repeated, undeterred.

'Well, for both our sakes I'm off now. Goodbye.'

"Allo.'

'Hello. Talking to yourself?'

This time the disembodied voice had a local accent. Swinging round, I saw a man materialising from the mist, an expensive camera on a tripod over his shoulder.

'No, to a grouse actually,' I offered, as though that justified it.

'Well, this weather can seep into the brain, I suppose.'

It turned out that he was from Stoke but a regular on The Roaches, first for the tough terrain in marathon training and nowadays as a photographer.

'Not very good for photos today,' I suggested.

'Fabulous day in fact,' he countered. 'Got a few shots from up in the light with the low sun cutting across billowing fog below. Bit like standing on an island with the waves breaking.'

'Will it last?'

'The fog? Shouldn't think so. Where are you going?'

'Beyond Buxton.'

'Oh, you'll be fine. Finer still if you get a cooked breakfast from The Winking Man.'

With this advice, Stoke Snapper loaded his car and drove off, leaving me alone again, the talking grouse having also disappeared safely into the heather. The eastern road around the base of the Roaches soon dropped Tetley and me out of the mist to reveal a broad, undulating landscape of purples and greens that rose gradually to the north, where barren moorland filled the horizon. Out of view, among the dense woods that cling to to the sides of these high valleys, stood a church that isn't a church.

Thousands of years ago, just above the headwaters of the Dane to the west of the watershed, a huge slab of the gritstone fell away along the line of a fault. The gap this created is now a dark and eerie, moss-covered chasm over 100 metres long, wide enough to walk comfortably in but deep enough to fall to your death in. It's known as Lud's Church.

Now, since the day -- many years before -- when I'd walked through here with a local rambling group, I'd taken the name to be that of Ned Ludd, the machine-wrecking inspiration of the Luddites, the nineteenth-century movement against mechanisation in the textile industry around here. I'd had visions of Ludd addressing a secret assembly of fellow rebels right here in the bowels of remotest Staffordshire.

Not so, it seems. For a start, it appears to have been known as Lud's Church some 400 years before, when the Lollards, a group of church reformers officially condemned as heretics, used to meet there for worship. Another theory puts the origins even earlier, with pagans gathering in the chasm to worship a Celtic god called Lud. The final nail in the coffin of my errant imagination is that Ned Ludd wasn't even a leader of the Luddites, but rather a young and apparently rather simple lad from Leicestershire who'd smashed a couple of stocking frames in a fit of rage some years before and whose name was subsequently used as the nominal culprit in all such machine wrecking. There's no record of his ever having been up here at all.

*

The Winking Man, famed not only for its breakfasts but also, according to an elderly man clearing ditches in a nearby field, for its 'falling-down fluid', is an inn named after a small hole in Ramshaw Rocks on the opposite side of the road. As you travel south on the A53 -- and I can confirm this is true -- the hole passes in front of another rock and then clear of it again, so that the sky appears, disappears and then re-appears, in the manner of a wink. Why it should seem like a man doing it I've no idea. Today, pedalling in the opposite direction in search of refreshment, I arrived winkless at Flash.

We're in the land of the highests here. Flash, a tiny village just off the main road at an altitude of 463 metres, is the highest in England -- and possibly in Great Britain, though this is disputed by a village in Dumfries and Galloway. It boasts the third-highest pub in England (the Traveller's Rest on the main road), as well as the fifth-highest (the New Inn in the village). Whether the Flash Bar Stores is the highest coffee shop in England I don't know but, all pubs still being closed, it was to here I repaired in search of some overdue sustenance.

The manager, a talkative man of about forty, shared two attributes with me: a Derbyshire birthplace and a slightly over-indulgent interest in confectionery. (Derbyshire folk generally eschew the current fad for acknowledging 'passions'. We don't do passion up here.) So we talked cakes: an overdue pastime in my case as, since the Northamptonshire seedcake incident, my search for locally named cakes had drawn a blank. Several times through Staffordshire I'd enquired in cake shops after the renowned Staffordshire oatcake, only to be met with definitive shakes of the head until, a few days before this stage, in Leek's Market Kitchen Cafe, I'd finally discovered why: it's not a cake after all. It's not overly endowed with oats either. The Staffordshire oatcake is a small pancake -- perfectly tasty with bacon and cheese in the Leek version, but definitely well outside any cake category. It's a point I raised with the manager of the Flash Bar Stores.

'Ah, no,' he said, wiping his hands on his apron. 'Neither is your Derbyshire oatcake.'

'What? Never heard of them. Ashamed to say.'

'Well, you'd better try one then. I'll warm one up. They're a bit thicker than the Staffordshire version, naturally.'

'Ah, you mean "Derbyshire born, Derbyshire bred, strong in the arm and thick in the 'ead".'

'Exactly. But they're more pikelets than pancakes, really.'

'Oh, pikelets are great. What do you have on them?'

'Jam and clotted cream or sometimes honey and ice cream.'

'I have Marmite.'

'What?' he exclaimed. 'Sweet and savoury together?!'

'Ah, well, I'm not very good at tastes,' I admitted. 'But I like it when the Marmite sinks through the holes.'

'What holes?'

'The pikelet's holes.'

'Pikelets don't have holes. Look.'

He showed me a packet of pikelets, which were effectively even smaller pancakes, before confusing me further by handing me the Derbyshire oatcake.

'You'd better sit down and concentrate on it,' added my advisor.

With a dollop of honey on top, it proved quite filling, slightly chewy and pretty tasty. After admitting that I'd confused childhood memories of pikelets and crumpets, I explained my current cakely mission.

'So you'll be including a Bakewell pudding then.'

'Certainly will. Of course,' I added, though now rather hesitant in any unjustified assertion, 'it's not really a pudding, is it?'

'No, it's a cake.'

'And a Bakewell tart?'

'A tart, of course. Which is a kind of cake.' And then, after a moment: 'We do Flash puddings here too...'

'Oh, I'll have one.'

'... but not today. Raspberries are too expensive at the

moment.'

'Is it a pudding, a tart, a cake, an oatcake or a pancake?'

My host looked me in the eye.

'Come back another day and try it, sir.'

And I shall.

*

As I ended up sampling the local toffee cake and sausage rolls as well, it was a slightly bloated cyclist that finally emerged, keen to get some more exercise.

Flash is the last village in Staffordshire, a position that explains its contribution to the English language. In the eighteenth century a local counterfeit gang is reputed to have exchanged its illegal coins just outside the village at Three Shire Head, where Staffordshire, Derbyshire and Cheshire meet, a location convenient for rapid escape across a county boundary should the forces of the law be on their trail. The counterfeit money was therefore called 'Flash money', the term since having expanded to cover anything or anyone regarded as a little showy or even vulgar: a flash car or Flash Harry, for instance.

Soon I was whizzing with a whoop past the sign announcing the entry into Derbyshire, my home county and the the last one on this journey. Even though I was born within the low-lying, urban end of the shire, this wild, high land still felt like home, so closely do most of the English identify with their county. It was a grand day to be up here, the smooth, blue-brown moors of Axe Edge looming to my left, the wide green fields of the upper Dove Valley stretching far to the right, its occasional white farmhouses tinier and tinier as the horizon approached Longnor and Hartington in the land of day-trippers and tea shops.

At the remote road junction where two or more sources of

the Dove gurgle just below the roadway, I pulled over with a decision to make. The watershed follows a high line to the north-west, before swinging east again beyond Buxton. It's a route that's not only uncyclable but also unwalkable by all but the most foolhardy. The two cyclable options were a zigzag route that twice crossed the watershed, but otherwise went nowhere near it, and the main road through Buxton. The main road went directly downhill from here. It was tempting. I took it.

My next coffee stop, therefore, came after a headlong descent into England's highest market town and was as different as could be from Flash Bar Stores: an outdoor seat among crowds of day visitors in the balmy surrounds of Buxton's Pavilion Gardens. The geothermal spring that the Romans knew and around which Victorians and Edwardians developed their resort town still bubbles up at St Ann's Well on The Crescent. While that elegant street and the Opera House would have been twin magnets for the Edwardian social elite, the Pavilion Gardens where I sipped my coffee (and scoffed a last cake before Kinder) would also have seen smartly dressed ladies wandering up and down, parasols protecting their complexion from the searing Derbyshire sun. As I listened to today's strollers discussing their plans for the afternoon (almost all concerning Christmas shopping -- in mid-October), I wondered if one of the town's sons, comedian Tim Brooke-Taylor, had also sat here to pick up the incredible accent of his best-known character, Lady Constance de Coverlet, in radio's *I'm Sorry, I'll Read That Again*. With radio DJ Dave Lee Travis and Robert Stevenson, the director of *Mary Poppins*, also born in Buxton, the town seems to have all cultural bases covered.

Being slightly off route and at the bottom of a hill, I couldn't afford to hang around and so soon found myself pushing Tetley up the northbound A6, doing my best to keep a few inches between Tetley's pedals and every passing HGV.

*

In 2001 a BBC radio poll voted Dove Holes the ugliest village in England. Having seen a few stinkers myself, but with no recollection of this one, I was intrigued to get to the top of the slope from Buxton and have a look for myself. Julie, on the other hand, knew it only too well, as the prospect of a summer jazz festival had, several years before, brought her and a dozen friends to a campsite here. I'll let her take up the story...

'To say it was cold and wet would be an understatement. I'd cooked and frozen a huge casserole to feed us all, but after a day's drive it was still half-frozen. Even after chipping away at it over a campfire, it was still quarter-frozen. That's Derbyshire in July for you. Suffice to say we ate late. And it rained like I'd never seen rain before. Mud everywhere, ugly buildings everywhere else, cold as hell -- and the music wasn't much cop either.'

I'd heard that those who endured this outing still refer to the village, years later, not as Dove Holes but -- rather predictably -- as A*** Holes. Technically they're not far from the truth, for 'Dove' is a Celtic river name meaning dark or black. Dark Black Holes: ugly or not, this would surely score as the worst address in England. On my route along the watershed I'd passed a few genuine addresses where you might think twice about buying a house. What about Waste Lane in Warwickshire? Or the more dangerous Cut Throat Lane nearby? Personally I'd prefer either of them to the unfortunate Twatling Lane near Lickey. Cold Slad in Gloucestershire doesn't strike a particularly homely note, but could be safer than Nutterswood just to the north. For a negative house name, you can't beat The Wrongs, near Sibbertoft in Northamptonshire. But if you really do fancy a dodgy address, then in Staffordshire you'd be spoilt for choice: Grub Street, near Woodseaves, is closely followed by The Bogs and only that morning I'd pedalled between Bent End Farm and Old Hag. You couldn't make it up.

So it wasn't with much hope of beauty that I swung into Dove Holes and I wasn't disappointed. While Cotswold Stone seems to mellow the light before reflecting it gently back to the eye, the local stone used throughout Dove Holes removes all hint of sunlight before chucking it back at you like a slice of dark November sky. And the houses themselves appear to have been designed as part of an intelligence test where you can use no more than ten lines. They're just boxes. Even the new houses dotted here and there are the same. Surely this would be a case where planning restrictions could state 'No similarity at all to existing structures in the village will be accepted'.

And yet I feel sure I've seen worse places in England. After all, Dove Holes has no cooling towers looming over it, no nuclear power station, no thundering motorway. And those green hills at the end of each side street are real hills, not the eerie artificial versions that surround old mining towns. No, I'm sorry: it may be in the bottom ten per cent, but Dove Holes is nowhere near the ugliest village in Britain. The vote must have been rigged, possibly by the residents of Dove Holes themselves to generate some public investment.

*

Last cake, last tea room, last village... and now the last pub before Kinder Scout. In the tiny hamlet of Sparrowpit (named after a pit of fluorspar rather than a pit of small birds) sits the intriguingly named Wanted Inn. I wanted in.

While downing my last beer before Kinder (a rich, thirst-quenching glass of Unicorn from Robinson's Brewery in nearby Stockport), I learnt the story behind the name. It's simpler than I'd imagined. Having been owned by the Duke of Devonshire for many years and under several unremarkable pub names, the inn was put up for sale in 1950 to help the duke pay off some death duties. Alas, it was 'unwanted' for six years before eventually being sold to new owners who confirmed it was now 'wanted' by changing its name again. Obvious really.

After licking the last remnants of ale from my lips, I could put it off no longer: to reach Julie and the car, I had to push up Rushup Edge. A particularly inappropriate name: Crawlup Edge perhaps? With Tetley weighing in as heavily as ever, my steps got shorter and shorter, my breathing faster and faster. At one stage I thought I was hallucinating as I saw a field of woolly brown llamas by the road... except it *was* a field of woolly brown llamas. Yesterday the Andes, today the Peak District.

It was with such random thoughts that I finally emerged on the Chapel-to-Castleton road, busy with heavily shod and warmly clad hikers scurrying between parked cars and the network of paths and bridleways that spread out from here like black streams on a green delta. This was the start of the High Peak, a wild landscape that barely tolerates walkers, let alone cyclists.

And so Julie, fresh from a day's shopping in Leek and Buxton, dashed out of the warm car to help me stable the bike. While I still had a day to go, this was the end of the road for good old Tetley. Apart from one small misdemeanour in Dorset, he'd stayed as faithful and puncture-free as ever. I really ought to treat him to a clean one day.

Stage 26: Small Brown Planet

Rushup Edge to Edale via Kinder Scout

Several weeks had passed before we returned to Rushup Edge, weeks waiting for the rain to stop and autumn mists to clear. By the time a bright dawn broke over the Midlands it was December, it was minus two and I'd taken part in that sleepy, ten-minute ritual familiar to winter car commuters all over England: window scraping in the dark. Two hours later we were crawling at five miles an hour across Winnat's Pass, trying to avoid sheep apparently nibbling the road surface, and a quarter of an hour after that I was waving goodbye to Julie at the Rushup Edge lay-by.

Turning round, I found myself waving goodbye as well to the group of four women walkers who'd set off from the lay-by just ahead of me. While they continued north-eastwards in the direction of Mam Tor, I turned north-west towards the distant wall of a railway air shaft. They'd be the last humans I'd see for about two hours.

It's not that this wasn't popular walking territory. Quite the contrary. The proximity of Sheffield, Manchester and The Potteries helps make the Peak District one of the most heavily visited national parks in the world -- though evidently not on chilly Tuesday mornings in December. Before me spread an empty wasteland, gently curving in all directions from a low rise a mile or two ahead. Echoing our experience at Abbotsbury Castle on Day One, it was once again as though I was pacing across the surface of a small, deserted planet, this time a brown one, speckled with frosty diamonds sparkling in the low sun and lined with narrow streaks of white as though a small spacecraft had briefly touched down before realising there was nothing on the planet to look at and rapidly taken off again.

The streaks of white in fact marked worn-down tracks where snow from the past few days still lay undisturbed by wind or warmth. My own path ahead, following the watershed between the westbound Roych Clough and the headwaters of the eastbound River Noe, was thus revealed as clearly as anywhere on this journey. After half an hour's walking, though, I was no longer using it. Tramping along this line of virgin snow, I'd suddenly seen one leg disappear from view up to the calf before emerging to my cry of 'Idiot!', now with a neat tide line between upper leg, blue with denim, and lower leg dripping black with cold, clammy mud. Boot off, sock off. My, it *is* cold. Two soakings in the last three days. At least I finally got to use the Swiss Army knife I'd been carrying for the last 450 miles -- to scrape a thick layer of Derbyshire mud from everything it had touched.

Not wanting to end up like Stapleton in Conan Doyle's Grimpen Mire, and with no Holmes nor Watson to haul me free, I henceforth picked a route parallel to the sunken path, stepping gingerly from frosty tussock to frosty tussock, my stick prodding tentatively ahead. I'd therefore averaged barely a mile an hour before I poked my way to a snack stop at the concrete trig point atop the summit of this brown knoll, named by a previous, no-nonsense generation as 'Brown Knoll'.

*

At 569 metres, this slight rise was enough to bring distant horizons back into view. To the east the green bowl formed by the Vale of Edale swept up to the peak of Lose Hill, to the south the low sun picked out a silhouette of trees somewhere above Sparrowpit, but it was to the west that the view was grandest. Just a few hundred metres away the light brown vegetation, as rough as a giant ginger biscuit, fell away to reveal once again the broad, misty swathe of the Cheshire Plain, which I'd been skirting for more travelling days than I could remember. This time though, I could see fifty kilometres or more, beyond Stockport, beyond Wilmslow, way beyond Manchester Airport to an horizon dominated by the huge, vertical clouds rising from the cooling towers of a power station that must have been somewhere near the Mersey estuary. Recalling that I'd yet to see the sea since the Dorset Downs, I trained my small binoculars on this horizon, but mist and cloud merged into an unvariegated blue-white haze. It was to be my last chance.

Sitting on the step of the trig point, sipping hot vacuum-flask coffee and chewing a cold Marmite cob, I realised the sounds of my snack were the only sounds there were. On this stillest of days on a remote, treeless Derbyshire hill, no blade of grass rustled, no bird sang, no mammal scurried. While below the surface busy trains rattled their way through Cowburn Tunnel from Sheffield to Manchester, while the distance views reflected earnest industrial activity, up here on Brown Knoll, nothing stirred. For minutes I simply sat and stared about me, for minutes more I could have stayed in the same semi-trance, but, with progress having been slow and the day one of the shortest of the year, I reluctantly packed up my things and pressed on.

As I walked carefully across the frozen wastes that encircled the white post, the cracking of ice beneath my boots echoed across the silence until I reached a T-junction in the paths. While I could see the inviting flagstones of what was clearly a better-used path, between me and it stretched a wire fence unbroken as far as I could see in either direction. My inside leg measurement is 74 cm. I can tell you that at its lowest the fence rose at least 80 cm from the highest tufts of grass. Eventually I minced onto the flagstones and turned right.

After a few hundred yards, at Edale Cross, where more tracks merged, a human being -- a man of about forty, sporting green woolly hat, green waterproof and smart pair of gaiters -- was walking smartly up from Edale.

'Oh! Good morning!' he said, evidently as startled as I was to see another living thing. 'What a morning.'

After we'd swapped route details -- Gaiters was doing the west-to-east, Edale-to-Hayfield path at right angles to mine -- I raised the question of the distant power station whose clouds were still visible in the west.

'Oh, there's a big 'un at Fiddler's Ferry near Widnes,' he said. 'Could be that one.' If he was right, it was nearer 60 than 50 kilometres away.

Thanking Gaiters for the information, I set off to the north aware that, but for the coincidence of our meeting at the crossways, we would each have probably passed an entire morning without human contact. As it happened, I'd another two hours before my next, but animal contact I did soon experience at Edale Rocks, where a familiar, and yet also slightly unfamiliar, greeting awaited.

'Ayup!'

'What?'

'Ayup!'

This time the red grouse had popped up from behind a rock rather than a clump of heather and seemed to have a more northern dialect than his Staffordshire cousin.

'Oh, you again,' I said out loud.

'Ayup!'

'Well, I can't stand here all day chatting to you. Toodle-oo then.'

Eyeing me with a mixture of disappointment and suspicion, the grouse bid me a predictable farewell:

'Ayup!'

*

Plain sailing now. From Edale Cross, I hadn't even bothered to glance at the map, for not only was the route laid out before me by a path of flagstones visible even as it passed in and out of the thickening snow cover, but also I'd passed the magic sign. The wooden fingerpost at Edale Cross bore the two words that had been at the back of my mind since that February morning on Chesil Beach, in fact since the moment I'd first hatched the idea of this watershed walk. The words were 'Pennine Way'.

For 429 kilometres from just around the corner at Edale all the way to the Cheviot Hills of Northumberland, the Pennine Way follows a line along 'the backbone of England', as the Pennines are so often described, more or less parallel to the English watershed, if not -- as here -- actually on it. Among those who register an assault on the entire route with www.nationaltrail.co.uk, the average time for completion is 16 days. In 1989 one Mike Hartley *ran* the Way in 2 days 17 hours 20 minutes and 15 seconds. Good on you, Mike. With my dodgy knee, you could give me 16 years and I'd still be in hospital before Scotland.

No. This brief experience -- my first ever -- of the Pennine Way would be enough. And how rare it must be to walk the Way up from Edale Cross to Kinder Scout with just a red grouse for company. Just beyond Edale Rocks the final trig point for which I'd been scanning the horizon sneaked out from behind a rock.

'Whoo-hooo!' I heard myself shout.

Steady on, Guise. Looking round to confirm I was still alone, I followed my poking stick across the black-and-white landscape until it clattered against the solid white column marking, at 633 metres, the highest point in the Peak District and in Derbyshire. And another 'Marilyn' to boot. With the same linguistic perversity that terms the uplands of southern England the Downs, this spot is called Kinder Low. Though born and bred in Derbyshire, I'd never set foot here -- unlike Julie, who several years before had reached here amid what she describes as a frenzy of walkers mashing up the mud in all directions.

What a privilege to be here today, quite alone.

And yet in a sense I wasn't. For the only time on this entire journey (to my knowledge) I was following in the footsteps of another watershed walker. Some five years before, writer Andrew Bibby had set off from Mam Tor, joining the same route as mine from Rushup Edge via Brown Knoll up here to Kinder Scout. Unlike me, however, Andrew was literally following the actual line of the watershed along its every twist and turn, whether it coincided with a path or not. Oh, and he continued top do so all the way to the Scottish border. The beautiful and informative book of his journey, *The Backbone of England* (see Selected Sources), is what I recommend to any reader who wants to continue the route. And it doesn't stop there, for tales of walks along the even more exhausting Scottish watershed route from the border all the way to the north coast are available at www.gdl.cdlr.strath.ac.uk/hewwat (by Dave Hewitt) and at www.watershedepic.org.uk (by Peter Wright). Perhaps the combination of their accounts and my own will inspire someone young enough to tackle the entire south-north watershed of Great Britain.

*

For my own part, before I left the magic moonscape of

Kinder I had another loose end to tie up. It was cake time.

Cake decision time in fact. Of the locally named cakes sampled en route, I'd selected as finalist the soft and scrumptious Dorset Apple Cake, scoffed in a Wessex meadow in springtime. The other place in the final was still to be decided between the two confections I now pulled out of my knapsack as I sat on a frosty rock in gritstone country: a Bakewell Pudding and a Bakewell Tart.

Both had been bought at the famous Old Original Bakewell Pudding Shop, tucked in the centre of that small village on the Wye some 30 kilometres from here. I'd been surprised -- shocked even -- to be able to buy both versions there for, as a child in the Sixties, it had been made clear to me that, while the pudding version was the real deal, the tart version was merely a sticky imitation passed off to *hoi polloi* at the Co-op. I'd raised this question with the shop assistant.

'Well,' said the smart young man, 'I've never heard that. We've been selling tarts as long as I've been here.'

'How long's that?'

'Fifteen years.'

So, still with a pang of conscience, I'd purchased both and now placed them carefully on the shiny grey rock. What unites the two is the egg and almond mixture, which the cook who first made the cake at a Bakewell Inn in 1820 was supposed to have combined with the pastry but instead spread on top of the jam. The mistake proved so tasty that an entire business eventually developed from it. I sunk my teeth into the Bakewell Pudding, the happy mistake. It's best eaten hot, but even cold the plum and raspberry jam squidged lusciously from the sponge, but was kept just under control by the almond sponge and flaky pastry. Stretching my legs towards a nearby bank of black peat, I let the textures roll around my palette before swallowing.

Next, the Bakewell Tart -- now, it seems, perfectly acceptable in polite Derbyshire society. After removing the glacé cherry from the top, I sampled the last cake of my journey. Mmm, drier, crunchier, quite almondy, less jammy. Different shortcrust pastry too. Definitely moreish though. Wiping the last crumb off my lips, I stood up, balanced on a frozen divot of mud, threw the cherry in the air and caught it in my mouth. OK, I thought, it's the Bakewell Pudding that gets to the final.

Dorset Apple Cake versus Bakewell Pudding. South versus north. Soft versus hard. (All right, hard*er*). Home-made versus shop-bought. It had to be done from memory. Meadow versus moorland. Brook versus bog... oh, hell, it's obviously Kate's apple cake. Sorry, Derbyshire. Kate Paterson's recipe for her delicious Dorset Apple Cake appears at the end of this book.

*

The trundle back down to Edale was a slightly more populated one. As I passed Edale Rocks, four male hikers were scrambling up to the top and I called up to the last one, who seemed reluctant to use his walking pole.

'Great day to be up here!'

'Aye, but it's the night we're after.'

'How's that?'

'Photographs. Looks like a fabulous sunset and then there's the stars.'

Of course. Though I didn't envy them their cold evening camped up here, this dark spot -- the Dark Peak is what the area's called -- must be a sensational place to observe the night sky. The 'pole' he shouldered up the slope was a tripod of course. Let's hope their torch batteries were well charged.

Not just people but some extra sounds on the way too, for

the creaking of ice below my boots was now accompanied by the grinding of knees above them as they negotiated the down slope. A waterfall near Jacob's Ladder, the rushing of the River Noe, scuffling sheep -- a positive cacophony of noise ending, eventually, in the lounge of the Old Nag's Head in Edale village, where a log fire crackled away and where Julie, who'd found Glossop's shops a rather limited source of retail distraction, was glad to be rescued from the Mountain Rescue.

From not by. What must have been the local Mountain Rescue's Christmas lunch had featured an impromptu competition in tales of extreme danger, a competition that was only ever going to be won by one man. Whichever cave his colleagues had ventured into, he'd been in a deeper one; whichever cliff, he'd braved a more precipitous one; whichever windswept peak, he'd hung on to a wilder one. It was close to sunset when I turned up and he was still at it.

'If you're in a force nine, where you don't want to be is off the Needles...'

I suppose they could have been practising for their own version of Monty Python's 'Four Yorkshiremen' sketch at the Emergency Services Christmas party. 'That's nothing. I was blown completely off the face of the planet and still fought my way back to save a hundred people, a dozen alligators and a dinosaur before the pubs opened.'

Of course I'm sure they all do a fine job and was glad I hadn't needed their help on this day or any other on my wiggly way through England. As I hope I've demonstrated, both to myself and to you, there's no need to go to dangerous extremes to have an adventure. The only danger was that I simply wanted to do it all over again. Crunch along Chesil Beach, stride over the Downs, swing around Salisbury Plain, pedal along quiet Cotswold lanes, follow Cromwell's path to Naseby, scan the horizon from the Lickeys, float under Dudley, tackle the Roaches and Kinder;

exchange banter in Dorset, sample cakes in Gloucestershire, down too many pints in Oxfordshire, learn maritime law in Warwickshire, reassess history in Staffordshire, sort out confectionery confusion on the borders of Derbyshire... I'm sure any out-of-the-way route across England would throw up equally unpredictable experiences, but the wandering watershed line seemed to have generated contacts that were particularly kaleidoscopic.

The outside world is as much on the doorstep as on the other side of the planet. A day out can be as much fun as a year away. My dad was right: as long as we're able, we should get out in the fresh air and experience it.

Dorset Apple Cake

Here is the recipe for the winner of the 'Best Locally Named Cake En Route' competition: Dorset Apple Cake. Both cake and recipe were kindly supplied by Kate Paterson.

Ingredients:

225 g cooking apples, peeled , cored and chopped

Juice of half a lemon

225 g plain flour

1.5 tsp baking power

115 g butter, diced

165 g soft, light brown sugar

1 egg, beaten

2 to 3 tbsp milk

0.5 tsp ground cinnamon

How to make it:

1. Preheat the oven to 180 degrees C.
2. Grease and line a 7-inch round cake tin.
3. Toss the apple with the lemon juice and set aside.
4. Sift the flour and baking powder together and then rub in the butter, until the mix resembles breadcrumbs.
5. Stir 115 g of the sugar, the apple and the egg, mix well, adding a little of the milk at a time to make a soft, doughy mix.
6. Transfer into your tin.

7. In a bowl, mix the remaining sugar and cinnamon and sprinkle it over the cake mix.
8. Bake for 45 to 50 minutes.
9. Leave to cool in the tin for 10 minutes and then transfer to a wire cooling rack.
10. Enjoy when cooled.

Stage by Stage: Distance and Toughness

The stages are numbered from south to north. Nine were walks, while seventeen were bike rides. My route distances were calculated from maps and signposts rather than an odometer.

Stage	From	To	Mode	Km	Ml	Comment
1	Chesil Beach	White Hill	Walk	6	4	Rural. Some steep.
2	White Hill	Powestock Common	Walk	15	9	Rural. Easy.
3	Powerstock Common	Leigh	Bike	27	17	Rural. Tough.
4	Leigh	Jack White's Gibbet	Bike	39	24	Rural. Easy.
5	Jack White's Gibbet	King Alfred's Tower	Walk	14	9	Rural. Easy, except steep for last two kilometres.
6	King Alfred's Tower	Devizes	Bike	60	37	Rural. Easy. Some dirt tracks.
7	Devizes	Cherhill White Horse	Walk	8	5	Rural. Some steep.
8	Cherhill White Horse	Trouble House	Bike	55	34	Rural. Easy. Some dirt tracks.
9	Trouble House	Seven Springs	Bike	32	20	Rural. Easy.
10	Seven Springs	Moreton-in-Marsh	Bike	47	29	Rural. Easy.

11	Moreton-in-Marsh	Edgehill	Bike	37	23	Rural. Easy.
12	Edgehill	Kilsby	Bike	44	27	Rural. Easy, except for one stiff ascent.
13	Kilsby	Thornby	Walk	16	10	Rural. Easy, but some busy roads.
14	Thornby	Husbands Bosworth	Walk	14	9	Rural. Easy.
15	Husbands Bosworth	Willey	Bike	23	14	Rural. Easy
16	Willey	Corley Moor	Bike	34	21	Rural. Easy.
17	Corley Moor	Meriden	Walk	6	4	Rural. Easy.
18	Meriden	Lapworth	Bike	21	13	Rural. Easy.
19	Lapworth	Lickey	Bike	29	18	Mostly rural. Easy.
20	Lickey	Frankley Green	Walk	9	6	Rural. Easy.
21	Frankley Green	Billy Wright's statue	Bike	24	15	Urban. Some steep.
22	Billy Wright's statue	Man-Monkey Bridge	Bike	38	24	Rural. Easy.
23	Man-Monkey Bridge	Keele	Bike	36	22	Rural. Easy.
24	Keele	Biddulph Moor	Bike	31	19	Mostly rural. Hilly.

25	Biddulph Moor	Rushup Edge	Bike	42	26	Rural. Some steep. Distance excludes tough 2 km walk over The Roaches.
26	Rushup Edge	The Old Nag's Head, Edale	Walk	13	8	Via Kinder Scout. Down tougher than up.
		Total		**720**	**447**	

Best stretches:

Chesil Beach, Dorset. A place just to sit and listen to the rhythm of wave on shingle.

Martin's Down, Dorset. Fresh air and freedom in the footsteps of our ancestors.

Imber Range Perimeter Path, Wiltshire. Mystery and history on one side, stunning views on the other.

Hay Wood, Warwickshire. Peace and tranquillity.

Lickey Hills, Worcestershire. A classic piece of English landscape between the conurbation and the countryside.

Clough Hall Drive, Kidsgrove, Staffordshire. A secret gem of scenic woodland on the edge of The Potteries.

Axe Edge, Derbyshire. Wide open moorland under endless skies.

Kinder Scout, Derbyshire. At its best on a quiet, clear winter's day.

Best pub: Falkland Arms, Great Tew, Oxfordshire.

Best pint: Three Sheets Ale, from Ringwood Brewery, at The Swan, Forton, Staffordshire.

Selected Sources

Books:

Bibby, Andrew *The Backbone of England* (2008, Frances Lincoln).

Brown, Ivor *The Heart of England* (1935, B.T. Batsford).

Crane, Nick *Two Degreees West* (1999, Viking). Entertaining and informative account of his walk along England's 'prime meridian', from Berwick-upon-Tweed to Dorset.

Hippisley Cox, Robert *The Green Roads of England* (2010, The Lost Library). A guide to the ancient trackways of southern England, originally published in 1914. As this book is itself pretty ancient, treat its interpretations with care.

Ingram, J.H. *North Midland Country* (1947, B.T. Batsford).

Massingham, H.J. *Cotswold Country* (1937, B.T. Batsford).

Massingham, H.J. *English Downland* (1936, B.T. Batsford).

Mills, A. D. *Oxford Dictionary of British Place Names* (2003, Oxford University Press). Comprehensive.

Phythian-Adams, Charles (Editor) *Societies, Cultures and Kinship 1580-1850: Cultural Provinces and English Local History* (1996, Leicester University Press). Phythian-Adams reveals that the frontiers between England's medieval 'cultural provinces' more or less follow the major watersheds.

Roberts, David *Rock Atlas* (2011, Clarksdale). An intriguing guide to pop music-related locations in Britain and Ireland.

Upton, Clive and Widdowson, J. D A. *An Atlas of English Dialects* (1996, Oxford University Press). Fascinating.

Websites:

www.archeoscan.com. Updates on the archaeological excavation of the Roman site near Tetbury, Gloucestershire, where we dug.

www.bbc.co.uk/birmingham/voices2005/stats.shtml. Report on the 2005 accent survey.

www.dailymail.co.uk. 13th June 2011. 'The wifelets of Bath, an 'immaculate conception', a catfight and a broken nose'. Article on the goings-on at Longleat House.

www.domesdaymap.co.uk. Free, easy access to data from *Domesday Book* (1086).

Half the net royalties received by the author from sales of this book will go to **Arthritis Research (UK)**. For more information, go to www.arthritisresearchuk.org or www.justgiving.com/Richard-Guise.

For up-to-date news on Richard Guise's travel writing, go to www.facebook.com/richard.guise.7.

www.ingramcontent.com/pod-product-compliance
Ingram Content Group UK Ltd.
Pitfield, Milton Keynes, MK11 3LW, UK
UKHW021052270726
13967UKWH00012B/582